THE STORY OF RUSSIA

Peasant Russia, Civil War: The Volga Countryside in Revolution,
1917–21
A People's Tragedy: The Russian Revolution, 1891–1924
Interpreting the Russian Revolution: The Language and Symbols of
1917 (with Boris Kolonitskii)
Natasha's Dance: A Cultural History of Russia
The Whisperers: Private Life in Stalin's Russia
Crimea: The Last Crusade
Just Send Me Word: A True Story of Love and Survival in the Gulag
Revolutionary Russia, 1891–1991
The Europeans: Three Lives and the Making of a Cosmopolitan
Culture

THE STORY OF RUSSIA

ORLANDO FIGES

BLOOMSBURY PUBLISHING
LONDON · OXFORD · NEW YORK · NEW DELHI · SYDNEY

BLOOMSBURY PUBLISHING
Bloomsbury Publishing Plc
50 Bedford Square, London, WC1B 3DP, UK
29 Earlsfort Terrace, Dublin 2, Ireland

BLOOMSBURY, BLOOMSBURY PUBLISHING and the Diana logo are trademarks of
Bloomsbury Publishing Plc

First published in Great Britain 2022

A catalogue record for this book is available from the British Library

ISBN: HB: 978-1-5266-3174-9; TPB: 978-1-5266-3176-3; EBOOK: 978-1-5266-3167-1;
EPDF: 978-1-5266-5689-6

2 4 6 8 10 9 7 5 3 1

Typeset by Newgen KnowledgeWorks Pvt. Ltd., Chennai, India
Printed and bound in Great Britain by CPI Group (UK) Ltd, Croydon CR0 4YY

To find out more about our authors and books visit www.bloomsbury.com
and sign up for our newsletters

For Stephanie.
Again. Always.

Contents

Russia in Europe

✂ Battle
━━━ USSR (1945–91)

0   100 200 300 400 500 km

FINLAND

Pustozersk

White Sea

Arctic Circle

Solovetsky

Archangelsk

White Sea Canal (Belomorkanal)

Staraya Ladoga

Solvychegodsk

Ustiug

Cherdyn

Ladoga

Volkov

Volga

Kostroma

R U S S I A

Perm

Tyumen

Klin

Sergiev-Posad

Suzdal

Nizhny Novgorod

Ekaterinburg

Borodino (1812) ✂

Tushino

Moscow

Vladimir

Kazan

Chelyabinsk

Novo-Ogarevo

Sviazhsk

Kama

Arzamas

Oka

Ardatov

Alatyr

Ufa

U R A L   M O U N T A I N S

Kaluga

Kostanay

Tula

Riazan

Staraya Riazan

Bezdna

Magnitogorsk

Orel

✂ Kulikovo (1380)

Simbirsk

Kozlov

Belinsky

Penza

Samara

Kursk

Tambov

Ardym

Voronezh

Saratov

Orenburg

Belgorod

Don

Volga

Uralsk

Aktobe

UKRAINE

K A Z A K H S T A N

Volgograd

Kalka

3

2

Novocherkassk

Sea of Azov

Azov Fortress

New Sarai

Old Sarai ?

Atyrau

BAYKONUR

Aral Sea

Astrakhan

Itil

Stavropol

UZBEKISTAN

Black Sea

Beslan

Chech-nya

Aktau

Caspian Sea

Sukhumi

4

GEO-

5

R G I A

Batumi

Gori

Tbilisi

Erzurum

ARM

AZERBAIJAN

Yerevan

6

Baku

TURKEY

TURKMENISTAN

Ashgabat

I R A N

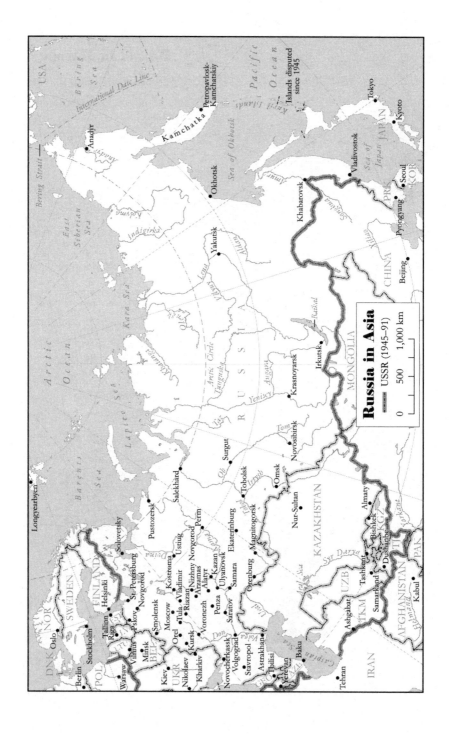

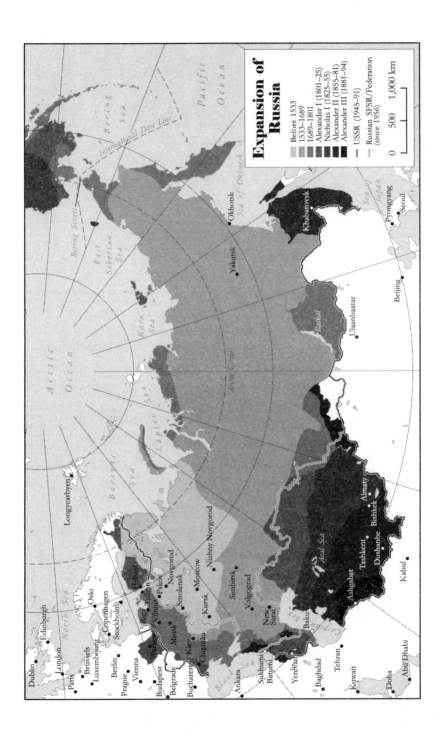

INTRODUCTION

On a cold and grey November morning, in 2016, a small crowd gathered on a snow-cleared square in front of the Kremlin in Moscow. They were there to witness the unveiling of a monument to Grand Prince Vladimir, the ruler of Kievan Rus, 'the first Russian state', between 980 and 1015. According to legend, Vladimir was baptised in the Crimea, then part of the Byzantine Empire, in 988, thus beginning the conversion of his people to the Eastern Orthodox Church. Russia's main religious leaders – the patriarch of Moscow and All-Russia, the Catholic ordinariate, the grand mufti, the chief rabbi and the head of the Buddhist Sangha – were all in attendance in their multicoloured robes.

The bronze figure, bearing cross and sword, stood at over twenty metres tall. It was the latest in a long series of elephantine shrines to Vladimir, all erected since the fall of Communism in the same kitsch 'Russian' national style developed in the nineteenth century. Other Russian towns – Belgorod, Vladimir, Astrakhan, Bataisk and Smolensk – had built monuments to the grand prince with funding from the state and public subscriptions. The Moscow statue was financed by the Ministry of Culture, a military history society and a motorcycle club.[1]

Another Vladimir, President Putin, gave the opening address. Even as he spoke he managed to look bored. He seemed to want the ceremony to be done as soon as possible – perhaps the reason why it started earlier than planned, when the film director Fedor

Bondarchuk, who had vocally supported the recent Russian annexation of Ukrainian Crimea, invited Vladimir Vladimirovich to the microphone. Reading in a flat tone from his script, Putin noted the symbolism of the date for this unveiling, 4 November, Russia's Day of National Unity. The grand prince, he proclaimed, had 'gathered and defended Russia's lands' by 'founding a strong, united and centralised state, incorporating diverse peoples, languages, cultures and religions into one enormous family'. The three modern countries that could trace their origins to Kievan Rus – Russia, Belarus and Ukraine – were all members of this family, Putin continued. They were a single people, or nation, sharing the same Christian principles, the same culture and language, which, he suggested, formed the Slavic bedrock of the Russian Empire and the Soviet Union. His point was echoed by the patriarch Kirill, who spoke next. If Vladimir had chosen to remain a pagan, or had converted only for himself, 'there would be no Russia, no great Russian Empire, no contemporary Russia'.

Natalia Solzhenitsyn, the writer's widow, gave the third and final speech, short and different in tone. The traumatic history of Russia's twentieth century had, she said, divided the country, and 'of all our disagreements, none is more divisive than our past'. She ended with a call to 'respect our history', which meant not just taking pride in it but 'honestly and bravely judging evil, not justifying it or sweeping it under the carpet to hide it from view'.[2] Putin looked uncomfortable.

The Ukrainians were furious. They had their own statue of the grand prince, Volodymyr as they call him. It was built in 1853, when Ukraine had been part of the Russian Empire, high up on the right bank of the Dnieper River overlooking Kiev, the Ukrainian capital. After the collapse of the Soviet Union in 1991, the statue had became a symbol of the country's independence from Russia. Within minutes of the ceremony's closing in Moscow, Ukraine's official Twitter account posted a picture of the Kiev monument with a tweet in English: 'Don't forget what [the] real Prince Volodymyr monument looks like.' The Ukrainian president, Petro Poroshenko, elected in the wake of the 2014 Maidan revolution, accused the Kremlin of appropriating Ukraine's history, comparing its 'imperial' behaviour to the Russian annexation of the Crimea, part of sovereign Ukraine, just before his election.[3]

Kiev and Moscow had been fighting over Volodymyr/Vladimir for several years. The monument in Moscow had been made a metre taller than the one in Kiev, as if to assert the primacy of Russia's claim to the grand prince. While Putin had enlisted Vladimir as the founder of the modern Russian state, the Ukrainians claimed Volodymyr as their own, the 'creator of the medieval European state of Rus-Ukraine', as he had been described by Poroshenko in a 2015 decree on the millennium of the grand prince's death in 1015 (the fact that the term 'Ukraine' would not appear in written sources until the end of the twelfth century – and then only in the sense of *okraina*, an old Slav word for 'periphery' or 'borderland' – was conveniently overlooked). A few months later, Poroshenko added that Volodymyr's decision to baptise Kievan Rus had been 'not only a cultural or political decision, but a European choice' by which Kiev had joined the Christian civilisation of Byzantium.[4] The message was clear: Ukraine wanted to be part of Europe, not a Russian colony.

Both sides were calling on the history of Kievan Rus – a history they share – to reimagine narratives of national identity they could use for their own nationalist purposes. Historically, of course, it makes little sense to talk of either 'Russia' or 'Ukraine' as a nation or a state in the tenth century (or indeed at any time during the medieval period). What we have in the conflict over Volodymyr/ Vladimir is not a genuine historical dispute, but two incompatible foundation myths.

The Kremlin's version – that the Russians, the Ukrainians and the Belarusians were all originally one nation – was invoked to validate its claim to a 'natural' sphere of interest (by which it meant a right of interference) in Ukraine and Belarus. Like many Russians of his generation, schooled in Soviet views of history, Putin never really recognised the independence of Ukraine. As late as 2008, he told the US president that Ukraine was 'not a real country' but a historic part of greater Russia, a borderland protecting Moscow's heartlands from the West. By this imperial logic Russia was entitled to defend itself against Western encroachments into Ukraine. Russia's annexation of the Crimea, the start of a long war against Ukraine, derived from this dubious reading of the country's history. The invasion was Russia's response to the 'putsch' in Kiev, as the Kremlin called the Maidan uprising, which had begun as a popular revolt against the pro-Russian government of Viktor Yanukovich after it had stalled negotiations with the European Union for an Association Agreement promising to bring Ukraine into the Western sphere. Poroshenko meanwhile used the myth of Ukraine's 'European choice' to legitimise the revolution, which had brought him into power, and his later signing of that EU agreement. The people of Ukraine had made their 'European choice' in the Maidan uprising.

'Who controls the past... controls the future: who controls the present controls the past,' George Orwell wrote in *Nineteen Eighty-Four*.[5] The maxim is more true for Russia than for any other country in the world. In Soviet times, when Communism was its certain destiny and history was adjusted to reflect that end, there was a joke, which perhaps Orwell had in mind: 'Russia is a country with a certain future; it is only its past that is unpredictable.'

No other country has reimagined its own past so frequently; none has a history so subjected to the vicissitudes of ruling ideologies. History in Russia is political. Drawing lessons from the country's past has always been the most effective way to win an argument about future directions and policies. All the great debates about the country's character and destiny have been framed by questions about history. The controversy between the Westernisers and the Slavophiles, which dominated Russia's intellectual life in the nineteenth century, came down to a conflict over history. For those who looked to the West for their inspiration, Russia had been strengthened by the Westernising reforms introduced by Peter the Great in the early eighteenth century; but according to the Slavophiles, Russia's native culture and traditions, its national cohesion, had been undermined by Peter's imposition of alien Western ways on the Russians.

Today the role of history in such debates is more important than ever. In Putin's system, where there are no left–right party divisions, no competing ideologies to frame debate, and no publicly agreed meanings for key concepts like 'democracy' or 'freedom', the discourse of politics is defined by ideas of the country's past. Once the regime lays its meaning on an episode from Russian history, that subject is politicised. This is nothing new. Soviet historians were even more the hostages to changes in the Party Line, particularly under Stalin, when history was falsified to elevate his own significance and discredit his rivals. Some were forced to 'correct' their work, while others had their works removed from libraries or were banned from publishing again.

Even before 1917, history was carefully censored. It was a question not just of preventing the publication of ideas and facts that could be politically dangerous (anything that portrayed the autocracy unfavourably) but of making sure that the official story of the country's past was not undermined in a way that challenged current policies. Ukrainian historians were particularly closely watched because of their presumed sympathy for European principles. They were not allowed to publish in Ukrainian, encourage nationalist feelings for Ukraine, or to promote a sense of grievance against Russia.[6]

Beyond such controlling narratives, history-writing in Russia, since its beginning in medieval chronicles, has been intertwined in mythical ideas – the myths of 'Holy Russia', the 'holy tsar', the 'Russian soul', Moscow as the 'Third Rome' and so on. These myths became fundamental to the Russians' understanding of their history and national character. They have often guided – and misguided – Western policies and attitudes towards Russia. To understand contemporary Russia we need to unpack these myths, explain their historical development and explore how they informed that country's actions and identity.

The great cultural historian of Russian myths, Michael Cherniavsky, proffered a persuasive explanation for their extraordinary power and resilience over many centuries:

It has been observed by many that myths, rather than approximating reality, tend to be in direct contradiction to it. And Russian reality was 'unholy' enough to have produced the 'holiest' myths of them all. The greater the power of the government, the more extreme was the myth required to justify it and excuse submission to it; the greater the misery of the Russian people, the more extreme was the eschatological jump the myth had to provide so as to justify the misery and transcend it.[7]

Many writers have observed the Russian people's need for transcendental myths promising a better version of Russia. In Dostoevsky's novels, where suffering and salvation are such frequent themes, it appears as the essence of the Russian character. The endurance of these myths explains much in Russia's history: the lasting force of Orthodox beliefs; the people's search for a holy tsar, the embodiment of their ideals, to deliver them from injustice; their dreams of building heaven on this earth, a revolutionary utopia, even when this dream turned out to be the nightmare of the Stalinist regime.

All of which is to explain why this book is called *The Story of Russia*. It is as much about the ideas, myths and ideologies that have shaped the country's history, about the ways the Russians have interpreted their past, as it is about the events, institutions, social groups, artists, thinkers and leaders that have made that history.

The book begins in the first millennium, when Russia's lands were settled by the Slavs, and ends with Putin, in the third, examining the myths of Russian history which he has used to bolster his authoritarian regime. Its underlying argument is simply put: Russia is a country held together by ideas rooted in its distant past, histories continuously reconfigured and repurposed to suit its present needs and reimagine its future. How the Russians came to tell their story – and to reinvent it as they went along – is a vital aspect of their history. It is the underlying framework of this history.

The cult of the grand prince Vladimir, 'Equal of the Apostles', as he's called, is an illustration of this reinvention of the past. Almost nothing about him is known. There are no contemporary documents, only later chronicles by monks, hagiographic legends of his conversion, which served as a sacred myth legitimising his descendants, the rulers of Kievan Rus. Vladimir was one of many princes to be made a saint in the medieval period. But it was only later, from the sixteenth century, that his cult assumed a more important status, when Ivan IV ('the Terrible') promoted it as the basis of his bogus claim, as Moscow's tsar, to be the sole legitimate successor to the Kievan rulers and the emperors of Byzantium. The myth was used as part of Russia's struggle against Poland and Lithuania, which possessed parts of what had once been Kievan Rus. From Ivan's reign, Vladimir was hailed as 'the first Russian tsar', the holy 'gatherer of the Russian lands', in a legendary narrative whose purpose was to trace the roots of Moscow's growing empire to Kievan Rus and Byzantium as its sacred foundations.[8]

This foundation myth was fundamental to the Romanovs, who had no descendance from the Kievan princes on which to base their fragile dynasty, founded after years of civil war in 1613. To symbolise a Kievan legacy and strengthen Moscow's claim to rule Ukraine, Mikhail, the founder of the dynasty, had the relics of Prince Vladimir (except for his head) brought from Kiev to Moscow, where they remained in the Kremlin's Dormition Cathedral until 1917. As the Russian Empire grew, swallowing most of Ukraine in the eighteenth century, the cult of Vladimir became the focus of its justifying myth. His life was venerated as a symbol of the empire's sacred origins and the united 'family' or 'nation' of Russians – the Great Russians, the Little Russians (Ukrainians) and the White Russians (Belarusians) as they were called in this imperial discourse. This was the intended Russian meaning of the Kiev monument to Vladimir when it was unveiled in 1853, although by the end of the nineteenth century it was already being contested by Ukrainian nationalists, who, like Poroshenko, claimed the statue as their own – a symbol of their European nationhood.[9]

Along with the myths that have shaped Russia's past, there are a number of recurring themes in *The Story of Russia*. These themes reflect the structural continuities of Russian history – geographic factors, systems of belief, modes of rule, political ideas and social customs – which remain so important for an informed understanding of Russia today. Contemporary Russian politics are too often analysed without knowledge of the country's past. To grasp what Putin really means for Russia and the broader world, we need to understand how his governance relates to the long-term patterns of Russian history, and what it means to Russians when he appeals to those 'traditional values'.

These deep structural continuities will become apparent in my narrative, but it is worth making one or two clear right from the start. The first is the most obvious: Russia's vast size and geography. Why did Russia grow so big? How was it able to expand so far across Eurasia and incorporate so many different nationalities (194 were recognised by the first Soviet census in 1926)? What was the impact of Russia's size on the evolution of the Russian state? The eighteenth-century empress Catherine the Great maintained that a country as big as Russia needed to be governed by autocracy: 'Only swiftness of decision in matters sent from distant realms can compensate for the slowness caused by these great distances. Any other form of government would be not merely harmful, but utterly ruinous for Russia.'[10] But did this have to be the case? Were there not other forms of representative or local government that might have taken the place of an autocratic state?

Russia developed on a flat and open territory without natural boundaries. Its position made it vulnerable to foreign invasion but also open to the influence of the surrounding powers – Khazars, Mongols, Byzantines, Europeans and Ottomans – with which its relations were defined by trade. As the Russian state grew stronger, a process we should date from the sixteenth century, its main focus was the defence of its frontiers. This priority involved certain patterns of development that have shaped the country's history.

It entailed the subordination of society to the state and its military needs. Social classes were created and legally defined to benefit the state as taxpayers and military servitors. It also meant a policy of territorial aggrandisement to secure Russia's frontiers. From the rise of Muscovy, or Moscow, the founding core of the Russian state, to Putin's wars in Ukraine, history shows that Russia tends to advance its security by keeping neighbouring countries weak, and by fighting wars beyond its borders to keep hostile powers at arm's length. Does this mean that Russia is expansionist in character, as so many of its critics in the modern age have said? Or should its tendency to push outwards and colonise the spaces around it be viewed rather as a defensive reaction, stemming from its perceived need for buffer states to protect it on the open steppe?

The nature of state power is the other theme worth mentioning here. Catherine the Great was in the habit of comparing Russia to the European absolutist states. But the Russian state was not like them. It had evolved as a patrimonial or personal autocracy, in which the concept of the state (*gosudarstvo*) was embodied in the person of the tsar (*gosudar*) as the sovereign lord or owner of the Russian lands. In medieval Europe the legal separation of the 'king's two bodies' – his mortal person and the sacred office of the monarchy – allowed for the development of an abstract and impersonal conception of the state.[11] But that did not happen in Russia. From the reign of Ivan IV, the tsar and state were seen as one – united in the body of a single being, who, as man and ruler, was an instrument of God.

The sacralisation of the tsar's authority, a legacy of Byzantium, was both a strength and a weakness of the Russian state. The myth of the tsar as a sacred agent was, on the one hand, essential to the cult of the holy tsar that underpinned the monarchy until the twentieth century, when the myth was at last broken by Nicholas II's repressive measures against popular protests. On the other hand, the same myth could be used by rebel leaders, as it was by the Cossack-led rebellions of the seventeenth and eighteenth centuries, to subvert the tsar's power. In the popular imagination the holy tsar was the deliverer of truth and social justice (*pravda*) to the people. But if the tsar brought injustice, he could not be the 'true tsar' – he was perhaps the Antichrist sent by Satan to destroy God's work in the 'Russian holy land' – and as such should be opposed. By claiming they were fighting to restore the true tsar to the throne, the Cossack rebel leaders were able to attract a mass following in protest movements that shook the state at crisis moments in its modern history.

Similar ideas of truth and justice would underpin the Russian Revolution of 1917. The myth of the holy tsar would also give way to the leader cults of Lenin and Stalin, whose statues would appear on every square. Putin's regime draws from this monarchical archetype of governance, giving the appearance of stability based on 'Russian traditions'.

Putin's cult has not been set in stone. There are no statues of him yet in public squares. But some wits said on the unveiling of the Moscow monument to Prince Vladimir that a statue of his namesake, the Russian president, would soon appear by the Kremlin wall.

Kievan Rus
11th century

0   100   200   300 km

I

ORIGINS

All countries have a story of their origin. Some invoke divine or classical mythologies, stories linking them to sacred acts of creation or ancient civilisations, but most, at least in Europe, have foundation myths generally invented in the eighteenth or early nineteenth centuries. This was a time when nationalist historians, philologists and archaeologists sought to trace their nations back to a primeval ethnos – homogeneous, immutable, containing all the seeds of the modern national character – which they saw reflected in whatever remnants they could find of the early peoples in their territories. The Celts, the Franks, the Gauls, the Goths, the Huns and the Serbs – all have served as the ur-people of a modern nationhood, although in truth they were complex social groups, formed over centuries of great migrations across the European continent.[1]

The origins of Russia are a case in point. No other country has been so divided over its own beginnings. None has changed its story so often. The subject is inseparable from myth. The only written account that we have, the *Tale of Bygone Years*, known as the *Primary Chronicle*, was compiled by the monk Nestor and other monks in Kiev during the 1110s. It tells us how, in 862, the warring Slavic tribes of north-west Russia agreed jointly to invite the Rus, a branch of the Vikings, to rule over them: 'Our land is vast and abundant, but there is no order in it. Come and reign as princes and have authority over us!'[2] Three princely brothers, the

Rus, arrived in longboats with their kin. They were accepted by the Slavs. Two brothers died but the third, Riurik, continued ruling over Novgorod, the most important of the northern trading towns, until his death in 879, when his son Oleg succeeded him. Three years later, Oleg captured Kiev, according to this story, and Kievan Rus, the first 'Russian' state, was established.

The *Primary Chronicle* reads more like a fairy tale than a work of history. It is a typical foundation myth – composed to establish the political legitimacy of the Riurikids, the Kievan ruling dynasty, as God's chosen agents for the Christianisation of the Rus lands. Much of it is fictional – stories patched together from orally transmitted epic songs and narrative poems (known in Russian as *byliny*), Norse sagas, Slav folklore, old Byzantine annals and religious texts. Nothing in it can be taken as a fact. We cannot say for sure whether Riurik even existed. He may have been Rörik, the nephew, son or possibly the brother of the Danish monarch Harald Klak, who was alive at the right time. But there is no evidence connecting him to Kiev, so the founder of the dynasty may have been a different Viking warrior, or an allegorical figure.[3] The Kievan monks were less concerned with the accuracy of their chronicle than with its religious symbolism and meaning. The timescale of the chronicle is biblical. It charts the history of the Rus from Noah in the Book of Genesis, claiming them to be the descendants of his son Japheth, so that Kievan Rus is understood to have been created as part of the divine plan.[4]

The *Primary Chronicle* was at the heart of a debate on Russia's origins that goes back to the first half of the eighteenth century, when history-writing in Russia was in its infancy. The new academic discipline was dominated by Germans. Among them was Gerhard Friedrich Müller (1705–83), who at the age of twenty had joined the teaching staff of the newly founded St Petersburg Academy of Sciences. Müller was the founding editor of the first series of documents and articles on Russian history, the *Sammlung Russischer Geschichte* (1732–65), published in German to inform a European readership, which knew almost nothing about Russia and its history. The peak of his career came in 1749, when he was tasked with giving an oration for the Empress Elizabeth on her name day. His lecture was entitled 'On the Origins of the Russian People and their Name'.

In it Müller summarised the findings of other German scholars, who had concluded from their reading of the *Primary Chronicle* that Russia owed its origins to the Vikings. The Rus, he said, were Scandinavians, whose tribal name derived from *Ruotsi*, a term used by the Finns to describe the Swedes from Roslagen. But this was not the moment to suggest that Russia was created by the Swedes, or any other foreigners. Russia's victory in the recent war against Sweden (1741–3) had bolstered patriotic sentiments, which extended to the country's past. Müller's lecture was roundly criticised at the Academy. A scrutiny committee was appointed to decide whether it could be delivered – if not on the empress's name day on 5 September then on the seventh anniversary of her coronation on 25 November – without bringing Russia 'into disrepute'. Mikhail Lomonosov, Russia's first great polymath, led the attack on the German, accusing him of setting out to denigrate the Slavs by depicting them as savages, incapable of organising themselves as a state. The Rus, he insisted, were not Swedes but Baltic Slavs, descendants of the Iranian Roxolani tribe, whose history went back to the Trojan Wars. National pride coloured Lomonosov's criticisms, along with a personal dislike of the German. He wrongly claimed that Müller was unable to read Russian documents, that he made gross errors as a consequence and that, like all foreigners, he could not really know the country's history because he was not Russian.

Six months of academic arguments ensued. On 8 March 1750, the scrutiny committee banned Müller's lecture and confiscated all the printed copies of it in both Russian and Latin. Lomonosov took part in the raid. The German was demoted to a junior post and barred from working in the state archive, supposedly to defend the Russian Empire from his attempts to 'besmirch' its history. Müller's academic career never fully recovered, but he published many books, including *Origines gentis et nominis Russorum* (1761), which developed the ideas of his lecture. Published first in

Germany, *Origines* did not appear in Russian until 1773, a decade after Lomonosov's *Ancient Russian History*, a book written as a refutation of Müller's argument.[5]

The debate on Russia's origins has continued to this day. Known as the Normanist Controversy (because the Vikings were Normans), it is highly charged with politics and ideology. The question at its heart is whether Russia was created by the Russians or by foreigners.

In the final decades of the eighteenth century, Müller's 'Norman theory' gained acceptance in the St Petersburg Academy, where German-born historians were dominant. They propagated the theory that Riurik had belonged to a Germanic tribe of Scandinavia and that Russia as a state and culture had thus been founded by Germans. Catherine the Great (herself German-born) supported their position, because it suggested that the Russians were of European stock, a viewpoint she promoted in her many works. In German hands the Normanist position entailed sometimes racist attitudes towards the Slavs. Typical is this passage from a study of the *Primary Chronicle* by August Ludwig von Schlözer in 1802:

> Of course there were people there [in Russia], God knows for
> how long and from where they came, but they were people
> without any leadership, living like wild beasts and birds in their
> vast forests ... No enlightened European had noticed them or
> had written about them. There was not a single real town in
> the whole of the North ... Wild, boorish and isolated Slavs
> began to be socially acceptable only thanks to the Germans,
> whose mission, decreed by fate, was to sow the first seeds of
> civilization among them.[6]

The Norman theory appealed to defenders of autocracy, supposing as it did that the warring Slavic tribes were incapable of governing themselves. Foremost among them was Nikolai Karamzin, Russia's first great writer and historian, who leaned heavily on Schlözer's work in his *History of the Russian State* (published in twelve volumes between 1818 and 1829). Before the establishment of foreign princely rule, Karamzin declared, Russia had been nothing but an 'empty space' with 'wild and warring tribes, living on a level with the beasts and birds'.[7]

These views were challenged in the nineteenth century by philologists and archaeologists. Often motivated by nationalist pride in Russia's ancient Slav culture, they looked for evidence that underlined its advanced social life in the first millennium. The anti-Normanists, as they were called, argued that the Rus were not from Scandinavia (they were not mentioned in the Old Norse sources or sagas) but were Slavs, whose name, they argued, had appeared in Greek sources from the second century and in Arab from the fifth. The Rus homeland, they maintained, was in Ukraine and was marked by Slavic river names (Ros, Rosava, Rusna, Rostavtsya and so on). Excavations of their settlements revealed that they were built in a defensive circle, in stark contrast to the Vikings' open settlements, and that they had attained a high level of material culture from their contacts with Hellenic, Byzantine and Asiatic civilisations long before the Vikings had arrived.

The fortunes of the anti-Normanists rose in line with the influence of nationalism on the Russian state. They peaked in Stalin's time, particularly after 1945, when a Great Russian chauvinism, boosted by the victory over Nazi Germany, was placed at the heart of Soviet ideology. The ethno-archaeology of early Slavic settlements became heavily politicised. Massive state investments were made in excavations whose remit was to show a 'Slavic homeland' stretching from the Volga River in the east to the Elbe River in the west, from the Baltic in the north to the Aegean and Black Seas – in other words the area that Stalin claimed as a Soviet 'sphere of influence' during the Cold War. The idea that Russia owed its origins to any foreign power – least of all to the 'Germanic' Vikings – became inadmissible. Scholars who had dared to suggest so were forced by the Party to revise their work.[8]

The Soviet view of Russia's origins was thus entangled in a concept of ethnicity, in which the *ethnos* was regarded as an ancient core of national identity, persisting throughout history, despite changes in society. At a time when Western scholars were coming to the view that ethnic groups were modern intellectual constructions, invented categories imposed on complex social groups, their Soviet counterparts were analysing them as primordial entities defined by biology. Through the study of ethnogenesis they traced modern Russia to a single people in the Iron Age, claiming that the Russians were descendants of the ancient Slavs.

This approach resurfaced with an even greater force after the collapse of the Soviet Union, when Russian, Ukrainian and Belarusian nationalists competed with each other for an ethnic claim of origin from the Kievan legacy. Here was Putin's purpose in his speech on the unveiling of the Moscow monument to Prince Vladimir. Asserting Russia's inheritance from Kiev, he invoked the old imperial myth that the Russians, the Ukrainians and the Belarusians were historically one people, three ethnic sub-groups of a single nation, thus establishing a 'natural' sphere of influence for today's Russia in its original 'ancestral lands'. History of course is more complex – even if it is a story too.

Russia grew on the forest lands and steppes between Europe and Asia. There are no natural boundaries, neither seas nor mountain ranges, to define its territory, which throughout its history has been colonised by peoples from both continents. The Ural mountains, said to be the frontier dividing 'European Russia' from Siberia, offered no protection to the Russian settlers against the nomadic tribes from the Asiatic steppe. They are a series of high ranges broken up by broad passes. In many places they are more like hills. It is significant that the word in Russian for a 'hill' or 'mountain' is the same (*gora*). This is a country on one horizontal plain.

On either side of the Urals the terrain is the same: a vast steppe, eleven time zones long, stretching from the borderlands of Russia in the west to the Pacific Ocean in the east. This territorial continuum is made up of four bands or zones that run in parallel from one end to the other, more or less. The first of these zones, around one-fifth of Russia's land mass, is above the Arctic circle, where the treeless tundra remains under snow and ice for eight months every year. Nomadic reindeer-herders, fur- and walrus-hunters were the only people to inhabit these regions until the twentieth century, when the discovery of coal, gold, platinum and diamonds in the permafrost led to the Gulag's colonisation of the Arctic zone, where 2 million Russians live today. Most of them are descendants of the Gulag's prisoners.

Moving south, we come next to the taiga forest zone, the largest coniferous forest in the world, stretching from the Baltic to the Pacific. It is made up of pine trees, spruce and larch, interspersed with marshes, lakes and gentle-running rivers, the fastest means of travel in this zone until the nineteenth century.

Pine forests give way to mixed woodlands and open wooded steppelands to the south of Moscow, where the rich black soil is in places up to several metres deep. This third band of Russia's land, known as the central agricultural zone, is wide at the western end, where it merges into the Hungarian plain, but narrows in the east, towards Siberia, where the taiga takes over. The fertile zone was secured by the Russians from the sixteenth century.

Finally, in the far south, we come to the Pontic steppe, the semi-arid grasslands and savannas running from the Black Sea's northern coastline in the west to the Caspian Sea and Kazakhstan in the east. The area was conquered by the Russians from the nomadic Turkic tribes only from the eighteenth century. It forms the religious fault line between Russia and the Muslim world.

The earliest recorded settlers in the lands that became known as Kievan Rus were the Slavs, although there were Finno-Ugric tribes, such as the Estonians, in the northern forest zones from the middle of the first millennium. According to the story told by most historians, the Slavs were forced to flee to the forests of the north by the Turkic tribes, whose military power gave them control of the grasslands further south. The Slavs spread out through the great primeval forests in small groups, clearing trees and burning their debris to sow crops in the ashen ground (a method known as slash and burn). Farming in the northern forest zone was arduous. A strong collectivism was essential to survive. Labour teams were needed to clear the trees, and to sow and harvest all the crops during the short growing season between the thaw and spring

floods of April and the beginning of the winter freeze in October.
The soil is poor, sandy, thin, on top of rock. Only rye, among the
cereals, could be grown here, and the harvest yields were low. Yet
the forests gave the peasants other means of livelihood: furs, honey,
wax, fishing, carpentry.

The Slavs lived in settlements enclosed by wooden walls.
Democratic in their character, they were governed by assemblies of
the adult men (the Byzantines considered their democracy 'disorder
and anarchy').⁹ Masters of the axe, the Slavs were skilled in turning
trees into buildings, longboats and canoes, meaning they were
able to add fishing and trade along the rivers to their means of
livelihood. Their numbers grew, forcing the Finno-Ugric tribes to
retreat deeper into the forest. By the end of the first millennium,
the Slavs had developed a durable, adaptive peasant culture, based
on collectivism and a spirit of endurance which have characterised
the Russians for much of their history.

The Vikings came to Russia, not to loot, as they did in England
(Russia was too poor for that), but to use its many waterways for
long-distance trade between Europe and Asia. The name of the
Rus was probably derived from the Old Norse word *róa*, which
means 'to row', suggesting that the Rus were known as boatmen
and most probably were quite diverse in ethnic terms. They were
not a tribe united by a common ethnic origin but an army based
on a common business enterprise. They sailed in their longboats
from the eastern Swedish coast to the mouth of the Neva River,
the location of St Petersburg today. From there they rowed up
the Neva to Lake Ladoga, an important trading post, where they
obtained slaves and precious furs from the Slavs and other peoples
of the north (the words 'Slav' and 'slave' became synonymous in
the Viking lexicon). The cargo was transported south along the
Dnieper, Don and Volga rivers, across the Black Sea and the
Caspian, to the markets of Byzantium and the Arab caliphate,
where slaves and furs were highly prized. The Rus returned with
silver coins, glass beads, metalwares and jewellery – artefacts
retrieved by archaeologists from graves at Old Ladoga, thought
to be the earliest Viking settlement, dating back to the eighth

century. The graves also contained leather shoes, combs made of bone and antlers, runic amulets and wooden sticks of a kind found in Scandinavia too.[10]

The Rus quickly settled down and assimilated into the Slav populace. Settlements like Old Ladoga were polyethnic communities with a Viking warrior elite, Slav and Finnic farmers and craftsmen. The Rus adopted the Slavs' language, names, customs and religious rituals, a process of assimilation accelerated by their shared conversion to Christianity during the tenth century. For this reason there are few Scandinavian traces in the Russian language or place names in Russia – a marked contrast with the heavy Viking influence on both language and place names in England and Germany.[11]

The Rus made a strong impression on the Arabs who encountered them. Ibn Fadlan met a group of merchants at Itil, on the Volga near the Caspian Sea, in 921:

> I have seen the Rus as they came on their merchant journeys and encamped by Itil. I have never seen more perfect physical specimens, tall as date palms, blond and ruddy; they wear neither tunics nor kaftans, but the men wear a garment which covers one side of the body and leaves a hand free. Each man has an axe, a sword, and a knife, and keeps each by him at all times. Each woman wears on either breast a box of iron, silver, copper, or gold; the value of the box indicates the wealth of the husband. Each box has a ring from which depends a knife. The women wear neck-rings of gold and silver. Their most prized ornaments are green glass beads. They string them as necklaces for their women.[12]

Itil was the capital of the Khazar state, or khaganate, a multi-confessional trading empire, headed by a Turkic warrior elite, which extended from the Aral Sea to the Carpathian Mountains, from the Caucasus to the upper Volga forest lands. It had an ordered government, efficient means of tax collecting and the military power to protect the river trading routes against the nomadic tribes, the most dangerous being the Polovtsians (also known as Kipchaks or Cumans). Founded as a series of scattered settlements in the middle of the first millennium, Kiev had developed as a Khazar stronghold controlling the Dnieper River on the trading route between the Baltic and Byzantium.

The Khazar influence on the development of Kievan Rus is a matter of controversy. Some scholars think that Khazars played a more important part than the Vikings or the Slavs.[13] Byzantine and Arab writers described the Rus as vassals of the khaganate, linked to it through marriages. The first Rus rulers called themselves khagans, suggesting that they derived their authority from the Khazars. They certainly had better relations with the Khazars than allowed by the medieval chronicles, which paint a picture of unending raids and violence by the Turkic-speaking Khazar tribes against peaceful Russian settlers. Historians of Russia in the nineteenth century relied completely on these chronicles. They told a story of the nation's beginnings as an epic struggle by the agriculturalists of the northern forest lands against the horsemen of the Asiatic steppe. This national myth became so fundamental to the Russians' European self-identity that even to suggest that their ancestors had been influenced by the Asiatic cultures of the steppe was to invite accusations of treason. In fact raids by the steppeland tribes were infrequent, and there were long periods of peaceful coexistence, trade, cooperation, social intermingling and even intermarriage between the Slavs and their nomadic neighbours on the steppe. The influence of the steppeland tribes was manifested in the Rus elite's adoption of their dress and status symbols, such as the wearing of belts studded with heavy metal mounts and bridles with elaborate sets of ornaments.[14] We need to think of early Rus, not as a story of hostile confrontation between the forest settlers and steppe nomads, but as one of largely peaceful interaction between all the peoples of Eurasia. We should think of it, perhaps, not in terms of ethnic groups at all, but as a trading union of diverse groups – Slavs, Finns, Vikings and Khazars.[15]

Kievan Rus emerged as the Khazar state declined. The growing military power of the Rus enabled them to free themselves from paying taxes to the khaganate; it also allowed them to assume the latter's role as the protector of the northern borders of Byzantium, a role which brought them rich rewards in the form of trade concessions in Constantinople, the Byzantine capital. As their power grew, the Rus warriors attacked the Khazar tribute-paying lands between the Volga and Dnieper. In 882 they captured Kiev, which became the capital of Kievan Rus.

Under the first Rus princes Kiev developed into an important trading centre between the Black and Baltic seas. In the Podol district of the city archaeologists have found large quantities of Byzantine coinage, amphoras and the weights of scales, as well as the remains of log houses built in a technique (without using nails) associated with the Russian north. To grow the population and tax base of the new state the grand prince Vladimir forcibly transported entire Slav communities from the northern forests to the regions around Kiev. It was the start of a long tradition of mass population movements enforced by the Russian state.[16]

Establishing their power-base in Kiev entailed two important changes for the Rus. First there was a shift in focus from long-distance trade to the business of collecting tribute, from which they had seen the Khazars thrive. Lands once controlled by the khaganate were now taxed by Kiev, which built forts and towns to protect its dominion of the western steppe. Secondly, the main flow of trade moved from the Volga and the Muslim world to the Dnieper and Byzantium. This turn to the south was consolidated by a series of commercial treaties between Kievan Rus and the Byzantine Empire. Each was preceded by a Rus attack on Constantinople whose aim was to force the Byzantines to open up their markets and improve the terms of trade. The first of these treaties, in 911, made generous concessions to the Rus traders.

Through trade and diplomacy pagan Rus was drawn into the Christian civilisation of the Byzantine Empire. Princess Olga, who reigned as a regent of Kievan Rus between 945 and 960, led the way. She had herself baptised in Constantinople, where she cemented a military alliance with the emperor by adopting for herself the same name as the reigning empress Helen (Elena in Russian). Her son

Sviatoslav remained a pagan, but her grandson, the grand prince Vladimir, had not just himself but all his realm converted to the Eastern Orthodox Church in 988.

According to the *Primary Chronicle*, Vladimir's conversion was the outcome of his search for the True Faith. The story goes that he was visited by representatives of the neighbouring states, each one seeking to convert him to their religion. First came the Islamic envoy of the Volga Bulgars, who enticed Vladimir with promises of carnal satisfaction in the afterlife (this was a man who, according to legend, had 800 wives), but put him off entirely with the Muslim ban on alcohol ('Drinking is the joy of the Rus. We cannot live without it,' the prince declared). Next came the German papal emissaries, followed by a Khazar delegation of rabbis (the Khazar leaders had embraced Judaism during the ninth century). Neither impressed Vladimir. Finally the Byzantines arrived. Their arguments persuaded him to send his envoys to observe the various faiths in their own environment. Among the Volga Bulgars they found only 'sorrow and a dreadful stench'. In Germany they 'beheld no glory'. But in the Hagia Sophia of Constantinople, 'We knew not whether we were in heaven or on earth,' they reported on the liturgy in the basilica, 'for surely there is no such splendour or beauty anywhere on earth. We cannot describe it to you. We only know that God dwells there among men. For we cannot forget that beauty.'[17]

Like the rest of the *Primary Chronicle*, the story is apocryphal. Vladimir's conversion had more to do with statecraft and diplomacy than with the aesthetics of religious rites. The acquisition of a single, unifying religion could help to legitimise the Kievan state and extend its authority throughout its multi-ethnic territory, where various beliefs and pagan cults militated against princely rule. The existence of a readily translated Church Slavonic literature – enabling the dissemination of its teachings over a large area – gave the Orthodox Christians a clear advantage over other religions whose scriptures were not yet in Slavonic. The key factor here was the work of the brothers Cyril and Methodius, the ninth-century missionaries sent by the Byzantine emperor to spread Christianity among the Slavs. They had translated the Greek Gospels into the Glagolitic script (an early version of Cyrillic, named after Cyril by his followers). This had made it possible to have a Christian service in the Slavic tongue rather than in Greek, which the population did not understand.[18]

At this point in the *Primary Chronicle* we are told that Vladimir converted in the Crimea, where he had gone with 6,000 of his warriors to crush a rebellion against the Byzantine emperor Basil II. The prize for his service was the hand of Anna, the emperor's sister, upon his conversion to Christianity. After he had put down the revolt, the *Chronicle* informs us, he had to threaten an attack on Constantinople before Basil honoured his end of the bargain and the marriage was secured. All this may be nothing but legend, a story later told by the monks in Kiev to depict Vladimir and therefore Kievan Rus as an equal to Byzantium, instead of a vassal state. It is just as likely that Vladimir had put down the uprising as an agent of the Byzantines, and as such had been made to convert before his departure for the Crimea.[19] Instead of the act of self-determination celebrated by the modern Russian and Ukrainian states, Vladimir's conversion to the Eastern Church may have been a declaration of his kingdom's subjugation to the Byzantine Empire.

Vladimir's conversion brought Russia into the cultural orbit of Byzantium. This involved a revolution, not just in the country's spiritual life but in its art and architecture, literature, philosophy, in the symbolic language and ideas of the state.

Byzantium was a universal culture, a 'commonwealth', to adopt the term of its great Anglo-Russian scholar Dimitri Obolensky. Its peoples were united by the dual symbolic power of the emperor (the *basileus* in Greek or *tsar* in Church Slavonic) and the ecumenical patriarch of Constantinople, who appointed Kiev's metropolitan, the head of the Russian Church.[20] The role of Byzantium was thus similar to that of Rome in the Latin West. Just as the Latins looked to Rome as the centre of their civilisation, so the Russians saw Constantinople (which they called Tsargrad, the Imperial City) as their spiritual capital.

Through Byzantium the Russians were connected to the Greeks, Bulgarians, Serbs, Albanians and Romanians, all affiliated to the Eastern Orthodox Church. Through its broader links to Christendom, they also entered into closer contact with Europe, becoming conscious of themselves as Europeans belonging to a common faith. As Obolensky put it, 'Byzantium was not a wall, erected between Russia and the West: she was Russia's gateway to Europe.'[21]

Although Vladimir had converted Rus to Christianity, it was his son Yaroslav who built most of its first great churches as grand prince of Kiev from 1019 to 1054. Having fought his brothers for the throne, Yaroslav had come to see that building churches would advance his prestige and secure his power-base in Kiev. The most important was the Church of St Sophia, closely modelled on the Hagia Sophia in Constantinople with its simple cross-in-square formation, Greek inscriptions, monumental frescoes and colourful mosaics, dominated by the massive, solemn face of Christ Pantokrator staring down from the heaven of the central dome. Beneath him are mosaics of the apostles, the Mother of God and the Eucharist, the three avenues by which the holy spirit descended to the earth, symbolising Christ's incarnation in nature.

Like other Russian churches, St Sophia had a row of icons on a low screen between the altar and the worshippers. Later it would be replaced by a high wall of icons, the iconostasis, whose visual beauty is a central feature of the Eastern Church. Seeing is believing for the Orthodox. Russians pray with their eyes open – their gaze fixed on an icon, which serves as a window on the divine sphere.[22] The icon is the focal point of the believers' spiritual emotions – a sacred object able to elicit miracles. Icons weep and produce myrrh. They are lost and reappear, intervening in events to steer them on a divine path. Not only paintings had this status in Russia: wood carvings, mosaics, even buildings could be icons too.[23] In contrast to the Western Christian mind, where the divine existed only in the heavens, in Russia the divine was immanent in worldly existence. Here were the roots of the utopian consciousness which lay at the heart of the Russian peasant religion: the belief in the certainty of building heaven on this earth, and specifically on Russian soil, according to the early Christian myth of Holy Russia, a new land of salvation where Christ would reappear.

Icons came to Russia from Byzantium. To begin with, they were painted by Greek artists, and remained austerely Greek in style. It was only from the thirteenth century that a more distinctive Russian style appeared. This native mode was distinguished by a simple harmony of line and colour, graceful movements and a skilful use of inverse perspective (where lines seem to converge on a point in front of the picture) to draw the viewer in and guide him in his prayers by symbolising how the icon's sacred action takes place in a sphere beyond the normal laws of existence.[24]

A similar transition towards Russian native forms can be seen in literature. Church Slavonic became the foundation of a literary language in Russia. Based on the South Slav dialect spoken around Thessaloniki, where Cyril and Methodius had lived, it followed Greek syntax – an influence that flowed into Russian. But the Greek influence was not entirely dominant. In the *Primary Chronicle* there is a distinctly Russian ideology.

At the heart of the *Primary Chronicle* is a myth that was to play a central role in the Russian political consciousness. Its basis is the sacred nature of the prince who dies as a martyr for the 'Holy Russian land'. The origins of this idea can be traced back to the cult of Boris and Gleb, the first saints of the Russian Church. The two brothers had been killed in the dynastic wars following the death of their father Vladimir in 1015. But their hagiographers, beginning with Nestor in the *Primary Chronicle*, presented them as 'passion-sufferers' (*strastoterptsy*), who had willingly laid down their lives for the salvation of the Russian land, as Christ had done for Palestine. Their sacrifice was venerated by the Church as the forging of a covenant between God and the newly baptised Rus, a new *Terra Sancta*, which was thus endowed with special grace (the origins of 'Holy Rus' and the 'Holy Russian land'). Churches of Boris and Gleb were built. The two saints were venerated in icons. They gave their name to monasteries and towns (and much later on to tsarist dragoon regiments, Soviet airbases and submarines). From the worship of these 'saintly princes', the cult of the holy prince or ruler would develop in Russia (as would the cult of the revolution's fallen heroes, who were also venerated as the 'people's saints' during 1917).[25] Of the 800 Russian saints created up until the eighteenth century, over a hundred had been princes or princesses.[26] No other country in the world has made so many saints from its rulers. Nowhere else has power been so sacralised.

Christianity was slow to spread through Kievan Rus. Long after Vladimir's conversion, paganism remained deeply rooted in the countryside and many towns. In 1071, when the clergy came to Novgorod and threw the pagan idols into the Volkhov River, there was a popular rebellion. The uprising was suppressed and a wooden church of St Sophia built; but only slowly did the Novgorodians exchange the amulets they wore to ward off evil spirits for crucifixes and icons.

Pagan idols were not gods in the Greek sense but natural forces and spirits, which appeared in ordinary people's daily lives. There was Perun, god of lightning and thunder; Volos, protector of the herds; Rozhanitsa, goddess of fertility; Mokosh, goddess of the earth (reincarnated as Mother Russia later on); Dazhborg and Khors, who were both sun gods. With the arrival of Christianity these gods did not disappear but were incorporated into the new system of beliefs and rituals. Saints and natural deities were frequently combined in the peasants' Christian–pagan religion. Poludnitsa, the old pagan goddess of the harvest, was worshipped through the placement of a sheaf of rye behind an icon; Volos morphed into St Vlasius; and Perun became St Elias. The Christianisation of the pagan deities was practised by the Orthodox Church itself. At the core of the Russian faith is a distinctive stress on motherhood which never really took root in the Latin West. Where the Catholic tradition placed its emphasis on the Madonna's purity, the Russian emphasised her divine motherhood (*bogoroditsa*). This is reflected in the way that Russian icons tend to show her with her face pressed tight against the infant's head in maternal devotion. It may well have been a conscious effort on the Church's part to supplant the pagan mother cults of Rozhanitsa and Mokosh.[27]

This 'dual belief' (*dvoeverie*) can be seen most clearly in the burial rites of the Russians during the medieval period. In the Upper Volga region, for example, archaeologists have excavated thirteenth-century barrow graves or mounds, the old pagan funeral practice, in which the dead were buried with both pagan amulets and Christian artefacts such as crosses and icons.[28] Pagan rituals continued to be practised in the Russian countryside for centuries. Soviet ethnographers found evidence of them in the 1920s, and there are parts of the Russian north where they can be found today.

From the beginning of his reign, Grand Prince Vladimir had placed his sons in charge of the various principalities within his realm. Each prince was equipped with an army or *druzhina* of a few thousand horsemen led by warriors, known as boyars, who received part of the prince's land. These landowners came to play a leading role in government through the Boyars' Council, which advised the prince, eventually forming something like an oligarchy of the major boyar clans. They were in charge of tax collection, military recruitment and justice in the provinces. The boyars were army men, often absent on campaigns; they took little interest in their land, which was farmed by the peasants in exchange for dues in labour or in kind. Land was plentiful but labour scarce – that was the basic fact of the seigneurial economy which guaranteed the peasants' access to the land and their freedom of movement, until the imposition of serfdom from the sixteenth century.

On the death of the grand prince or one of his sons there was a reshuffling of the principalities held by the remaining kin. Normally the throne of the grand prince would pass, not from father to son, but from the elder brother to the younger one (usually until the fourth brother). Only then would it pass down to the next generation. When the eldest brother took the throne in Kiev, all the others moved up to the principality on the next step of the ladder. It was a system of collateral succession not found elsewhere in Europe.[29]

Because there were no clear rules of primogeniture, family squabbles were a major source of instability during the eleventh century. It was not until the Liubech Conference, in 1097, that a set of principles was finally agreed, and then only because unity was seen as essential by the princes for the defence of their realms against the external threat of the Polovtsians and other warring tribes. The conference confirmed that all the princely brothers were collectively responsible for defending Kievan Rus. But otherwise their principalities became patrimonial domains (*otchiny*), ruled as extensions of their household property, and belonging solely to their own branch of the dynasty. Only Kiev remained subject to collateral succession, the principle of passing power from one brother to another in order of their seniority.

Kievan Rus was a loose dynastic federation of principalities rather than a kingdom in the European sense. Kinship not kingship was its constitutional principle. The grand prince was not the equal of a king, but *primus inter pares*, a figurehead of unity. Outside Kiev itself, in the principalities, his authority was limited. This was a polycentric state, in which every prince was in theory equal, although hierarchies did emerge as some principalities became more successful than others. Novgorod emerged as a growing economic force and potential rival to Kiev because of its access to the Baltic Sea and flourishing commerce with the Hanseatic Germans and Europe. Located on Lake Ilmen, an important waterway, it was the main transit point for the east–west river trade. It grew in wealth by collecting taxes from the furs and slaves that went from northern Russia to the West, and imposing duties on the cloth, wool, salt and metal goods that went the other way. Vladimir, Suzdal, Riazan, Polotsk, Smolensk, Chernigov, Galich and Vladimir-Volhynia all emerged as independent economic centres during the eleventh century.

Much has been made of these separatist tendencies. They have been blamed for the disunity of Kievan Rus that supposedly led to its destruction by the Mongols in the early thirteenth century. Many historians have argued that Kiev went into decline before the Mongol invasion. Their argument is based on three main points: chronicle accounts of petty wars between the principalities and regular incursions by the Polovtsians; the idea that the trade along the Dnieper to Byzantium declined after 1204, when the Fourth Crusade attacked Constantinople, leading to a shift in commerce from the Dnieper to the West; and the nationalist assumption that a European country such as Kievan Rus would not have fallen to the Asiatic Mongols if it had not been already weakened from within. Their arguments do not stack up. The rise of thriving centres such as Novgorod was a sign not of the weakening of Kievan Rus, but of its regional prosperity.[30] It was the wealth of these trading towns that helped them to become more independent of the political centre. Kievan Rus fell victim to its own success.

All the indications point to a flourishing economy and culture during the twelfth century. In the major towns churches and cathedrals were being built in stone instead of wood. Monasteries were established. Kiev's trades and crafts were doing well, judging from the large amounts of glazed pottery, ceramic tiles, glassworks, jewellery, metal locks and looms found by archaeologists. Birch-bark writings (carved into the inside of tree bark) suggest a thriving urban life and widespread literacy in towns such as Novgorod, where these fragments have been best preserved because of the muddy soil. Nothing indicates that any of the towns were in decline prior to the Mongol invasion. Kiev had a population of 40,000 people, more than London and not much less than Paris, at the start of the thirteenth century.[31]

Links to Europe were developing. In Novgorod, heavily involved with it through trade, Anglo-Saxon and German coins have been found in far larger quantities from the twelfth than from any earlier century. Kiev was increasingly connected to the European dynasties through marriages: Vladimir Monomakh was married to the daughter of the English king Harold, killed at the Battle of Hastings in 1066; his son was married to the daughter of the Swedish king; and his grandson to the daughter of the Serbian prince.

Politically, Kievan Rus was moving along European lines. The landowning rights of the boyar class gave it the potential to become an independent aristocracy as a counterbalance to the power of the crown. There was a kernel of democracy in the *veche* or town assembly, at which the freemen were allowed to speak and vote on civic appointments, domestic laws and taxes, even questions of war and peace. The *veche* was particularly powerful in Novgorod, where from 1126 it was responsible for electing the city's mayor or *posadnik*, previously appointed by the prince. The *posadnik*, once elected, acted as a check on monarchical power. Ten years later, the city also won the right to choose its prince and define his powers in a contract drawn up by the *veche*. Here was a city state similar to Venice and other city republics where the ruler was elected, and his powers checked, by a council of the leading men. The democratic potential of Novgorod captured the imagination of succeeding generations in Russia. In the nineteenth century the long-lost freedoms of the city were an inspiration to republicans and democrats.

How does the period of Kievan Rus connect with the rest of Russian history? Is there any meaningful sense in which modern Russia can lay claim to it as the foundation of its nationhood, as Putin did at the unveiling of the monument to the grand prince Vladimir? Russian historiography has taken it for granted that Muscovy was the successor to the Kievan state. This assumption is rooted in the writings of Moscow's churchmen and imperial ideologists from the later fifteenth century. After the capture of Constantinople by the Turks, in 1453, they had asserted Moscow's claim to inherit the authority of the Byzantine Empire, including all the lands of Kievan Rus. But the claim was based on myth, a story of succession to buttress the imperial pretensions of the tsar of Muscovy. In fact, politically, Muscovy was different from Kievan Rus. Two hundred and fifty years of Mongol occupation had created a fundamental break between the two.

The lasting legacy of Kievan Rus was in religion and the cultural sphere, where Byzantium would permanently mark Russian civilisation. Some of the fundamental ideas that would shape the course of Russian history – the idea of Holy Rus, the sacred status of the monarchy, the principle of oligarchic power – can be traced back to the Byzantine inheritance. But it is absurd to claim that Kievan Rus was the birthplace of the modern Russian or Ukrainian state. Perhaps, in the end, we should look at Kievan Rus as part of Russia's 'ancient history' – a period related to its later history in the same sense as Anglo-Saxon Wessex is part of English history or Merovingian Gaul is linked to modern France – namely as a source of the country's religion, its language and its artistic forms. The rest of the Kievan heritage in Russia has been lost.

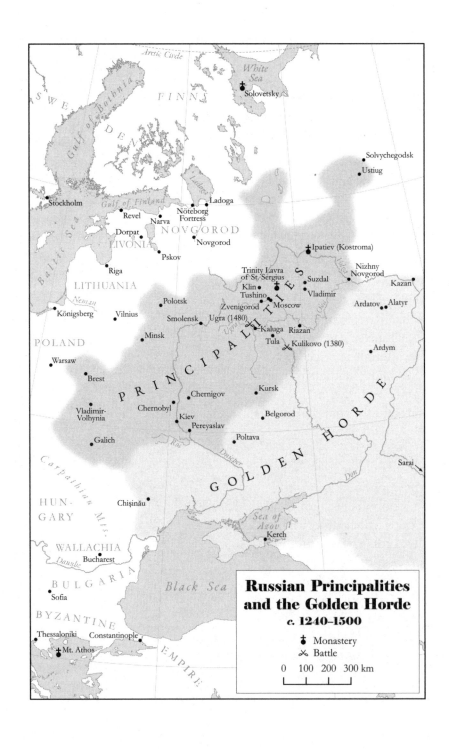

Russian Principalities and the Golden Horde

Arctic Circle

White Sea

⚓ Solovetsky

SWEDEN

Gulf of Bothnia

FINNS

Solvychegodsk

Ustiug

Stockholm

Gulf of Finland

Ladoga

Ladoga

Revel

Nöteborg Fortress

NOVGOROD

Ipatiev (Kostroma)

Narva

Dorpat

Novgorod

Nizhny Novgorod

Baltic Sea

LIVONIA

Pskov

Trinity Lavra of St. Sergius

Suzdal

Kazan

Riga

Klin

Vladimir

LITHUANIA

Tushino

Ardatov

Alatyr

Neman

Polotsk

Zvenigorod

Moscow

Vilnius

Smolensk

Ugra (1480)

Volga

Königsberg

Kaluga

Riazan

Ardym

Minsk

Tula

Kulikovo (1380)

POLAND

Oka

Warsaw

PRINCIPALITIES

Brest

Chernigov

Kursk

Vladimir-Volhynia

Chernobyl

Belgorod

Galich

Kiev

Pereyaslav

Poltava

GOLDEN HORDE

Ros

Dnieper

Don

Carpathian Mts.

Sarai

HUN-GARY

Chişinău

WALLACHIA

Sea of Azov

Danube

Bucharest

Kerch

BULGARIA

Black Sea

Sofia

BYZANTINE

Thessaloniki

Constantinople

⚓ Mt. Athos

EMPIRE

Russian Principalities and the Golden Horde
c. 1240–1500

⚓ Monastery
⚔ Battle

0   100   200   300 km

THE MONGOL IMPACT

In 1223, a new army appeared on the southern steppe. Its horsemen quickly overran the Polovtsian lands and headed west, easily defeating a combined force of the Rus princes on the banks of the Kalka River, just north of the Azov Sea, before retreating east with equal speed. They arrived and disappeared so fast, leaving so much devastation in their wake, that the Russians were dumbfounded. 'We know neither from whence they came nor whither they have gone,' recorded a chronicler. 'Only God knows that, because he brought them upon us for our sins.'[1]

The mysterious raiders had been sent on a reconnaissance by Chingiz Khan, chief of the Mongolian tribes, whose armies had already conquered China, Central Asia and the Caucasus. In 1237, they appeared again, this time in much greater numbers, around 50,000 warriors, not just Mongols but with Polovtsians and other Turkic tribes absorbed into their army, under the command of Batu Khan, the grandson of Chingiz Khan, who had died ten years previously. They were driven west by ideas of a world empire, by the aim of controlling the Eurasian trade routes and by the prospect of war booty. The horsemen destroyed Riazan, Suzdal, Vladimir and other northern Russian towns, before turning south to capture Kiev on 6 December 1240, an event that marked the end of Kievan Rus, and continuing on their westward path on to the Hungarian plain. From this resting place, where they could feed their horses, the Mongol army was in a good position to conquer Europe, whose disunited countries had little chance of withstanding the onslaught. But the West was saved by the death of the great khan Ögedei, the favourite son of Chingiz Khan, in December 1241. When Batu received the news, the following spring, he called off the western offensive and took his army back to Karakorum, the empire's capital on the Mongolian steppe, to stake his claim to the succession.[2]

In their accounts of the Mongol invasion the Russian chronicles invariably emphasised how heavily the Russians were outnumbered by their Asiatic conquerors. It was the only way they were prepared to explain their defeat. But the Mongol victory had less to do with numbers – the Kievan princes had twice as many warriors at their disposal – than with the superiority of the Mongol cavalry. It was the best mounted army in the world. From early childhood their horsemen had been trained to ride at speed and accurately shoot with a reflex bow and arrow by standing semi-erect in a high stirrup. Their skills had been perfected by hunting, an important means of livelihood in nomadic societies, through which young boys were also trained to scout new territory. The seasonal migrations of the Mongol clans, when they would move with their cattle over thousands of kilometres, had endowed their horses and riders with extraordinary stamina. They could ride for days without food or rest, undeterred by heat or frost (the Russian winter was no obstacle to them because their horses had been trained to paw the snow-covered ground like reindeer to reach the grass beneath). They preferred indeed to fight in the winter when the rivers and marshlands – the main impediment to their horses – were frozen. Their success on the battlefield was explained by the well-drilled flanking movements the Mongol horsemen used to surround the enemy – something they had practised all their lives by hunting animals – before sending in the heavy cavalry to finish them with sabres, lances, battle axes and lassos. Although new to siege warfare, they had copied the designs of catapults and battering-rams captured in their conquest of China, where they had also learned to use gunpowder for incendiary missiles.[3] Their machines were too powerful for the fortifications of wood and beaten earth built by the Russians to protect their towns.

The destruction caused by the invasion was immense, although not as great as claimed in the later chronicles, whose accounts of atrocities were integral to their religious narrative about Holy Russia being punished by the Tatar infidels for its sins (they called them the 'Tartars', with an extra 'r', to associate them with Tartarus, the Greek name for 'hell'). In Riazan, the first town they sacked, the Mongols 'burned this holy city with all its beauty and wealth', according to *The Tale of the Destruction of Riazan by Batu*. 'And churches of God were destroyed and much blood was spilled on the holy altars. And not one man remained alive in the city. All were dead ... And there was not even anyone to mourn the dead.'[4]

An estimated two-thirds of the towns of Kievan Rus were totally destroyed. Their populations disappeared, killed or taken off as slaves, or fleeing to the forests where the Mongols did not go. So many craftsmen were captured by the Mongols that practically no stone or brick buildings were built in the half-abandoned towns during the next fifty years.[5]

Batu Khan did not succeed the great khan Ögedei but returned to the Russian steppe a few years later to establish his own dynasty, the Golden Horde, which ruled the western sector of the Mongol Empire from the Urals to Bulgaria. The focus of the Golden Horde was not the Russian forest lands (they had no use for them) but the grassland pastures of the southern steppes and the trading routes connecting Central Asia and Persia to its capital Sarai, on the lower Volga near the Caspian Sea. The revenue the Mongols could derive from the Russian river trade with Europe was relatively minor compared to the wealth that flowed into their coffers from the silk routes between Samarkand, Baghdad and the Black Sea. The European trade was not enough to warrant the expense of ruling Russia directly. Instead the Mongols remained on the steppe, where they could graze their horses and cattle, and did not settle in the forest zone, which they ruled indirectly from Sarai. They collected tribute from the Russian lands, over which they exercised their dominion through a network of officials (*baskaki*) stationed in strategic positions with military detachments, which carried out ferocious raids to punish towns if they were slow to pay their dues, and set an example to others. Almost every year, there was an attack on at least one Russian town. Vladimir and Suzdal were each sacked five times during the last quarter of the thirteenth century.[6]

One of Batu's first moves was to summon the Russian princes to Sarai to swear an oath of allegiance to the Mongol khan. These trips became a regular phenomenon, for no prince could rule without a patent (*yarlyk*) from the khan. The prince was forced to dress in Mongol clothes and undergo a ritual that involved passing between flames and kneeling at the feet of his sovereign to beg for his patent. If there was more than one candidate, the *yarlyk* would be given to the prince who promised the most revenue, offered the most soldiers for the Mongol army and gave the best assurance of maintaining order over his people. To fix the tax and number of recruits from each region the Mongols instituted censuses – a practice they had learned from the Chinese – which the *baskaki* and their military units oversaw. The general Mongol practice was to take one-tenth of everything, 'men and girls as well as possessions', according to a papal missionary who passed through Russia on his way to Karakorum in 1245–6.[7]

The Russian princes and boyars went along with the Mongol system, helping it to carry out the censuses and enforce the taxation. To resist meant inviting destruction. Their collaboration posed difficulties for the Russian chroniclers, who told a story of the saintly princes as the helpless victims of the infidels (almost all the princes killed in battle by the Mongols were later canonised). The most problematic example was Alexander Nevsky, prince of Novgorod and Pskov. Nevsky was a Russian hero for his leading role in the defeat of the Swedes on the Neva River (from which he received his name Nevsky) in 1240. Two years later, he defeated the Teutonic Knights, German crusaders, in a battle on the ice of Lake Chud near Livonia – a victory that looms large in the national consciousness because it forms the central episode of *Alexander Nevsky* (1938), Sergei Eisenstein's great patriotic film, which was seen by millions in the Soviet Union during the war against Hitler.

In 1252, Nevsky travelled to Sarai, where Batu Khan appointed him the grand prince of Vladimir, the most senior of the princes following the fall of Kiev. He acted as the Mongols' loyal servant, suppressing a rebellion in Novgorod and other towns against their census officials. Nevsky's collaboration was no doubt motivated by his mistrust of the West, which he regarded as a greater threat to Orthodox Russia than the Golden Horde, generally tolerant of religions. He recognised the Mongols as powerful protectors of the lucrative north Russian trade with the Baltic Germans and Sweden. But Nevsky's realpolitik caused a problem for the chroniclers, particularly after he was made a saint by the Russian Church in 1547, for in their terms he had colluded with the infidel. They got around the issue by presenting his collusion as a gracious sacrifice – imitating Christ in his humility – to save Holy Russia from an all-conquering 'Eastern tsar' sent by God to punish Russians for their sins.[8] Nevsky's sacrifice would also feed into the myth of Russia saving Christendom. By placating the Mongols, he had stopped them from progressing further west.

The Church too collaborated with the Golden Horde. The khan exempted it from taxation, protected its property and outlawed the persecution of all Christians, on condition that its priests said prayers for him, meaning that they upheld his authority. These dispensations allowed the Church to thrive. Under the Mongols it made its first real inroads into the pagan countryside. Peasants flocked to the church lands where they were free from Mongol taxes and military service. It was at this time that the most used word in Russian for a peasant changed from *liudi*, a general term for 'people', to *krestianin*, derived from *khristianin*, meaning a Christian.[9] Monasteries grew as landowners bestowed estates on them in the belief that it would save their souls – and save themselves from the infidels. Around thirty monasteries were founded during the first century of Mongol rule, and five times that number in the second century.[10]

An important part of this monastic movement was led by men of deep religious feeling who rebelled against the worldly hierarchies of the Orthodox Church and went into the wilderness to live an

ascetic life of private prayer and contemplation, book-learning
and manual work. They took their spiritual guidance from the
hesychasm of Byzantium, a contemplative mysticism (from the
Greek *hesychia*, meaning 'quietude') founded on the idea that
the way to God was through a life of poverty and prayer under
the guidance of a holy man or elder. The centre of the movement
was Mount Athos in northern Greece, a monastic retreat since the
early Christian era, whose hermitic monks inspired imitators in
Russia. The most important was Sergius of Radonezh, who in 1337
established a church of the Holy Trinity at Sergiev-Posad, north-
east of Moscow, which became a monastic community populated
by his followers (today it is known as the Trinity Lavra of St Sergius,
the spiritual centre of the Russian Church). By his death in 1392,
Sergius's pupils numbered several hundred monks, who went on to
found new monasteries, many in the remote north-east regions of
Russia, which in this way were colonised, as peasants went where
the monks led. Among these colonial missionaries were Stephen of
Perm, the bringer of Christianity to the Komi people, who fought
hard to defend their animist beliefs (the artist Kandinsky found
them still in existence when he visited the remote Komi region in
1889), and the elder Zosima, who went as far as the White Sea to
found a monastery on Solovetsky Island (converted into a prison
after 1917, it is better known today as the prototype of Stalin's Gulag
labour camps).

The religious arts flourished, icon painting in particular. In these
years of isolation from Byzantium, icon painters developed a more
specifically Russian style characterised by greater animation and
plasticity, warmer colours, simpler lines and softer tones than those
found in the Greek tradition they had previously followed. That
style reached its supreme heights in Andrei Rublev's icons of the
early fifteenth century. No other icon painter could match their
poetic qualities – their graceful harmony and sense of movement,
their transparency of colour that makes their sacred figures appear
illuminated from within. A notable example is the *Trinity* he
painted for the Holy Trinity Church in Sergiev-Posad between
1408 and 1425.

The miracle of Rublev's art occurred as Russia was emerging from two centuries of Mongol rule. It became a marker of the nation's spiritual unity in later stories of this period. What defined the Russians, what became the focus of their spirit of endurance at this dark moment in their history, was their Christianity. Readers may recall the final glorious scene of Andrei Tarkovsky's film *Andrei Rublev* (1966), in which a group of craftsmen, led by the orphan of a bell maker, cast a giant bell for the town of Vladimir, sacked many times by the Mongols. The first ringing of the bell, watched by a delegation of Italians, along with the grand prince and people of the town, is a moment of pure joy, a symbol of the ways in which the Russians have survived through their spiritual strength and creativity.

The Mongol conquest destroyed Kievan Rus and turned its princes into vassals of the Golden Horde. The leadership of Kiev was replaced by that of Vladimir, whose grand prince was appointed by the khan. The contenders travelled to Sarai to pledge their allegiance to the Golden Horde and plead their case, as they did for the patent to their principalities. The successful candidate was accompanied by the khan's ambassadors to Vladimir, where they installed him on the throne.

Within a century of the Mongol invasion the make-up of the lands once constituting Kievan Rus had changed dramatically – so much so that neither modern Russia nor Ukraine nor Belarus can lay any general claim to them. Kievan Rus was cut in two by the Mongol occupation, with each half set upon a different path of political development. The south-western principalities (Polotsk, Vitebsk, Minsk, Chernigov, Kiev, Volhynia and Galich) were drawn into the orbit of Poland and Lithuania, which offered them protection from the Mongols and continued access to the West. These lands' political development was later shaped by the Polish–Lithuanian Commonwealth, a constitutional monarchy with an elected king and parliament dominated by the local landed nobles, which would rule this polyethnic area from the sixteenth to the eighteenth century. The north-eastern (Russian) half of Kievan Rus followed a quite different path. The six principalities conquered by the Mongols (Moscow, Tver, Vladimir, Novgorod, Rostov-Suzdal and Riazan) were sub-divided into fourteen fiefdoms (known as apanages) with their own tax systems and armies. In each of these domains the ruling prince was deemed to own the realm (and all the land and people within it) as his patrimonial property. These lands would form the nucleus of Muscovy, where patrimonial autocracy emerged from the Mongol occupation as a ruling principle.

The apanage system had begun in Kievan Rus, but it was reinforced by the Mongols, who found it advantageous to have small but stable principalities headed by a strong but compliant grand prince based in Vladimir. Tver and Moscow were to play key roles. Tver was the patrimonial property of the descendants of Iaroslav Iaroslavich, the younger brother of Alexander Nevsky, whom he had succeeded as grand prince of Vladimir in 1263. Moscow, meanwhile, belonged to the heirs of Daniil Alexandrovich, the Daniilovichi as they are called. Daniil Alexandrovich was Nevsky's youngest son (he was only two when his father died) and was given Moscow as (at that time) the least significant of all his lands.

Moscow is first mentioned in the chronicles in 1147. It was just a village on the western border of the principality of Rostov-Suzdal. By the time of the Mongol conquest, it had grown in size and become fortified. But it was only in the second half of the thirteenth century that it became a major force among the Russian principalities. Geography was part of its success. Located on the Moscow River, which connected it to the Volga and Oka, it was at the centre of the Russian river network, which allowed it to become an affluent commercial hub. It had a natural defence system in the dense forests and marshlands around it, making it attractive to peasants fleeing the Mongols in the east and south. As Moscow grew in population and military strength it annexed nearby principalities. By the mid-fourteenth century, it had become so rich that its prince, Ivan Daniilovich, popularly known as Kalita ('Moneybags'), purchased further territories or made them loans enabling him to annex them when they were unable to repay their debt. Thus began a process that would become known as Moscow's 'gathering of the Russian lands'.

The only serious rival to Moscow was Tver, the domain of the Iaroslavichi. Only Tver and Moscow had the economic base to compete for control of the Grand Principality of Vladimir. Like Moscow, Tver was favoured by geography. Located on the Volga, it was well connected by its river network to the most important trading towns of the Russian forest zone. While it had few natural defences, its relative remoteness from the Mongol forces, allied to its good communications, enabled Tver to sustain a growing population in the century following the invasion.

At the beginning of the fourteenth century, when their rivalry began, Moscow and Tver were more or less equal. But by the end of the century there was no doubt that Moscow was the supreme force – the only Russian principality capable of challenging the Golden Horde. What were the reasons for its victory?

The outcome of their rivalry was ultimately decided by the Golden Horde, whose policies were guided by divide and rule. Wanting neither Tver nor Moscow to become too powerful, the khan would always back the weaker of the two. Diplomacy was therefore more effective than military strength in winning favour from Sarai. Ivan Kalita was more shrewd and cravenly submissive in his dealings with the Mongols than his rival, Prince Mikhail of Tver, who led his city in a failed rebellion against a combined Muscovite and Tatar force in 1317. Kalita cultivated his relations with Khan Uzbek, who reigned from 1313 to 1341. He travelled at least five times to Sarai, collected Mongol taxes with efficiency and led his army against other principalities showing any sign of rebellion against the Golden Horde. After his suppression of a second Tver uprising, in 1327, Kalita was promoted by Uzbek to the title of grand prince of Vladimir, the most senior Russian power in the former lands of Kievan Rus. When Kalita put down a rising in Smolensk, in 1339, the khan rewarded him by giving legal sanction to his will, conferring the succession of his sons to the Moscow throne.[11] The office of grand prince of Vladimir was henceforth held by the Daniilovichi. It was incorporated into the all-Russian powers of the grand prince of Muscovy.

The Mongols' growing fear of Lithuania was also an important factor in their promotion of Moscow. In the early fourteenth century the Lithuanians were steadily expanding their control to the former western lands of Kievan Rus. Where they were unable to annex them by pressure or persuasion, the Lithuanians turned to religion. They established a separate metropolitan to prise away the western territories from the rest of Orthodox Russia. By the 1330s, Smolensk, Novgorod and Tver were all close to throwing in their lot with Lithuania; Moscow was struggling to rein them in through military threats; and the Mongols were confronted by the danger of a powerful new state appearing on their western frontier that might undermine their empire in the Russian lands. Building up the power of Moscow to resist the Lithuanians was the khan's best policy. It was also successful. Novgorod was brought back into Moscow's fold. Tver disintegrated into warring boyar fiefdoms. And Smolensk was annexed by Moscow in 1352.

As Moscow grew in power, the Mongols tried to contain it by divide and rule again. In the west they encouraged it to grow as a buffer state against Poland and Lithuania, but in the north and east, where their own control depended on its weakness, they encouraged anti-Moscow elements. By the second half of the thirteenth century, it was too late for the Golden Horde to contain the rise of Moscow, however. The city had become an important trading hub, thanks in large part to the Mongols' protection and encouragement of international trading routes via Moscow's waterways. The European trade through Novgorod alone brought great wealth to Muscovy, which kept a good share of the taxes it collected for the Golden Horde. New towns appeared, large stone churches were constructed and Moscow's crafts and industries revived. The first stone walls and churches of the Moscow Kremlin were built around this time – the walls by order of the grand prince Dmitry in 1366–7. Over 50,000 cubic metres of stone were hauled from distant quarries by massive teams, far larger than the labour forces that Europe's rulers were able to obtain for projects of this kind. The building of the Kremlin was a symbol of the power of Moscow.

It was also the result of a new deal with the Church, which allied itself to Moscow's cause as a national power centre to liberate the Orthodox from Mongol rule. The alliance had begun in 1325 when the Metropolitan of Kiev and All Rus, Peter II, moved his see from Vladimir to Moscow at the request of Ivan Kalita. To mark his arrival Ivan promptly ordered the construction of the Dormition Cathedral in the Kremlin, the first stone church within its walls. From this point, Ivan endowed the Church with large estates. These lands became so extensive that a contract was drawn up to define the obligations of the metropolitan to the ruling dynasty. It confirmed his position as a vassal, in effect, to the grand prince.[12]

Moscow's standing with the Church was boosted by its military defeat of a large Tatar army in 1380. It was the first time a Russian force had scored any kind of victory against the Mongols. The conflict had its roots in the Golden Horde's demands for tribute payments from Moscow. Mamai Khan was counting on the grand prince Dmitry to deliver ever greater revenues. But Moscow's income was suffering at this time from a trade dispute between Novgorod and its partners in the West. Matters came to a head in 1378, when Sarai was attacked by a rival Mongol khan, forcing Mamai to supplement his army, at that time depleted by the plague, and demand an extra payment from Moscow. A Mongol force of 30,000 men was sent to collect it from Moscow. Dmitry raised an army of equal size, marched it south to meet the Mongols and defeated them at Kulikovo near the River Don. The victory earned him his nickname, Dmitry Donskoi (meaning 'of the Don').[13]

To celebrate the victory the Church in Moscow introduced an annual holiday on the Day of St Dmitry, the grand prince's patron saint. From that point Kulikovo featured in the national story as the start of Russia's liberation from the Tatar infidels, later as the moment of its 'national awakening'. Kulikovo is still celebrated in Russia. Putin has frequently referred to it as evidence that Russia was already a great power – the saviour of Europe from the Mongol threat – in the fourteenth century. This idea – Russia as a guard protecting Europe from the 'Asiatic hordes' – became part of the national myth from the sixteenth century, as Muscovy began to see itself as a European power on the Asian steppe. The idea reached its apogee with the 'Scythian' poets in the early twentieth century, among them Alexander Blok, who reproached a thankless Europe for its failure to recognise that Russia had protected it from the Asiatic tribes:

> Like slaves, obeying and abhorred,
> We were the shield between the breeds
> Of Europe and the raging Mongol horde.[14]

Today the Kulikovo victory is linked in the nationalist consciousness to other episodes when Russia's military sacrifice 'saved' the West, in 1812–15 (against Napoleon) or 1941–5, for example; each time its sacrifice had been unthanked, unrecognised by its Western allies in these wars. The country's deep resentment of the West is rooted in this national myth.

Kulikovo had shown that the Mongols could be beaten on the battlefield. But their defeat was not the end of Mongol rule. Moscow suffered heavy losses in its victory. Two years later it was too depleted to defend itself when Tokhtamysh, the new khan, sent his army to exact revenge. After three days of fighting, the Mongols sacked the city, killing half its people.[15] Moscow's status was weakened. Acknowledging their defencelessness, the Russian princes hurried to Sarai to pledge their submission to the Golden Horde.

Just as the Mongols were dealing with the challenge from Moscow, they faced a new threat from the Central Asian empire that was then emerging under the command of Timur, better known as Tamerlane. Timur's army conquered Persia and the Caucasus and then went on to destroy the key trading bases of the Golden Horde, which began a slow but terminal decline. The weakening of the Horde, however, was due less to outside military threats than to the Black Death, which began on the Central Asian steppe in the mid-fourteenth century. The pandemic turned trade routes into plague routes, devastating the economy and killing perhaps half the population of the Golden Horde, which over the next century broke up into three khanates (Kazan, Crimea, Astrakhan). None of them was powerful enough to threaten Russia as the Golden Horde had done.

Muscovy remained a vassal of the khans until 1502. Long before, however, it began to act as if it were an independent state. In 1480, in a bid to reassert his dwindling authority, Khan Ahmed advanced with his army on Moscow. The Muscovites assembled their own troops and met the Mongols at the River Ugra, south of Moscow, where the two sides faced each other for two weeks, without any arrows being fired, the Muscovites on the west bank, the Tatars on the east. Finally, the Mongols turned around and retreated. The Russian chronicles would tell the story of the 'Great Stand on the Ugra' as the 'overthrow of the Tatar yoke', an event of world historical significance. In fact it was a relatively minor episode, similar to many such encounters in the past, different only because it would be the last.

The Mongols stayed in Russia for more than three centuries. It was not until the 1550s that the khanates of Kazan and Astrakhan were finally defeated by Ivan IV (the khanate of Crimea survived until 1783). How much impact did these centuries have on the course of Russian history?

There are three main Russian views. In most accounts, the Mongol impact is entirely negative. This was a time of suffering and sacrifice, humiliation and oppression. Russia languished under the 'Tatar yoke', which prevented its progression on the European path. In this narrative the Mongols have been blamed for everything that held Russia back. They isolated it from Europe and the cultural advances of the Renaissance. They plunged Russia into its 'Dark Age', coarsening every aspect of the Russian way of life. The literary critic Vissarion Belinsky made a list in 1841:

> The seclusion of women, the habit of burying money in the ground and of wearing rags from the fear of revealing one's wealth, usury, Asiaticism in the way of life, a laziness of the mind, ignorance, contempt for oneself – in a word, all that

Peter the Great was uprooting, everything that was in Russia opposed to Europeanism, everything that was not native to us but *had been grafted* on to us by the Tatars [emphasis in original].[16]

A second view was advanced by a number of Slavophiles, the nineteenth-century nationalists opposed to Russia's following the Western model of development. While accepting the destructive impact of the Mongols on Russia, they saw the period of Mongol occupation as one in which there had been some positive developments for the foundation of the later Russian state. In particular, Russia's isolation from the West had allowed it to preserve its Byzantine inheritance, its old Slavonic culture and its Orthodox beliefs, untouched by the secular and individualistic trends of Renaissance humanism in Europe.

A third, more common view was to deny that the Mongols had an influence at all: they came, they terrorised and they plundered, but then they left without a trace. Karamzin, for example, in his *History of the Russian State*, did not write a word about the cultural legacies of Mongol rule. 'For how', he asked, 'could a civilised people have learned from such nomads?' This remains the dominant perspective of the Europeanised intelligentsia, which sees Russia facing west. 'From Asia we received extraordinarily little,' wrote the revered historian Dmitry Likhachev in his book *Russian Culture* (2000). He had nothing more to say about the Mongols or any other oriental influence on Russia's cultural history.[17]

This denial of the Mongol legacy is rooted in a sense of national humiliation that a European country such as Russia should have been subjected for so long to the domination of an Asiatic empire, deemed by the Russians to be culturally inferior. It can be traced from the medieval chronicles, which portrayed the Mongols as plunderers of Russia (sent by God to punish Russians for their sins) but not as its conquerors.[18] Russia's first historians were heavily dependent on the chronicles. Grounded as they were in the Eurocentric views of the Enlightenment, they took little interest in the Mongol state or Mongol–Russian relations, which barely featured in their histories. In his *History of Russia from the Earliest Times* (published in twenty-nine volumes between 1851 and 1879), the great historian Sergei Solovyov dismissed even the possibility of 'any Mongol influence on Russia's internal administration, because we do not see any trace of it'.[19] Vasily Kliuchevsky, who had studied under Solovyov, hardly mentioned the Mongols in his five-volume *History of Russia* (1904–11), preferring to explain the development of Russia at this time exclusively in terms of its own internal changes rather than through foreign influence (a rule he broke for the influence of Europe from the eighteenth century).[20]

It was only at the end of the nineteenth century that Russian archaeologists, ethnographers and orientalists began to take a serious interest in the Mongols and their influence. Archaeological excavations showed that Sarai had not been a settlement of tents, as imagined by the Russians until then, but a large medieval city of 75,000 people with stone buildings, well-laid-out streets and hydraulic systems, craft workshops and schools.[21] Philologists established the Tatar origins of many of the basic Russian words in administration and finance – *dengi* (money), *kazna* (treasury), *tamozhna* (customs duty), *barysh* (profit) – suggesting that the Mongols had an impact in these spheres.

Many Russian families had Tatar names. Some descended from the Mongols who had stayed in Russia and entered into service in the Moscow court following the break-up of the Golden Horde. According to one estimate, 156 of the 915 noble families in the service of the tsar in the 1680s were of Tatar or other Asiatic origins. They were not as many as the Lithuanian and western European families, which made up almost half the noble class. But the true figure was probably higher because many Tatars Russified their names when they entered the nobility. Among these were some of the most famous names in Russian history: writers (Karamzin, Chaadaev, Turgenev, Bulgakov), composers (Rimsky-Korsakov), tsars (Boris Godunov) and revolutionaries (Bukharin).[22]

It was not just the elites that stayed behind in Russia when the Mongols left. What we call 'the Mongol invasion' was in fact a gradual migration of nomadic tribes. They came in search of new pastures because of overpopulation in Mongolia. The populations of Uzbekistan and Kazakhstan are of mainly Mongol origin. But the nomads also settled further west. Some gave up their herds and became peasant farmers in Russia. Others took up trades and crafts, particularly those that serviced livestock herds, in which many of the basic Russian words have Tatar origins – *loshad* (horse), *bazar* (market), *bashmak* (shoe) and so on. Many towns in southern Russia and the Volga lands still have Tatar names – among them Penza, Chembar, Ardym, Anybei, Ardatov and Alatyr.

These deep Asian elements of Russian culture were the main concern of the Eurasianists, a diverse group of émigré scholars scattered over Europe and America after 1917. In their first collection of essays, *Exodus to the East* (1921), Prince Nikolai Trubetskoi, a philologist, maintained that Russia was at root a Eurasian steppeland culture formed by the Russians' intermingling with the Finno-Ugric peoples, the Mongols and other Turkic-speaking tribes over many centuries. Byzantine and European influences, which had shaped the Russian state and its high culture, barely penetrated to the lower strata of Russia's folk culture, its music, dancing, belief system and psychology, which had all developed more through contact with the East. Russian folk song was derived from the pentatonic (five-tone) scale common to the music of Asia. Folk dance, too, according to Trubetskoi, shared much with the dancing of the East, especially the Caucasus, where, as in Russia, it was done by groups in lines and circles, its rhythmic movements performed by hands and shoulders as well as by the feet, rather than in pairs, as in the European tradition. All these cultural forms were, he said, expressions of an 'Eastern psyche' – an inclination for abstract symmetry, a tendency to contemplation and fatalistic attitudes, and the primacy of the collective over individual interests – which explained the sacred nature of monarchical authority and the Russians' willingness to submit themselves to it.[23]

Among the founders of the Eurasianist theory was George Vernadsky, an émigré historian, teaching then in Prague but soon to move to the United States, where he embarked on his six-volume *A History of Russia* (1943–69). Vernadsky presented the Mongol occupation as the key turning-point in Russian history. It set Russia on a path towards autocracy, serfdom and imperial expansion into Asia, although its effects would not become apparent until later in a process he described as 'influence through delayed action'. To overthrow the Mongols, he argued, the Russians had to absorb many features of their government: the dragooning of society into service to the state; the control of the steppe's nomadic tribes through imperial conquest. As he wrote in *The Mongols and Russia* (1953), 'Autocracy and serfdom were the price the Russian people had to pay for national survival.'[24]

One might question Vernadsky's theory of delayed influence. How could Russia's rulers borrow institutions that no longer existed? The link he made between the Mongols and the introduction of serfdom is particularly dubious, for while it may be true that the first restrictions on peasant movement were imposed in the Mongol period, the laws enforcing serfdom were not passed until 1649. Two hundred years is a long 'delay'. Nonetheless, Vernadsky's analysis has encouraged a more nuanced view of the Mongol impact than those contained in narratives about the 'Tatar yoke'.

In fact the impact of the Mongols was immense, and not long delayed at all. The adoption of Mongol political institutions began from as early as the first half of the fourteenth century. The Muscovite princes made frequent visits to Sarai, where they obtained first-hand knowledge of the Golden Horde's administrative practices, at that time far superior to anything developed in Russia. Most of the methods of the Golden Horde were adopted by Ivan Kalita when he replaced the Mongol *baskaki* with his own tax-collecting officials (known as *danschiki*) to collect tribute. The Mongol *tamga*, a customs duty, became the commercial tax of Muscovy.

One of the mechanisms used by tax collectors in Russia was known as *krugovaya poruka*, meaning joint responsibility. It was a method of collecting taxes in which a village or community was made collectively responsible for their payment. Although it had existed under Kievan Rus, the system emerged greatly strengthened from the period of Mongol rule. The Mongols employed coercive means, such as beating shins with rods or taking hostages until the tax was paid. *Krugovaya poruka* would be used in later centuries both by tsarist and (more coercively) by Bolshevik officials to squeeze taxes from a population barely able to pay them. To distribute the burden of these taxes fairly between their household members, communities developed institutions of self-government – the *veche* in the towns and the *mir* or peasant commune in the villages – which reinforced these collective practices.[25]

The Mongol period brought some positive advances for Russia. The postal system was the fastest in the world – a vast network of relay stations, each equipped with teams of fresh horses capable of carrying officials to all corners of the Mongol Empire at unheard-of speeds. It became the basis of the Muscovite system, which so impressed foreigners. Sigismund von Herberstein, an early sixteenth-century Habsburg envoy, was astounded by the speed of the post in Muscovy. A letter sent from Moscow would arrive in Novgorod, a journey of 660 kilometres, in less than three days. In sixteenth-century Germany a letter would have taken twice as long to travel that distance.[26]

Moscow's army also improved from its contacts with the Mongols, the best mounted forces in the world. It owed much to the Mongol military, from its flanking tactics in the field to its highly mobile cavalry formations, armour and weapons. Richard Chancellor, an English traveller to Muscovy in 1553, noted that the Russian horsemen rode half standing up in a 'short stirrup after the manner of the Turks'. He also remarked that, like the Mongol archers, they wore silk with their coat of mail. He thought they did so to display their wealth. But that was not the reason. The Russians had learned from the Mongols that the barbed tip of an arrow does not pierce through silk on entering the body. This meant it could be removed without worsening the wound.[27]

Economically the impact of the Mongols was not as harmful as once thought by Russian chroniclers of the 'Tatar yoke'. The Golden Horde was a powerful protector of the international trading routes that enriched Russia's towns. Money earned from trade and customs poured into the towns, which were rebuilt and re-energised once they had recovered from the devastation of the Mongol invasion. Novgorod and Moscow became large and rich cities, equal in their architecture and artistic riches to many other cities in Europe.

The legacy that dominates historical debates is the Mongol impact on autocracy. The Asiatic character of Russia's despotism became a commonplace of the Western-oriented intelligentsia. The nineteenth-century socialist Alexander Herzen compared the repressive Nicholas I (who reigned from 1825 to 1855) to 'Chingiz Khan with a telegraph'. The Bolshevik Nikolai Bukharin said that Stalin was like 'Chingiz Khan with a telephone'.

The Russian autocratic tradition had many roots, but the Mongol legacy did more than most to fix the basic nature of its politics. From the sixteenth century, the first tsars of Muscovy drew upon the Mongol imperial tradition, adapting it to their own purposes. Beginning with Ivan IV ('the Terrible'), they justified their claim to an imperial status not just on the basis of their spiritual descent from Byzantium but also on the basis of their territorial inheritance from Chingiz Khan. The title 'tsar' was used for both emperors – the Byzantine *basileus* and the khan of the Golden Horde – so the two became confused. Russian images of the Mongol khan depicted him in the regalia of the Byzantine emperor. There was equally confusion between the Russian terms for 'tsar' and 'khan', which for a long time were practically interchangeable. Even Chingiz Khan was rendered Chingiz Tsar.[28]

Moscow's princes emulated the behaviour of the khans when they drove them out of Russia and succeeded them as tsars. The khans had demanded, and mercilessly enforced, complete submission to their will from all classes of society – a principle continued by the Russian tsars. Along with the khans' despotic power came the idea of their ownership of all the land, an idea that the Mongols took from the Chinese. By the fourteenth century, this ideology of ownership had also entered Muscovy. It reinforced the patrimonial principle of princely power inherited from Kievan Rus. Now, more than before, the power of the state was invested in the person of the tsar as the lord or sovereign owner of the land. Like the Mongol khans, the grand prince claimed the domain he ruled as his household property. He was free to give his land (along with the dues owed by the peasants on it) to his servitors; and free to take it from them if they displeased him. Whereas previously, in Kievan Rus, the boyars owned their land as private property, which they kept if they left the service of the prince, henceforth they were deemed to own their land on condition of their service to the prince. They lost it when they left him. Here was the fundamental weakness of the Russian aristocracy. The most senior boyar clans – those who were closest through marriage or royal favour to the Moscow court – formed an oligarchic ruling class, which at times, when the grand prince was weak, might direct his government. But their wealth and power came from him. They kept them only for as long as they retained his protection. It was a system of dependency upon the ruler that has lasted to this day. Putin's oligarchs are totally dependent on his will.

The supporting structures of this patrimonial autocracy were also built in the period of Mongol rule. One was the system of *mestnichestvo* (literally 'placement') by which the princes and the boyar clans were ranked officially not just by their service record but by their genealogical relation to the ruling family. Because wealth and power came with rank, the boyars attached immense significance to their position in this ranking system, which affected every aspect of their lives, right down to their place at table during feasts (a matter of no little importance to the boyars, who were quick to take offence if seated lower than demanded by their rank). This hierarchy was more stable than the system that pertained in the princely courts of Kievan Rus, where the boyar clans had openly competed for positions and power, a system that could lead to bitter infighting and even civil war. In post-Mongol Muscovy only the Daniilovichi could hold the office of grand prince; the rules of dynastic succession switched to primogeniture; and the boyars closest to the throne occupied the senior positions in the state and military. It was like the Mongol system, on which it was probably modelled, where only Chingizids, the direct descendants of Chingiz Khan, could rule as the great khan of the empire, and where the ranking order of the Mongol clans was determined by their relation to the ruling family.²⁹

Another element of this emerging system of autocracy was the 'feeding' of officials from the land (*kormlenie*). The practice had its origins in Kievan Rus but became widespread in the Mongol period. Because he lacked the currency to pay his officials' salaries, the ruling prince allowed them to 'feed themselves' by extracting goods and money from the population under their control. This 'feeding' system was an easy means of self-enrichment for the boyars, who competed with each other to get their noses in the biggest trough. Their abuse of office was so rife that, even when the people complained to the prince about overfeeding by a district chief and succeeded in getting him removed, the replacement might be worse. The *kormlenie* system was formally abolished in 1556, but the corrupt practice which it legitimised would long be carried on by local officials through other means (taking bribes, extorting money from the population, pocketing state revenues, and so on). Here was the root of the corruption that has plagued the Russian state for centuries. Here indeed was the origin of the oligarchic system that operates today, in which the only way to become rich is to be a member of the highest ruling circles or enjoy their protection.

It was in the north and east of Russia, the domain of Muscovy, that the legacies of Mongol rule were most lasting. In the south and west, corresponding to Ukraine and Belarus, the Mongol hold was weaker and broken earlier, as most of these territories were drawn to Poland or Lithuania from the early fourteenth century. To some extent this greater freedom from the Mongol influence set the lands of Kiev on a different historical trajectory from Muscovy. The Kievan lands were more oriented to the West, less exposed to the institutions of patrimonial autocracy. But this contrast was not so great as to justify the claims of today's Ukrainian nationalists – namely that Russia became despotic and Asiatic, and its people servile, because of the 'Tatar yoke', whereas the Ukrainians were always freedom-loving and more 'European' because they had not been ruled by the Mongols. These are distinctions that belong to nationalist myth-making, although of course, like many myths, they contain elements of truth.

The Russian lands controlled by Muscovy emerged strengthened, their people toughened by the harsh experience of Mongol rule, better equipped to survive the hardships that awaited them and more united nationally than they had been previously. Only Moscow was now capable of liberating them from the Mongols, of ruling all the Russians in a single state. As Karamzin put it, 'Moscow owes its greatness to the khans.'[30]

3

TSAR AND GOD

On 16 January 1547, the grand prince of Moscow, Ivan IV, became the first tsar and autocrat of all Russia. Ivan the Terrible, as he is better known, was just sixteen when he was crowned in the Cathedral of the Dormition, the main church of the Moscow metropolitan Makary, head of the Russian Church. Most of the ceremony's ritual elements had been invented or adapted from the Byzantines. They signified a new imperial myth about Russia and its tsars.

On his entry to the candlelit cathedral, Ivan was greeted with a choral chant of *mnogoletie* ('many years') and a large assembly of the highest dignitaries. He climbed twelve steps to a dais where, in front of the high iconostasis, there were two thrones, one for Makary, the other for Ivan, symbolising the Byzantine ideal of a 'symphony' of Church and state ruling God's dominion. Ivan listed his ancestors, grand princes of Moscow and all Russia, and proclaimed his wish to be recognised 'with all our ancient titles'. Makary crowned him, blessed him with the cross and seated him upon his throne. At this point Ivan made a new demand to be crowned tsar 'according to our ancient custom'. Makary assented, proclaiming, 'Now thou art anointed and titled Grand Prince Ivan Vasilevich, God-crowned Tsar and Autocrat of all great Russia.'[1] The clergy broke into a sacred chant as Makary blessed him with a cross, anointed him with oil, conferring sacred charisma on him, placed a sceptre in his hand and crowned him with the Cap of

Monomakh, a golden skullcap trimmed with sable, inlaid with jewels and surmounted by a cross. Legend said that it had been presented by the Byzantine emperor Constantine IX Monomachos to his grandson Vladimir on his coronation as grand prince of Kiev. The cap was meant to symbolise the new tsar's claim to the imperial title of the Byzantines. In fact Vladimir was only two years old when his grandfather died, and would not be crowned grand prince of Kiev until almost fifty years later. As for the cap, it was almost certainly not Byzantine but from Central Asia, probably a gift from Khan Uzbek to the Daniilovichi in the early fourteenth century.[2] But facts were not really the point.

Makary gave a sermon on the tsar's sacred duties to protect the Orthodox by 'ruling with the fear of God'. Most of the sermon was taken from the *Patrologia Graecae*, a series of maxims addressed to Emperor Justinian by Agapetus, deacon of the Hagia Sophia in Constantinople, around the time of his coronation in 527. Makary emphasised the sacred source of the tsar's authority. In the coronation ceremony this was symbolised by the act of anointment linking Ivan to David, 'whom God anointed to be king over the people of Israel'. In the ideology of sacred kingship ('Wisdom Theology') embraced by Makary, the tsar, like Christ, contained within his body both the mortal and the divine. He had divine charisma, a gift of grace that made him appear in his power like a god. As it was expressed in the fourteenth-century Church Slavonic version of the Agapetus text which Makary used in his sermon: 'The Tsar's mortal body is like that of any man, but in his power he is like Almighty God.'[3] The lesson was self-evident: if the tsar embodied God on earth, it was heresy to oppose him.

The dual nature of the Christian ruler – fallible in his humanity but divine in his princely functions – was a common notion in Europe.[4] The tension it created in the monarch's image was resolved in western Europe by distinguishing between the mortal person and the sacred office of the king. This distinction would allow the concept of an abstract state to develop in the West as a counterbalance to the king. But that did not happen in Russia, where tsar and state were considered one – united in the body of a single mortal being, who as man and ruler was an instrument of God.

The title 'tsar', the anointment of Ivan, the Byzantine regalia and the sermon – these were modern reinventions of Byzantine traditions to create the aura of an ancient lineage and imperial status for Ivan. The legend of the Cap of Monomakh had circulated only from the early sixteenth century. It appeared in *The Tale of the Princes of Vladimir*, which spuriously claimed that Moscow's princes were descended from the Byzantine emperors through the grand prince Vladimir (the one who had converted to Christianity in 988). Illustrations of *The Tale* were carved in bas-relief on Ivan's throne in the Dormition Cathedral. *The Book of Pedigrees*, commissioned by Makary, went one step further in this invention of Moscow's past. It traced Ivan's descent from the Roman emperor Augustus, preposterously claiming that the Riurikids were descendants of the emperor's brother Prus, the Roman ruler of Prussia. Ivan was thus hailed as the blood heir to the emperors of Rome and their successors in Constantinople, the 'new' or 'second' Rome as it was called. By inventing this imperial heritage, Moscow claimed the right to rule the former lands of Kievan Rus that had been under the spiritual authority of the patriarch in Constantinople – including territories (in today's Ukraine and Belarus) that had since passed to Poland–Lithuania.

Ivan's elevation to the status of a tsar was a statement about Russia's status in the world. Derived from the Roman term 'Caesar', the title had been given by the Russians to the khan of the Golden Horde, the Ottoman sultan and the Old Testament kings. By being crowned a tsar, Ivan would become the equal of the Holy Roman emperor, the secular head of Western Christianity, rivalling his authority through his leadership of Eastern Christianity.

Ivan was the first of the grand princes to be crowned tsar, but the title had been used on occasion by his predecessors Ivan III (reigned 1462–1505) and Vasily III (1505–33) to aggrandise their status. They sought the recognition of Europe, and taking on the mantle of Byzantium was their way to achieve this. Through his marriage to Sophia Paleologue, the niece of the last Byzantine emperor, Ivan III had staked his claim to the imperial role vacated by the Paleologues. He made the double-headed eagle Russia's coat of arms, although this was in imitation more of the Habsburgs than of the Byzantines.[5] Ivan IV carried this claim for recognition to a higher level still. He insisted that European rulers call him 'tsar'. As his megalomania grew, he took it as an insult and broke off diplomatic relations if they did not. He looked down on monarchs like Elizabeth I, the English queen, who had to rule with the consent of their people. No such limits had been placed on him.

Crowning him as tsar was equally important to Makary's mission to promote Moscow as the last true seat of the Christian faith, the successor to Byzantium, following the conquest of Constantinople by the Turks. The Russian Church had been moving to the idea of this role since the Council of Florence (1438–9), when the Byzantine emperor and many other leaders of the Eastern Church had pressed for a reunion with Rome to secure the assistance of the Catholic powers against the Muslim infidels. In 1448, in a declaration of their independence from Constantinople, the Russian bishops took it on themselves to name Iona of Riazan their metropolitan, an office normally appointed by the patriarch of Constantinople. The fall of the Byzantine capital, only five years later, confirmed to the Russians that they had done well to create an independent national church. Their conviction grew in 1458, when Lithuania broke off its ecclesiastical relations with Moscow and placed its Orthodox population under the spiritual authority of the Uniate Church in Rome.

To defend its independence the Russian Church developed the idea that Moscow had replaced Constantinople as the authentic capital of Orthodoxy. Church leaders glorified the Muscovite grand princes as the only true defenders of the Christian faith, God's chosen saviours of humanity. By the 1530s the idea had been fleshed out in church tracts and legendary tales into what would later become known as the 'Third Rome doctrine'. It was best expressed by a monk named Filofei in a letter to Vasily III's representative in Pskov around 1523. Because both Rome and Byzantium had fallen into apostasy, Moscow's grand prince was 'the only Tsar for

Christians in the world'. Moscow had become the last capital of the true faith, Filofei argued, 'for two Romes have fallen, the Third stands, and there shall not be a fourth'.[6]

The Third Rome doctrine was quickly taken up by Russia's Church leaders, none more so than Makary, a champion of Moscow's imperial ambitions. He cited it in his sermon on Ivan's coronation to underline the sacred duties of the tsar to defend the purity of Russian Orthodoxy against foreign and internal heresies. If Ivan failed and Russia also fell into apostasy, as Rome and Byzantium had done, the end of the world, no less, would be the result, because, as Filofei had warned, there would not be a fourth Rome. Such apocalyptic warnings were to play a crucial role in Ivan's reign. He ruled with terror in the firm belief that the Day of Judgement was at hand, that the world would end and that it was his divine duty to purge the Russian land of sin in preparation for that end.

Ivan's elevation to the status of a tsar was also meant to help him reassert the crown's authority after fourteen years of boyar fighting for the throne during his minority. He was only three when his father, Vasily III, died in 1533. Ivan's mother, Elena Glinskaya, at first acted as regent, but she died, probably from poisoning, in 1538, whereupon the major boyar clans, the Glinskys, Belskys and Shuiskys, engaged in a brutal and chaotic struggle for power, in which there were fourteen murders, two forced depositions of metropolitans and three changes of the ruling clique before Ivan came of age in 1546. According to his own account, Ivan had a miserable childhood, neglected and mistreated by 'uncaring boyars', especially the princes of the Shuisky clan.[7] At the age of just thirteen, he took revenge on them by ordering the killing of Prince Andrei Shuisky, the last of the Shuiskys at his court. As soon as he came of age, Ivan took a wife to secure his dynasty by fathering an heir that might reach maturity before he died. Political stability depended on eradicating rival claims to the succession. His choice fell on Anastasia Romanova, the daughter of a boyar clan that had stood aside from the power struggles during his minority.

By promoting a neutral family to the highest rank at court, Ivan hoped to unite the boyar clans by giving them an undisputed heir to recognise. However much the clans might fight among themselves, they depended on stability to defend their oligarchic interests.

Stability was also crucial to the building of a centralised political system capable of governing the growing empire of Moscow. Like other European monarchs at this time, Ivan aimed to forge a single kingdom from the loose network of principalities, each one ruled by its own princes and boyars, which had developed in the fifteenth century as Moscow swallowed up new lands. This kingdom-building had begun in the reign of Ivan's grandfather Ivan III, and had been continued by his father Vasily. Between 1462 and 1533, the Muscovite state expanded more than three times in size and population, as it annexed and absorbed the principalities and republics of Iaroslavl (in 1471), Perm (1472), Rostov-Suzdal (1473), Tver (1485), Viatka (1489), Pskov (1510), Smolensk (1514) and Riazan (1521).

Its most important conquest was the city republic of Novgorod, with its extensive northern lands. Novgorod had signed a treaty recognising Moscow's sovereignty in 1456. But there remained a faction of its leaders that still looked to Lithuania to protect the city's liberties against Moscow. When Novgorod requested Lithuania's military help in 1470, Ivan III declared war on the republic and defeated it, forcing it to renew the 1456 accord. The city's patriots would still not submit, so, once again, in 1478, Ivan sent his armies in. This time Moscow annexed Novgorod, confiscating all its agricultural territories. In a symbolic act to underline the end of the city republic, the Kremlin's forces took away the bell that Novgorod had used to summon its *veche*, the assembly of its citizens.

Moscow was enriched by these conquests. By the end of the fifteenth century it had become one of the wealthiest trading cities in Europe. Merchants came from Germany, Poland, the Habsburg lands and Italy to buy its precious furs and the horses which were brought by Tatars to Moscow in their tens of thousands every year. Moscow itself had a population of perhaps 100,000 people by the early sixteenth century, almost twice as many as London. Although the houses were all built of wood, the city contained large stone churches, many in the Kremlin, whose thick stone walls were completed at this time.

The Kremlin was a symbol of Moscow's power and arrival on the European scene. Its vast complex of palaces and churches was constructed largely by Italians. The Hall of Facets (the tsar's palace) was the work of the Venetian architects Marco Ruffo and Pietro Antonio Solari, who built the Kremlin's walls in the style of the Sforza castle in Milan. Aristotele Fioravanti was responsible for the newly rebuilt Dormition Cathedral (1475–9) and Alevise Novi for the Archangel Cathedral, completed twenty years later. Over centuries many of the Kremlin's buildings became Russified – Russian architectural elements and ornaments were gradually added – so that today visitors will not easily recognise its Italianate character.

There was an important contrast between the Kremlin and the great Renaissance fortresses of northern Italy. The Kremlin's walls enclosed the city's most important churches, whereas the cathedrals of northern Italy were always built outside the castle walls. It was a symbolic difference. In Latin Europe the Church and state were close allies but separate entities, and sometimes in conflict, particularly when the pope attempted to depose or restrain kings, a right claimed and practised by the papacy before the rise of the absolutist state in the sixteenth century. But in Russia Church and state were meant to rule as one. The location of the tsar's palace next to the Dormition Cathedral may be taken as a symbol of this symphony between the two. They were united in a theocratic empire where the tsar in office was revered as sacred because his power came from God.

Autocracy in Russia developed differently from the European absolutist monarchies. If it took its theory from Byzantium, it owed more in practice to the legacies of Mongol rule. There were of course some common patterns of state-building shared by Russia and the West. From the reign of Ivan III, Moscow's aim, like that of any state, was to extend its power to all corners of the realm and roll back the powers of those princes and boyars who blocked a unified authority. As in Europe, the main function of this centralising state was to finance armed forces. The 'military revolution' of the early modern period – in which the medieval lance and pike were rendered obsolete by mobile siege artillery and gunpowder weapons – massively increased the cost of war. Monarchies built larger standing armies in their pursuit of territorial aggrandisement; they fought more wars; and they needed bigger and more centralised bureaucracies to collect the taxes that financed these wars. Muscovy was no exception to this European trend. It was in many way a typical example of the 'fiscal–military state' that emerged in Europe in the sixteenth century.

From the beginning of his reign Ivan IV set out to increase the powers of his state. He appointed his supporters to the Boyars' Council, or Duma, and created an Assembly of the Land (*Zemsky Sobor*) that brought together representatives of the three main social classes (the nobility, the clergy and the commoners) to consult on policies. He expanded the treasury bureaucracy by employing secretaries, scribes and clerks to manage tax collection; tightened Moscow's hold on the administration of the provinces by replacing boyar governors with centrally appointed officials; and introduced a new legal code to standardise the laws of the former principalities and make their rulers more dependent on Moscow. All these measures were in line with the reforms carried out by European monarchs to forge one kingdom from the various territories, each with their own legal structures and customs, which came under their control.

Other elements of Ivan's state-building were taken from the Mongols, however. There was nothing like them in the West. European visitors to Moscow were astounded by the extent of the tsar's power over his subjects, including the nobility. 'All the people consider themselves to be the slaves of their Tsar,' remarked Herberstein, who thought that 'in the sway which he holds over his people, he surpasses the monarchs of the whole world'.[8] Ivan referred to his servitors as 'slaves' (*kholopy*). Protocol required every boyar, even members of the princely clans, to refer to themselves as 'your slave' when addressing him – a ritual reminiscent of the servility displayed by the Mongols to their khans. This subservience was fundamental to the patrimonial autocracy that distinguished Russia from the European monarchies. The concept of the state was embodied in the tsar as sovereign or lord of all the Russian lands. The system placed his servitors at his mercy. If they displeased him, he could take away their land. They had no rights of property to protect them from their sovereign.

In 1556, Ivan decreed mandatory military service for all Russia's landowners – whether they were boyars, who had owned their land for centuries, or *pomeshchiki*, a new class of servitors rewarded by the tsar with grants of land (*pomeste*). For every 100 *chetverty* (55 hectares) of arable land in his domain, the landowner had to give one fully equipped soldier and one horse to the army. He also had to serve himself, or send a retainer in his place. There were laws like this in other countries in Europe, but what made this one different was its novel principle, unknown in the rest of Europe, that the landowner held his land on condition of performing state service. He did not own it as private property. Whatever land he had in his possession could not be sold or passed on to his sons without the service obligations attached to its ownership.

Through the system of *pomeste* the tsar was able to raise a force of 20,000 soldiers at short notice. The system was similar to one developed in the khanate of Kazan and was probably derived from it. There was nothing like it in the West where feudalism entailed private landed property with individual rights attached to it. The *pomeste* system had been inaugurated by Ivan III after the defeat of Novgorod in 1478. Lands confiscated from the city state were given as *pomeste* to the victorious servicemen, mostly sons of the low-ranking boyars, who thus became *pomeshchiki*. The tsar's granting of *pomeste* became widespread throughout Muscovy (except in the north where there was no foreign threat, so no militias were needed). Older forms of landed property (*votchiny*) were gradually eliminated by laws restricting their sale or inheritance. By the middle of the sixteenth century, the granting of *pomeste* had created 23,000 new landholding servitors, a number that would double over the next hundred years.[9] As this service class increased in size, the pressure on the state to find more land for it intensified. This became a major driving force of Russia's territorial expansion – the conquest of new lands for the military servitors.

One result of the *pomeste* system was the creation of a landowning service class with only weak ties to a particular community. The *pomeshchiki* were creatures of the state. Despatched from one place to another in the tsar's empire, they had neither time nor inclination to put down roots in one locality. The *pomeshchik* looked on his estate as a source of revenue and readily exchanged it for another closer to his place of service, if this was for any length of time. All the things that connected the nobility of feudal Europe to a village or county – networks of charity and patronage, parish life, corporate bodies and local government, in short everything that fosters regional identities and loyalties – were thus missing in Russia. It was only from the middle of the nineteenth century that these local networks and identities began to evolve – too late, as it turned out, to sustain the development of an independent civil society or a democratic form of government.

The persistence of autocracy in Russia is explained less by the state's strength than by the weakness of society. There were few public institutions to resist the power of the monarchy. The landowning class was overly dependent on the tsar. Its members were too supine and malleable to play the role of Europe's independent aristocracy, whose rights of landed property and standing as the leaders of communities enabled it to oppose the encroachments of the absolutist state and defend local liberties. The Boyar Councils and Assemblies of the Land cannot be compared to Europe's parliaments and estates general, which became national assemblies, eventually leading to democracy. The boyar assemblies were not representative, for no one had elected them. They had no power to restrain the tsar, who summoned them when he saw fit to consult them but did not have to follow their opinion. This imbalance – between a dominating state and a weak society – has shaped the course of Russian history.

The reign of Ivan the Terrible marked the start of Russia's growth as an imperial power. Between 1500 and the revolution of 1917, the Russian Empire grew at an astonishing rate, 130 square kilometres on average every day.[10] From the nucleus of Muscovy it expanded into the world's largest territorial empire. The history of Russia, as Kliuchevsky put it, is the 'history of a country that is colonizing itself'.[11]

How can we explain this extraordinary growth, unparalleled by any other power in the history of the world? From the early nineteenth century, when the European powers first began to fear it, the most common Western explanation was that Russia was expansionist in character. This has been a long-held view, reinforced in the Cold War when Soviet expansion into eastern Europe was explained in part by Russophobic stereotypes about the 'Russian menace' dating from the nineteenth century. But it cannot be applied so easily to the sixteenth century, when Russia's territorial spread was comparable in its ambition to that of other powers on the European continent, such as Poland–Lithuania and the Habsburgs, or to those with overseas empires, such as England, France and Spain.

Russia's enlargement in the sixteenth century was facilitated by the lack of any natural frontiers, which also made it vulnerable to attack. The greatest danger was in the west, where it was threatened by Poland–Lithuania (united in 1569), which blocked Russia's access to the Baltic Sea and claimed most of the former western territories of Kievan Rus. To the south, the khanate of Crimea was another major threat, not least because of its close alliance with the Ottoman Empire. The Crimeans blocked the Russians' access to the Black Sea and the Muslim world beyond. Their raids were a constant problem for the Russians on their southern frontier, which traversed the grasslands east of Kiev. They necessitated the construction of defensive lines and fortresses manned by a new border force made up of Cossacks.

The Cossacks' name derived from the Turkic word *qazaqi*, meaning 'adventurers' or 'vagrant soldiers' who lived in freedom as bandits on the steppe. Many of the Cossacks were remnants of the

Mongol army (Tamerlane had started out as a *qazaq*). They were joined by Russians from the north who fled in growing numbers to the 'wild lands' of the south because of the economic crises caused by wars, rising taxes and crop failures in the 'little ice age' of the sixteenth century. There was no ethnic barrier to 'cossacking'. Forming themselves into military fraternities, the Cossacks were recruited by the Lithuanians and then by the Russians to defend their southern borders against the Crimean Tatars, the Nogais and other steppeland tribes. For their services they were rewarded with money, grants of land, tax exemptions and other rights and privileges which they guarded jealously as symbols of their freedom and superiority to the farming peasantry.

Meanwhile, to the east, Russia's neighbour was the khanate of Kazan, which occupied the middle Volga lands between Viatka in the north and Saratov in the south. On its own it was not strong enough to threaten Moscow. But if it joined Crimea, the strongest of the khanates, it could form an advance base for an attack on Muscovy. The only way for Moscow to prevent this danger was to conquer Kazan first. Because Moscow was not strong enough to fight on two fronts at once, Ivan reasoned that he needed to eliminate the danger of Kazan before any clash with Poland–Lithuania, whose gunpowder army was a greater challenge than the khanates' bow-and-arrow cavalry.

Ivan led the first campaign against Kazan in 1547–8. The Russian archers were unable to defeat the khanate's cavalry and, with their supply lines overstretched, they had to retreat. For their second campaign, in 1552, the Russians changed their strategy. They switched to gunpowder war and established an advance fortress at Sviazhsk on the Volga near Kazan to maintain munition supplies. They used fixed artillery and musketeers (*streltsy*), newly formed as the first standing units of the Russian army, to deliver concentrated fire. They employed Dutch engineers to mine under Kazan's walls, where they managed to position forty-eight barrels of gunpowder, enough to blast a massive hole in the city's defences when they were exploded in the early hours of 2 October. The Russians stormed the city, killing everyone in sight.

The conquest of Kazan was celebrated as a providential victory for the Orthodox, the first against Islam since the fall of Constantinople almost a hundred years before. The Russian Church portrayed it as the start of a crusade. It called for the forcible conversion of the Muslim infidels. To mark the victory a large horizontal icon, *The Blessed Host of the Heavenly Tsar*, was painted facing the tsar's throne in the Dormition Cathedral. Known as *The Church Militant*, it shows the mounted figure of Ivan following the Archangel Michael in a procession of Russian troops from the hell-like burning city of Kazan to Moscow, depicted like Jerusalem, where they are received by the Madonna and Child. The iconography borrows from the Book of Revelation, in which Michael defeats Satan before the Apocalypse. Ivan appears as a new King David and the Russians as God's Chosen People, the new Israelites, reinforcing Moscow's mythic status and mission in the world as the Third Rome.[12]

Four years later, in 1556, the Russians scored another victory, this time defeating the khanate of Astrakhan. The tsar commemorated his triumph by ordering the construction of a new cathedral on Red Square in Moscow, so named because the word for 'red' (*krasny*) was connected to the word for 'beautiful' (*krasivyi*). The Cathedral of the Intercession on the Moat became popularly known as St Basil's. Loosely modelled on the Church of the Holy Sepulchre, it was meant to reinforce the notion of Moscow as the New Jerusalem. Its main chapel was devoted to Christ's entry into the Holy City on Palm Sunday. It became the focus of the annual Palm Sunday procession, when the tsar, on foot, led his people to the cathedral – a ritual to symbolise his divine role as the leader of the Orthodox – followed by the metropolitan, seated on a horse, as Christ had been on a donkey when he came to Jerusalem.

Completed in 1560, St Basil's was more than a symbol of Russia's victory over the khanates. It was a triumphant proclamation of the country's liberation from the Tatar culture that had dominated it since the thirteenth century. With its showy colours, its playful ornament and outrageous onion domes, St Basil's was intended as a joyful celebration of the Byzantine traditions to which Russia now returned (although it was more ornate and oriental in its style than any church to be found in Byzantium).

The dedication to St Basil was also rather strange, because Basil was the city's favourite Holy Fool (*iurodyvy*), a figure without parallel in the Orthodox or any other Christian tradition. In Russian folklore, the 'fool for the sake of Christ', or Holy Fool, held the status of a saint, though he acted more like a madman or a clown, dressed in bizarre clothes, with an iron cap or harness on his head and chains beneath his shirt, like the shamans of Asia. He wandered as a poor man round the countryside, living off the alms of villagers, who found portents in his strange riddles and believed in his supernatural powers of divination and healing. Unafraid to speak the truth to the rich and powerful, he was frequently received by the nobility and became a common presence at the court. Ivan enjoyed the company of Holy Fools.

The conquest of Kazan was of huge symbolic importance. It gave the tsar a new status, increasing his prestige among the steppe nomads as a legitimate successor to the Mongol khans, at the same time as confirming his imperial claim to be a universal Christian ruler, heir to the emperor of Byzantium. In 1557, Ivan requested confirmation of his title 'tsar' from the patriarch of Constantinople. It was recognition he had merited, he argued, as a liberator of Orthodoxy from Islam. His request was granted in 1561. To secure his dynasty Ivan also sent a long list of his ancestors and relatives to be sanctified as tsars by the patriarch, thereby inventing a genealogy that linked his family to the emperors of Byzantium stretching back to ancient times.

With Kazan in their hands, the steppelands to the east were opened up to the Russians. Their armies could push on to control the riches of Siberia and the trading routes to Central Asia and China. But the newly conquered Tatars were not so easy to control. There were revolts against the Russians and their religious missionaries. Moscow feared that the Ottomans and Crimeans would intervene to defend their co-religionists. The Russians backed off from forcible conversions and resigned themselves to a long period of pacification, while they built a defensive line of fortress garrisons and monasteries between Kazan and Arzamas.

Buoyed by their success in the east, Ivan turned his armies to the west, where Russia's access to the Baltic Sea was blocked by Sweden, Lithuania and the Livonian Order of Teutonic Knights. Capturing the Livonian territories (Estonia and the northern half of Latvia today) would allow Moscow to control the ports on Russia's European trading routes. With the acquisition of Kazan and Astrakhan, which had controlled the Volga route, such a victory would give the Russians the entire river network between the Baltic Sea and the Caspian, enabling them to profit from the silk roads between Asia and Europe.

In 1558, the Russians captured Narva, a crucial port on the Gulf of Finland, and seized Dorpat, deep in the Livonian lands. The other Baltic powers intervened to block the Russians' advance and obtain portions of Livonia for themselves. A local frontier war thus became a regional conflict in which Russia, Poland–Lithuania, Sweden, Denmark and Livonia were involved. The Crimean Tatars, smarting from the loss of Kazan to Russia, supported Poland–Lithuania, so that the Russians had to fight a two-front war. Twice the Crimeans attacked Moscow – in 1571, when they burned the wooden city to the ground, and the next year, when they were defeated by the Muscovites. The Crimeans would continue to harass the Russian lands in the 1570s. Under these conditions it was practically impossible for Moscow to sustain its early victories in the Livonian War. Without a Baltic fleet it could not hold on to Narva (which fell to the Swedes in 1579) nor take the ports of Riga or Revel (Tallinn) because any siege by land alone was bound to be defeated by defenders able to receive supplies and reinforcements from the sea. The war dragged on until 1583, when the Poles expelled the Russians from Livonia, which they then divided with the Swedes. Its economic cost to the Russians was immense. Entire regions of the country were abandoned by the peasants, who fled to the 'wild lands' of the south.

There was an important lesson to be learned from the Livonian War. Russia could more easily expand in Asia, where it was a

European power, than it could in Europe, where its western neighbours were stronger.

The long Russian conquest of Siberia began with the annexation of Kazan. After the downfall of the khanate of Kazan, its tributaries, including Udmurt and Bashkiria, recognised Ivan as their new khan. The Siberian khanate in Tiumen also began paying annual tribute to Moscow. Ivan was reluctant to send troops to occupy these lands. He did not want a war with the khanates. Instead he licensed private entrepreneurs to settle on the land, allowing them to exploit it for their own economic purposes and defend themselves with mercenary troops, usually Cossacks.

The Stroganovs were the first big beneficiaries of this colonial policy. A wealthy merchant family with interests in saltworks and mining, in 1558 they leased vast tracts of land on the Kama River between Kazan and Perm. Their only obligation was to report on any copper, gold or silver they might find. More grants of land were leased by them over the next decade, making the Stroganovs the masters of a domain not much smaller than England. As they explored and began to settle on the borderlands of the Siberian khanate, in the early 1570s, they were attacked by the khan's troops. A hundred settlers were killed in the first of these attacks, and with each assault the khan's forces seemed to grow.

The Stroganovs appealed to the tsar to let them take the fight into the heart of the khanate rather than continue fighting a defensive war. Angered by the killing of one of his envoys to the khan, Ivan gave them permission to conquer the Siberian khanate. At once he had second thoughts and reversed his decision, fearful that he might become embroiled in a general war if the Crimeans joined their co-religionists; but the Stroganovs ignored his counter-order and recruited Cossack fighters under the command of a chieftain known as Ermak to invade the khanate of Siberia.

Most of what we know about Ermak is derived from Russian folklore and legends. He is celebrated as a great hero, Russia's Columbus, for 'discovering' Siberia. All we know is that he had fought in the Livonian War and engaged in banditry along the Volga before he was recruited by the Stroganovs. His mercenary force of 540 Cossacks set off from Perm in 1582. Travelling by river, two months later they reached Qashliq, a fortress stuffed with furs, silk and gold near the modern city of Tobolsk, which they captured easily. Their muskets were too powerful for the Tatar cavalry. Ermak set up his base at Qashliq and set about the subjugation of the neighbouring tribes, forcing them to pay tribute. He was killed by Tatar forces loyal to the Siberian khanate in an ambush by the River Irtysh in 1585. It would take another fifteen years before the Siberian khanate was conquered, and another century before the Russians laid eyes on the Pacific. But Ermak's bold adventure would go down in the story of Russia as the 'conquest of Siberia'.[13]

We know very little about Ivan as a human being. There is no surviving letter or decree in his hand, so we cannot say for sure if he was even literate. We have no record of his personal relations with any of his seven wives or his children; no account of life at Ivan's court; and no authentic portrait of the tsar – for all such images in Ivan's lifetime were iconic and imaginary. In 1963, Ivan's bones were exhumed from his sarcophagus in the Archangel Cathedral in the Kremlin and used to reconstruct a 'virtual' bust, which confirms contemporary descriptions of the tsar as tall and strong with a high forehead, looking like an 'angry warrior'.[14]

Ivan became 'the Terrible' – in the sense we understand today – only in the eighteenth century. The epithet (*grozny*) was first applied to him in the early seventeenth century, when a rich folklore about the tsar was just developing. At that time the meaning of the word was closer to the sense of awe-inspiring and formidable rather than cruel or harsh – so basically positive. In folklore Ivan was portrayed as a strong tsar, a guardian of justice, who had protected the people by punishing the boyars for their sins. It was only a century later, once historians began to look more closely at the terror he unleashed, that the words 'Ivan the Terrible' became synonymous with executions, tortures, grisly massacres and a mad and monstrous tyranny that reason struggles to explain. This was the image of Ivan, terrible and fierce with his all-seeing eye, immortalised by Viktor Vasnetsov in his 1897 painting, *Tsar Ivan IV the Terrible*.

Perhaps his violence was rooted in his personality. It appears that Ivan was unhinged by the death, in 1560, of his wife Anastasia, who had had a calming influence on his tempestuous character. Ivan suspected the boyars of having poisoned her, a suspicion he connected to the 'boyar plot' of 1553, when he had been gravely ill and some of the leading boyar clans had failed to swear allegiance to his infant son Dmitry in the event of his death (Dmitry himself died when he was eight months old). The loss of his younger brother, the deaf and dumb Yuri, for whom he had displayed a tender affection, followed by the death of Makary in 1563, left the tsar even more isolated. But the straw that broke the camel's back was the defection of Prince Andrei Kurbsky, the tsar's old friend and commander of his armies in Livonia, who fled to join the king of Poland–Lithuania in 1564. Ivan now saw treason everywhere.

It was at this point that Ivan set up the *oprichnina* – a separate domain made up of lands confiscated from the princes and boyars. The land was given to *oprichniki*, a new class of loyal servitors, numbering perhaps 5,000 men, who formed his private army, charged with fighting internal sedition. Recruited on the basis of their loyalty to the tsar, the *oprichniki* were forbidden to have any contact with the nobles of the *zemshchina*, the lands that remained outside the *oprichnina*. They dressed in long black cloaks like a monk's habit and rode around the country on black horses with dogs' heads and brooms attached to their bridles – symbols of their mission to hunt out the tsar's enemies and sweep them from the land.[15]

The bloodletting began with the slaughter of those clans whose leaders had defected to Poland–Lithuania, the Belskys, Kurbskys and Teterins, and the kinsmen of advisers such as Adashev and Silvester who had fallen from favour. The system of collective responsibility was taken by the tsar to justify the killing of all traitors' families. From 1569, the scale of the repressions was increased to wholesale massacres in towns such as Tver, Klin, Novgorod and Pskov, which were deemed too independent and freedom-loving, and probably suspected by Ivan of sympathising with the Lithuanians and the Poles. Churches were looted, houses burned and 30,000 people perished by the sword or died from hunger and disease, which took hold of these towns once the raiders left.

The final scene of reckoning with the 'boyar traitors' took place on the Poganaya Meadow in Moscow on 25 July 1570. The tsar appeared on horseback dressed in black, accompanied by 1,500 mounted musketeers. Three hundred noblemen, in various stages of decrepitude suggesting the tortures they had undergone, were brought before Ivan. As an act of mercy, he released 184 of them, and then proceeded to supervise the killing of the rest. Some were tied to stakes and cut to pieces, others flayed or boiled in water. An old man who could barely walk was run through with a spear, stabbed and beheaded by Ivan. After a few hours of killing, the tsar had had enough and withdrew to his palace.[16]

In his correspondence with Kurbsky, Ivan justified this terror on the grounds that he was ordained by God. Any act of treason against him was a sin that he was free to punish in God's name. Citing Romans 13: 3–4,* Ivan maintained that a tsar 'beareth not the sword in vain, but to revenge evil-doers, and for the praise of the righteous'.[17] In his view the *oprichniki* were a religious instrument to chastise sinners and cleanse the 'Holy Russian land' in preparation for the Last Judgement. The brutal killing methods which he oversaw reflected his ideas of divine punishment. Most of his victims were murdered suddenly (often by beheading) so that they did not have time to receive the last rites and save their souls. Many of his favourite punishments (victims burned alive or devoured by wild animals) were meant to replicate the torments of hell.[18] Ivan saw himself as a sword-bearing archangel, an agent sent by God to protect the Orthodox and purge the world of infidels and sinners before the Apocalypse. In his personal mythology there was no contradiction between his

---

* 'For rulers are not a terror to good conduct, but to bad. Would you have no fear of the one who is in authority? Then do what is good, and you will receive his approval, for he is God's servant for your good. But if you do wrong, be afraid, for he does not bear the sword in vain. For he is the servant of God, an avenger who carries out God's wrath on the wrongdoer.'

status as a righteous Christian king and the cruel violence which he meted out as an expression of God's wrath.[19]

The terror ended suddenly, as terror often does, when the tsar had the main *oprichnik* leader, Alexei Basmanov, executed in 1570. Ivan had suspected him of working for the Poles and Lithuanians. A large-scale purge of the *oprichnik* leaders then followed. The *oprichnina* was abolished, never to be mentioned again in the tsar's presence. Always fearful of treason, Ivan continued to order executions of suspected boyar clans. But his main response to the dangers he perceived was to retire to his residence and surround himself with bodyguards. At one point, in 1575, he even abdicated from the throne and named as tsar his loyal retainer Semen Bekbulatovich, a Tatar descendant of Chingiz Khan.

Was Ivan remorseful in his final years? There is evidence that he tried to redress the injuries which he had caused, forgiving many people in disgrace, endowing monasteries and praying for the dead. In one draft of his will, probably dictated while seriously ill in 1579, the tsar described himself as the 'worst sinner on earth, corrupt of reason and bestial of mind'. But this may have been religious rhetoric. Throughout his reign, Ivan's moods swung between mad fits of temper and remorseful prayer. Sometimes he withdrew from public life and retreated to a monastery. He spoke of his desire to become a monk.

His last killing was the murder of his twenty-seven-year-old son and heir, the Tsarevich Ivan, in 1581. The story goes that he came across his son's wife in her chambers dressed only in her underwear. Considering her conduct indecent, he began to hit her with his staff. His son tried to stop him, only to be killed by a blow to his head. The horror of the scene was captured by Repin in his 1885 painting *Ivan the Terrible and his Son Ivan on 16 November 1581*, in which Ivan is shown consumed by remorse.

By one rash act, Ivan had jeopardised his dynasty, for the next in line, the Tsarevich Fedor, the sole surviving son of his first wife Anastasia, was mentally deficient, while his other son, born to Maria Nagaya, the last of his wives, was only one when Ivan died in 1584. The dispute over who should rule would lead to the civil war that engulfed Russia over the next thirty years.

Was Ivan that terrible? Was he any worse than, say, Cesare Borgia, King Henry VIII or Pope Julius II, *il Papa terribile*? In the Western mind the name Ivan the Terrible is synonymous with the 'barbaric' and 'despotic' nature of Russia. But were his methods any different to those advised by the great Renaissance thinker of Florence, Niccolò Machiavelli, in *The Prince*?

> Men have less scruple in offending one who makes himself
> loved than one who makes himself feared; for love is held
> by a chain of obligation which, men being selfish, is broken
> whenever it serves their purpose; but fear is maintained by a
> dread of punishment which never fails.[20]

Ivan may never have heard of the Florentine philosopher, but he shared his ideas of human nature and kingship, and certainly applied them in Russia.

The modern image of Ivan goes back to Karamzin's *History*, where he is portrayed as a tragically divided personality, torn and remorseful about the violence he was forced to use as a ruler. This was the dramatic conception of Eisenstein's *Ivan the Terrible* (1944–6), a cinematic commentary on the human costs of tyranny which the director intended as a moral lesson to Stalin. In the first part of the film Eisenstein depicts the heroic aspects of Ivan: his vision of a unified Russia; his state-building; his fearless struggle against the scheming boyars; his strong authority and leadership in the war against Kazan; his ambition to secure a Baltic coastline for the empire. All these virtues were accentuated in the Soviet cult of Ivan the Terrible that Stalin had been actively encouraging since the early 1930s.

In the second part the film switches from the public sphere to Ivan's inner world. The tsar now emerges as a tormented figure, isolated, paranoid, haunted by the consequences of his violence. The tsar's remorse was the central theme of a third (unfinished) part. The film was meant to end with a confession scene in which Ivan kneels beneath the fresco of the Last Judgement in the Cathedral of the Dormition and offers his repentance for the evils of his reign while a monk reads out an endless list of people executed on the tsar's command. Ivan bangs his forehead against the flagstones; his eyes and ears are filled with blood. 'Stalin has killed more people [than Ivan],' Eisenstein explained to the actor Mikhail Kuznetsov, 'and still he does not repent. Let him see this and he will repent.'[21]

Stalin liked the first part, which received the Stalin Prize. But when he saw a screening of the second part, in March 1946, he reacted violently. 'This is not a film, it is some kind of a nightmare!' He was particularly angered by the film's depiction of the *oprichniki* who, he said, appeared as 'the worst kind of filth, degenerates, something like the Ku Klux Klan', no doubt fearing that the viewing public would see in them a reference to his own political police. The film was banned and not shown publicly until 1958, ten years after the director's death.

In 1947, Stalin summoned Eisenstein to a late-night meeting in the Kremlin at which he subjected him to a revealing lecture on Russian history. Eisenstein's Ivan was weak-willed and neurotic, like Hamlet, Stalin said. But the real Ivan was great and wise. He was 'very cruel', and Eisenstein could show him in that light. 'But you have to show why he needed to be cruel'.

> One of Ivan the Terrible's mistakes was to stop short of cutting up the five key feudal clans. Had he destroyed them, there would have been no Time of Troubles [Russia's civil war after Ivan's death]. When Ivan had someone executed, he would spend a long time in repentance and prayer. God was a hindrance to him in this respect. He should have been more ruthless.[22]

4

TIMES OF TROUBLE

Four years after Ivan's death, in 1588, the Englishman Giles Fletcher, on a diplomatic mission to the Moscow court, observed that the late tsar's tyranny 'hath so troubled that countrey, and filled it so full of grudge and mortall hatred ever since, that it will not be quenched (as it seemeth now) till it burne again into a civill flame'.[1]

For the next quarter of a century Russia would be torn apart by civil wars and foreign invasion – a Time of Troubles (*smutnoe vremia*), as it would be known, subsiding only with the 'election' of Tsar Mikhail Romanov and the founding of his dynasty in 1613. But not all of Russia's troubles ended then. Over the next century, the time span of this chapter, the state's authority was shaken by a series of rebellions. They revealed the problems of establishing the tsar's authority in the eyes of the people, who believed only in a monarchy that represented their utopian ideals.

The problem had begun on Ivan's death with the rival claims of his two sons, Fedor and Dmitry, to the throne. Fedor succeeded as the eldest son, but was too feeble-minded for the tasks of government, which were assigned to Boris Godunov, his wife's brother. Descended from a Tatar prince, Godunov had joined Ivan's *oprichniki* and risen to become a senior boyar at his court. As one of the four regents to Tsar Fedor, he proved an able ruler. But from the start he faced the opposition of his co-regent Prince Vasily Shuisky (the grandson of the Shuisky executed by Ivan IV), a descendant of the Riurikids, who looked upon the 'low-born'

Godunov as an upstart. Reports of the eight-year-old Dmitry's death in an accident in 1591 led to rumours of his murder at the hands of Boris Godunov. These rumours grew after Fedor's death, when an Assembly of the Land elected Godunov as the next tsar.

Godunov was never able to establish his legitimacy as tsar. His authority was weakened by the economic crisis left behind by the Livonian War. Up to one-third of the country's population was lost through hunger and disease; many of the rest fled to the 'wild lands' of the south where the famine did not reach. The state was thus deprived of taxpayers, while its military servitors, the *pomeshchiki*, lost the peasants on whom they relied to work their land. It was in both their interests to stop the peasant flight. Boris tightened the existing laws restricting peasant movement and gave landowners increased powers to reclaim those peasants who had run away. It was a step towards the imposition of serfdom.

People saw the famine as God's punishment of Russia and its wicked Tsar Boris. Popular legends began to circulate about the reappearance of the 'true tsar Dmitry'. In some versions Dmitry had not been killed at all but had escaped. In others he was resurrected, like Jesus Christ, to deliver Russia from the usurper tsar and save the people from serfdom. In 1604, such a man appeared, a charismatic twenty-two-year-old, possibly a defrocked monk named Grigory Otrepov, who claimed to be Dmitry. Backed by the Poles to conquer Russia through a popular rebellion, he was supported (and manipulated) by the boyar clans opposed to Boris Godunov. With around 4,000 men, the pretender crossed into Russia from Kiev (then part of the Kingdom of Poland) and advanced towards Moscow. In town after town his authority was recognised as an expression of the people's hopes for freedom and justice, *volia* and *pravda*, the two basic concepts of their revolutionary utopia. As his army moved along the southern borderlands, the 'wild lands' of banditry and freedom, its ranks were swelled by Cossacks, peasants and townsmen, who joined its 'holy war' for the true tsar.

Here was the fundamental instability of the Russian monarchy. The tsar's authority was founded on the myth of his divine status as an agent of God's rule in Holy Russia, the last surviving seat of the true Orthodox faith in the Third Rome ideology. In the popular religious consciousness, always a medium for political ideas, Russia was the land of salvation, a new Israel where freedom, truth and justice would be given to the people by their holy tsar. As Mikhail Bakunin, the nineteenth-century revolutionary, wrote, 'The Tsar is the ideal of the Russian people, he is a kind of Russian Christ.'[2] The 'little-father tsar' or *tsar-batiushka* was revered in folklore as the people's protector, an avenger of the evils carried out by his boyars. By the logic of this belief system, if he acted as a 'tsar-tormentor' (*tsar-muchitel*), the Orthodox were justified in opposing him as a 'false tsar', as the Antichrist, perhaps, sent by Satan to end God's rule in Holy Russia, leading to the destruction of the world.[3] The crucial factor in the tsar's authority – his godlike personality projected through the myth of the holy tsar – could thus be turned against him if his actions did not meet the people's expectations of his sacred cult.

There were dozens of 'pretender tsars' (*samozvantsy*) who stirred the people to revolt by claiming they were the true tsar, the deliverer of God's justice. At least twenty-three of these pretenders have been documented before 1700, and there would be over forty in the eighteenth century.[4] Popular uprisings, by necessity, were monarchical in form. The *only* way the Russians could legitimise rebellion was in the name of the true tsar. No other concept of the state – neither the idea of the public good nor the commonwealth – carried any force in the peasant mind. This was the outcome of a patrimonial autocracy in which the state was embodied in the person of the tsar.

In April 1605, with the false Dmitry's forces encamped near Moscow, Boris died. His army soon went over to the rebel side. With the support of the boyar clans, the pretender entered Moscow, where he was crowned Tsar Dmitry, the only tsar raised to the throne by a popular rebellion. The hopes invested in Dmitry were soon dashed. Rumours spread about his heavy drinking and debauchery. His court was filled by Polish nobles. Suspicions of his Catholic persuasion grew when he announced his intention to marry a Pole without her first converting to the Russian Church.

Led by Shuisky, a boyar force broke into the Kremlin and murdered Dmitry in May 1606. Shuisky was crowned Tsar Vasily IV.

Once again, rumours circulated that Dmitry was not dead. New Dmitrys soon appeared (a dozen have been counted by historians), each one claiming to be the true tsar.[5] Many were proclaimed by Cossack bands to legitimise their banditry. The most dangerous was Ivan Bolotnikov, hailed in Soviet historiography as the first peasant revolutionary. In fact he was a small-scale landowner and military servitor who, like so many of his kind, had fallen on hard times and run away to join the Cossacks, living as a bandit on the steppe. In July 1606, he appeared with a rebel army of Cossacks, peasants and other southern frontiersmen, including small-scale gentry landowners. The army gathered more supporters, swelling to a force of 60,000 men, as it marched towards Moscow, claiming to be fighting for the restoration of the true tsar Dmitry. This was not a peasant or class war, a myth promoted in the name of Marxist ideology, but an uprising by the 'wild lands' of the southern frontier against Moscow.[6]

Bolotnikov was defeated, and in 1608 was killed. His gentry commanders went over to Shuisky's side, calculating that their own demands for better pay and tax exemptions were more likely to be met by his boyar oligarchy than by the 'rabble' that had joined Bolotnikov's rebellion. By this time, another false Dmitry had appeared. Known as Vor ('brigand'), the name given to him by Shuisky's government, he had ties to the Polish aristocracy, and was possibly an agent of the Polish crown, a suggestion disputed by historians. Certainly his army was joined by many Poles. As it advanced on Moscow, it was joined by the remnants of Bolotnikov's rebellion. In the summer of 1608 they established an armed camp at Tushino, just north of the capital, where they remained for a year with their own court and boyar council, dominated by the Saltykovs and Romanovs, Shuisky's bitter enemies.

With Russia torn apart by civil war, foreign powers intervened to advance their own interests. The Swedes and Poles were quick to take advantage of the chaos. Shuisky was desperate for Swedish help to defeat the Tushino rebellion. He agreed to cede the coastline of Karelia and Ingria to Sweden in exchange for mercenary troops. Part of the agreement involved Russia's commitment to supporting the Swedes in their long-running war against the Poles. Sigismund, the Polish king, took this as a pretext to send his armies into Russia. While the Swedes came to the aid of Moscow against the Tushino rebellion, the Poles crossed the border into Russia and laid siege to Smolensk.

Alarmed by the Polish invasion, the boyar clans in Moscow struck a deal with Sigismund under which his son, Prince Władysław, would become tsar after his conversion to the Russian Church. A Polish tsar, whose powers could be limited, was a price they were prepared to pay to consolidate their boyar rights. Deposing Shuisky in a coup, the Moscow boyar leaders swore their allegiance to Prince Władysław, and welcomed the arrival of the Polish troops, which had defeated the Tushino rebels on their advance to the capital. It now emerged that Sigismund intended, not to install Władysław, but to occupy the throne himself, ruling Russia with Poland as one Catholic kingdom. The boyar clans had been deceived.

The Muscovites rose up against the Poles in 1612. United by the defence of their Orthodox religion, their patriotic cause became a 'national' uprising when the humble citizens of Nizhny Novgorod and other Volga towns responded to the calls of Hermogen, the Russian patriarch, and organised 'militias of the land' to march on Moscow and expel the infidels. In Nizhny Novgorod it was a simple butcher, Kuzma Minin, who led the initiative to raise money for a militia by subscriptions and taxes. He appealed to other towns to do the same. Under the command of Prince Dmitry Pozharsky, scion of an ancient princely family, the militias, joined by Cossacks, liberated Moscow from the Poles – a victory that elevated Minin and Pozharsky to eternal heroes in the story of Russia.

On the bicentenary of these events, in 1812, another year of fighting against foreign invaders, this time Napoleon and his Grande Armée, a handsome monument to Minin and Pozharsky was funded by a public subscription in Nizhny Novgorod. Six years later, the statue was unveiled, not in Nizhny Novgorod, as had been planned, but in the middle of Red Square (in 1931 it was moved to its current position in front of St Basil's Cathedral to allow more space for military parades). From this point, the cult of Minin and Pozharsky was promoted by the state, which needed symbols of the patriotic sacrifice by ordinary Russians united by religion and devotion to the motherland. Their images appeared on coins, medals, postage stamps; books about their deeds were published for a wide range of readers; and films were made, including one by the great director Pudovkin, *Minin and Pozharsky* (1939). The film was launched and seen by millions during the Red Army's invasion of Poland, when the events of 1612 were constantly retold by Soviet propagandists to portray the Poles as aggressors, potential allies of Hitler, to justify the invasion. Putin has continued with this anti-Polish theme, using it to justify the Hitler–Stalin Pact and subsequent invasion of Poland as an act of self-defence, and has mobilised the myth of Minin and Pozharsky to add patriotic sentiment to his bogus argument. In 2005 he introduced a Day of National Unity on 4 November, the date of the expulsion of the Poles from Moscow in 1612, whose official celebration focused on the exploits of the butcher and the prince as a symbol of the people's unity against foreign aggression. It was for a clear symbolic purpose, then, that on his way to the unveiling of the statue to Prince Vladimir on the 2016 holiday, the event with which this book began, Putin stopped before the Minin and Pozharsky monument, where he posed with soldiers for photographers.

As Pozharsky led his forces to Moscow, a military council called on all the towns to send their representatives to an Assembly of the Land to elect a Russian tsar. Several hundred delegates appeared in Moscow for the vote on 7 February 1613. They represented a cross-section of society, from princes, boyars and landowning servitors to clergy, townsmen, Cossacks, even a small number of peasants. Mikhail Romanov was the candidate they chose.

There was nothing particularly distinguished about the man whose name would be given to the ruling dynasty for the next 300 years. Not yet twenty years of age, he was sickly, placid, poorly educated and, like many of his descendants, not especially intelligent. But his father, Filaret, the patriarch of Moscow, was popular with the Cossacks. Filaret had been the leader of the Russian Church at Tushino. He was a supporter of the tsar Dmitry, while his family's connections to Ivan IV, and the fact that Mikhail was the nephew of Fedor, the last tsar of Riurik's dynasty, made him seem a natural choice to those whose main priority was to restore the sacred form and content of the antebellum system and reunite the country around a Russian on the throne.

Attempts were made by the boyars to set limits on the tsar's power. By longstanding tradition the tsar had ruled in consultation with a group of senior nobles in the boyars' council – a tradition broken only by the tyranny of Ivan the Terrible. The leading boyars now sought to restore that principle. According to Kliuchevsky, they made Mikhail promise, among other things, not to make laws or wars on his own, without the consent of the Boyars' Council or Assembly of the Land. If this truly was a chance for a limited or oligarchic monarchy, it was a chance the boyars missed. The Assembly of the Land met frequently in the early years of Mikhail's reign (1613–45), when the tsar was struggling to establish his authority and needed it to restore order, impose unity and raise taxes. But later, when the dynasty became entrenched, the assembly declined in activity, meeting rarely and only when it had been summoned by the tsar to give formal consent to his laws. It failed to develop as a national assembly, a permanent body in the state order, such as one could find, to varying degrees, in Europe's parliaments. Russia remained on its autocratic path.

The new dynasty faced enormous challenges. Large parts of the country were still occupied by the Swedes and Poles – the former bent on gaining the north-western lands, including Novgorod and Pskov, the latter wanting nothing less than the Russian throne. It took more fighting and expensive treaties to convince them to retreat. The Russo-Swedish treaty of 1617 ceded to the Swedes complete control of the Baltic coast from Finland to Livonia, while the 1618 treaty with the Poles gave up all the western borderlands, including Smolensk and thirty other towns. The situation was no better in the south, where the Crimean Tatars were a constant threat with their raids on Russia's border towns. The tsar's ability to get the Crimean khan or his Ottoman protectors to curtail their raids was undermined by the actions of the Don Cossacks, who ignored his pleas to cease their raids on Crimean and Turkish territories. The Cossacks' capture of the Azov Fortress, in 1637, risked dragging Russia into war against the Ottomans, who suspected the Kremlin of supporting the attack on their northern garrison. The crisis was averted by Mikhail ordering the Cossacks to abandon Azov to the Turks in 1642. But the Tatar raids and Cossack counter-raids continued unabated on the southern frontier, where Moscow reinforced its defences by building yet more garrisons.

It was hard for an elected tsar like Mikhail Romanov to claim the title of autocrat and establish his authority. Pretenders to the throne continued to appear, especially among the Cossacks, who elected their own rebel tsars. Taxation was the hardest task. Russia was involved in thirty years of war between 1613 and 1682. Military costs almost tripled in this period, as Russia grew its standing army and paid for more advanced technologies to compete with the other powers of Europe. The bureaucratic state increased in size and stretched its reach into the provinces to raise more income from taxes. But there was a downturn in the agricultural economy which put a growing strain on the state's relations with society. It was part of a general crisis across Europe, where expensive wars brought states into conflict with their taxpayers, who were already under stress from crop failures, disease and other miseries.[7] The more the state encroached on people's livelihoods, the more it had to deal with popular revolts against taxes and the centralisation of power.

The first big wave of rebellions took place in response to a large increase in the salt tax in 1646. Salt was a basic household need, essential for preserving food. Under popular pressure the tax was quickly abolished, but it was replaced by other hefty taxes introduced by the young Tsar Alexei, son of Mikhail, who reigned from 1645 to 1676. The biggest protest occurred in Moscow, where the populace was angered by the tax exemptions enjoyed by foreign merchants and members of the ruling circles of the court. On 1 June 1648, returning from his annual pilgrimage to the Trinity-St

Sergei Monastery, Alexei was met on the outskirts of the city by a group of townsmen wanting to present him with a petition. They complained about the influence of 'powerful people' who 'by their destructiveness and greed are fomenting trouble between You, the Sovereign, and the whole land'.[8]

Petitioning the tsar had a long tradition in Russia. It continued through the Soviet period when millions of people wrote to Stalin for his help against the abuses of his officials, and can still be seen in Putin's annual TV programme *Direct Line* when viewers call in with their questions for the president. In Russia's patrimonial autocracy, where the state was embodied in the person of the tsar, it was the most obvious way for the people to seek redress against wrongdoing and injustices. The right to appeal directly to the tsar was fundamental to the myth of the little-father tsar, the *tsar-batiushka*, as a righteous and paternal protector of his people. 'The tsar is good but his boyars bad,' the Russian proverb said, meaning that the tsar was unaware of the injustices committed by his servitors but would correct them and punish his officials once he had been told of them. This was the idea of the petitioners who met Alexei on that day. On his coronation, they believed, he had kissed the cross and sworn an oath to protect the poor.

Imagine, then, the anger of the Moscow protesters when the young tsar brushed aside their petitions and ordered the arrest of the petitioners. The next day he was heckled by the crowd assembled on Red Square when he emerged from the Kremlin to attend a service in St Basil's Cathedral. Joined by many of the musketeers, who had mutinied when ordered to disperse them, the crowds broke into the Kremlin fortress, thronged in front of the tsar's palace and then went off to attack the mansions of the city's ruling magnates, some inside the Kremlin's walls, others in the nearby wealthy districts, before going on the rampage and putting wooden Moscow to the torch. Officials blamed for the salt tax were beaten by the mob. One was cut to pieces and thrown onto a pile of dung. In a desperate attempt to end the protests, the tsar ordered the execution of the head of the Artillery Chancellery, a scapegoat to pacify the musketeers. But the real hate-figure of the crowd, the boyar Boris Morozov, the tsar's childhood tutor and a leading figure in his government, escaped lightly with a short spell of exile in a monastery.

Revolts broke out in other towns – Kozlov, Kursk, Voronezh in the south, Solvychegodsk and Ustiug in the north, and in several districts of Siberia. Frightened of a full-scale revolution like the one in England led by Cromwell at that time, the tsar summoned an Assembly of the Land to introduce reforms. Its main result was a new Law Code (*Ulozhenie*) of 1649. Cobbled together from Lithuanian and Byzantine statutes, mixed with earlier Russian laws, it was the first such code to be published in Russia. Several thousand copies were rushed out to local governors so that they could let the people know that a new approach was being taken by the government to give every subject equal access to justice. The code's twenty-nine thematic chapters, covering every aspect of society, would remain the fundamental law until 1833. The fact that it survived so long did not 'testify to its merits', according to Kliuchevsky, but rather showed 'how long we Russians can survive without satisfactory law'.[9]

The *Ulozhenie* marks a shift towards the notion of a law-based state. It represents an early form of bureaucratic rule, in which virtually every matter would be regulated by the published law and no longer left to the discretion of the tsar. This was not what the protesters had been asking for. They had wanted the tsar to appoint more 'godly judges' and restore the proper functioning of the traditional system, in which the merciful and pious tsar was the highest judge of all. The Law Code swept away these customary norms. It stated, for example, that instead of writing to the tsar the people had to appeal to the relevant department of the state, the chancellery responsible for the matter they had raised. Anyone petitioning the tsar directly was to be punished by having the soles of their feet beaten with bastinadoes.[10]

The Legal Code was the underpinning for a huge expansion of the bureaucratic state. From a few hundred officials in 1613, the administration grew by the 1680s to over 2,000 secretaries and clerks working full-time in the various chancelleries of Moscow.[11]

Increasingly these officials came from a new class of men appointed on the basis of their literacy and numeracy, organisational skills and technical expertise, qualities distinctly lacking in most nobles at the court. Taking over more and more responsibilities, they extended the state's reach to almost every aspect of the people's lives. Before 1649 the ordinary Russian would have had little contact with the state; afterwards he felt its growing intrusion as new laws regulated everything from blasphemy to gambling, brewing alcohol, foreign travel, vagrants, wandering minstrels and musicians.

Russia was too big for the state to reach everywhere. On the provincial level it looked to appointed governors (*voevodas*) and magistrates to enforce its authority. In the rural localities it relied on the landowners to exercise judicial powers over the peasants. Further down, at the village level, it depended on the peasants' own communal institutions, overseen by the landlord's bailiff, to maintain basic order and collect the taxes levied on the village as a whole. The system of collective responsibility (*krugovaya poruka*), which we have encountered already, involved the peasants as collaborators in the tax-collecting and judicial functions of the autocratic state. The new Law Code extended their collective duty to mutual surveillance and denunciation of sedition to the state. Every subject of the tsar was legally obliged, under penalty of death, to inform the authorities about 'any plot or gathering or any other evil machinations against the tsarist majesty among the people'.[12] In one section worthy of the Stalinist regime, the code stated that the families of 'traitors', even children, were liable to execution if they failed to denounce their seditious relatives. Included in such crimes were expressions of intent to rebel against the tsar or public statements against him. The practice of informing became deeply rooted in society. By the late nineteenth century it was an effective tool of the police.

The Law Code divided the population into legally defined classes, known as estates (*sosloviia*), strictly ordered in a hierarchy according to their service to the state. Each class was closed and self-contained. The service nobles, townsmen, clergy and peasants could neither leave their class nor hope their children would. This regimentation of society had profound and long-term consequences for Russia's development. The social mobility that made Western societies so dynamic in the early modern age was basically absent in Russia. The town population in Russia was permanently fixed. Migration in and out of towns became a criminal offence. Urban taxpayers were obliged to live where they were registered in the tax census. Only they had a legal right to engage in urban occupations or even to own property in towns. It was a restriction that deprived Russia's trades and industries of the entrepreneurial energy introduced by immigrants to Europe's cities at this time. Russia's towns were inward-looking by comparison. In Moscow, for example, foreigners were legally forbidden to own houses or have their own church. It was a concession by the government to the petitioners of 1648 who had complained about the threat of foreigners to their livelihood and faith.[13]

The chief beneficiaries of the Law Code were the military servitors, on whom the state depended for its defence. The *pomeshchiki* had fallen on hard times. The custom of dividing their estates between their sons had reduced their average landholding. By the 1640s most only had enough land to support half a dozen peasant families. They could not stop the peasants from deserting them for better land and conditions in the south. Many were unable to equip themselves with full armour. They sold themselves as slaves to the richer servicemen, which meant fighting in their place. The struggling *pomeshchiki* begged the tsar to support them. They wanted stricter laws to bind the peasants to their land. The result of their pleas was the institution of serfdom under the provisions of the new Law Code.

Until the end of the fifteenth century the peasants had been free to move around, provided they had met their obligations to the landowner or, if they lived on the so-called black lands where there were no landowners, had paid their taxes to the ruling prince. Land was plentiful but labour hard to find – a basic fact of life in Russia – which meant that the peasants moved around, looking for the best landlords or settling on the 'wild lands' of the south. Peasant flight deprived the *pomeshchiki* of the labour they needed.

It also meant the state lost taxpayers. Laws were passed to restrict the movement of peasants. From the reign of Boris Godunov, they could leave their landlords only in a two-week period around St George's Day (25 November), and then only on condition that they paid an exit fee to compensate for the housing they had occupied. But these restrictions did not solve the underlying problem, which was peasant poverty.[14]

The settled peasantry fell into increasing debt, in part because of the general downturn in the agricultural economy, and in part because the flight of their fellows deprived them of the labour and taxpayers they needed. Because taxes were imposed collectively on the commune, the decline of the village population meant an increased burden on those peasants who remained. Many took out loans from the landowners which they contracted to repay by working on their land. These *kabala* contracts, as they were called (another word of Mongol origin), stipulated how many days each week they would work for the landowner, and how many years they would remain in his employ. Few peasants managed to repay the interest on the loan, let alone the principal. In effect they sold themselves into indentured servitude.

The *kabala* contracts were a decisive legal step in the direction of serfdom. They obliged the state to tighten its restrictions on peasant movement if it wanted to protect its military servitors from the risk of peasant flight – the simplest way the peasants had at their disposal to avoid repaying the *kabala* debt. From the 1580s, the state began to tighten up the laws, allowing greater leeway for the landowners to recapture peasants who had run away. In effect it recognised the peasant's labour as a form of property belonging to his landowner. This recognition was enshrined in the new Law Code of 1649. It bound the peasants to their landlord's land, without any right of departure, and made the state responsible for catching and returning runaways, now defined as criminals.

The laws of serfdom would remain in place until 1861. They applied to 90 per cent of the peasantry, the vast majority of the Russian population. Once they were no longer free to move, the serfs lost any means of leverage they had to protect their interests.

They were now subjected to increasing exploitation by their landowners, who made them work, on average, for three to four days every week in their seigneurial economy (a form of labour service known as *barshchina*), and made them pay a money rent (*obrok*) for their own peasant fields by earning cash from handicrafts. The landowners depended on this income for their wants and needs (their salaries as servicemen were too small), so they tried by every means to squeeze more money out of their peasants. Apart from the landlord's dues, the peasants had to pay their taxes to the state, both in labour duties and in cash. In economic terms they were worse off than most slaves, who did not pay state taxes.

In other terms they were no better off. Some landowners had a sense of paternal obligation to their serfs. But there was no control on their actions, so they were free to punish their serfs pretty much as they saw fit. This impunity was bound to have a coarsening effect on the landowners over time. Arbitrary beatings and floggings, rapes of women and the threat of separating families – these were the means by which they ruled their serfs. The mother of the nineteenth-century writer Ivan Turgenev, Varvara Petrovna Lutovinova, was a good example of the old-style Russian landowner, combining as she did a sense of charity with arbitrary acts of cruelty against her 5,000 serfs on various estates south of Moscow. Once she sent two household serfs into penal exile in Siberia for the sole reason that they had failed to remove their caps and bow to her in the appropriate manner.[15] It was the arbitrary nature of these punishments, as much as their violence, that built up peasant hatred of the landowners – a hatred expressed in the peasant violence of 1917.

Peasant flight was the main response to the coming of serfdom. Increasingly the peasants fled south-east, to the Volga lands and the lower Don, where the presence of the state was weaker than it was in the fortified frontier lands on the steppe south of Moscow. The Cossacks, too, were moving east, as it became more difficult for them to live from banditry on the steppelands. It was on the Volga and the Don that the largest popular uprising of the century began, the Razin rebellion, in May 1670.

Stepan Razin was a Cossack from an area of the Don overrun by peasant fugitives. The migrants were ready to become 'Cossacks', to live a life of freedom, without masters or taxes. The charismatic Razin, famous for his raids on the Turks and Persians, called on them to join his Cossacks in a war against the boyars and the landowners – a war to 'win the people's freedom' and put a just tsar (a Cossack) on the throne. Soviet historians presented the rebellion as a peasant war, but in fact the Razin army was made up of many elements – Cossacks, peasants, townsmen, poorer clergymen and Tatar, Mordvinian and Chuvash tribesmen who had lost their grazing lands to the Russians. It was a war between the have-nots and the haves.

For a year the Razin army caused havoc. Up and down the Volga River, town after town rose in revolt on his approach – Astrakhan, Tsaritsyn, Saratov, Samara – and in the countryside peasants burned the manors of their landowners. But after a long siege at Simbirsk the tsarist forces pushed the rebels back, and in a campaign of merciless repression, in which perhaps 100,000 rebel fighters lost their lives, reduced them to a handful of small and scattered bands.[16] Captured rebel leaders were impaled on stakes, nailed to boards, hung, drawn and quartered in town squares to teach the common people a lesson. Razin himself was captured. Chained to a scaffold on an open wagon, he was taken to Moscow, where he was brutally tortured before being executed on Red Square on 6 June 1671. For many years the legend of his immortality was retold by the peasants and Cossacks. They said that he was hiding in the wilderness, waiting for the moment when the people needed him, when he would reappear in the form of a black raven to deliver them from oppression. At the beginning of the twentieth century the raven image of Razin continued to be seen, flying up and down the Volga River, heralding the advent of the peasant revolutionary utopia.[17]

Russia doubled in size during the seventeenth century. It grew because it could. From the Mongol conquest it had learned that the best way to defend itself against the Tatar tribes was to control as much as possible of the Eurasian steppe – to conquer any territory from which it could be attacked. The collapse of the Mongol Empire and its successor states opened the Siberian steppe to Russian conquest and colonisation. There were no natural frontiers, no other powers except distant China to prevent the Russians' eastward march – only the Siberian tribes, the Khantys, Samoyeds, Tungus, Yakuts, Buriats, Chukchis, Daurians and other smaller tribes who were no match with their hunting bows and spears for the Russian muskets and artillery.

The Russians were driven east by fur, the 'soft gold' that accounted for one-third of the imperial coffers at the height of the fur trade in the 1680s. Close on the heels of the fur trappers came the Cossack mercenaries, who built wooden forts and exacted a fur tribute from the native tribes by taking hostages (usually women, children, tribal elders and shamans). Locked inside the forts, the hostages were shown to their tribesmen when they brought their tribute in sables, minks, ermines and foxes. The tribute-paying tribes were also made to help the Russians in their conquest of the neighbouring tribal areas by serving them as guides, interpreters, carters and fighters – a duty many tribesmen were eager to fulfil if it meant destroying their rivals.

Not all the tribes were easily subdued. There was stiff resistance from the Tungus and the Buriats, who were more developed in their metalworking crafts and social organisation than most other tribes. Terrible atrocities were carried out by the Russians – the burning of whole villages, executions, mass rape and enslavement of women. Some tribes fled or killed themselves en masse rather than submit to the Russians.

This violence has been played down in the Russian history books, where the conquest of Siberia is usually presented as a peaceful colonisation, in which the native tribes were 'civilised' as they were assimilated into Russian culture and society. In this myth the empire colonised or grew into itself, creating harmony between its peoples which in time would form the 'fraternity of nationalities' celebrated in the Soviet Union. The narrative the Russians have been taught represents a stark contrast to the violent empire-building of the European powers, which conquered and oppressed lands overseas. It also stands in contrast to America, a territorial 'empire' like Russia, where the conquest of the West, unlike the Russian conquest of Siberia, involved genocidal violence against the Native American tribes. This tale underpins the Russians' image of themselves as benevolent imperialists, 'naturally' suited to assume leadership in Asia because of their European character.

The vast size of Siberia was the most difficult obstacle to overcome. The further east the conquerors went, the harder it became for Moscow to control or support them. It took the best part of a year for a messenger to travel from the capital to Yakutsk, the main town in the eastern sector of Siberia, and at least another year to reach Okhotsk, the Russian base on the Pacific, so that an exchange of messages could take four years. Getting food and military supplies to the advanced forces was a logistical nightmare. The Russians could not feed themselves from the tundra and mountainous forests between Yakutsk and Okhotsk, so, beginning in the 1640s, they turned south to the Amur valley, believing that its fertile fields and fish-filled rivers would feed 20,000 Russians every year. Under their commander Khabarov (who would give his name to Khabarovsk, the largest city in Russia's Far East today), the Russian forces waged a ten-year war of terror, plunder and extermination against the Daurian tribes. In 1652, the Daurians called for help from the Chinese, the only power able and near enough to break the Russian hold on the Amur. Sporadic fighting between the Russians and Chinese continued until 1689, when by the Treaty of Nerchinsk the defeated Russians renounced all their claims to the Amur lands. They would not get them back until the age of steamships and railways.

Meanwhile, in the west, Russia was enlarged by its union with the Zaporozhian Host, a fledgling Cossack state ruled by a hetman or military commander, which in 1648 had called for Russia's help in its war of liberation against Poland. There had been a number of Cossack uprisings against the Poles in the early decades of the century – mostly in reaction to the settlement of Polish service nobles on the steppelands controlled by Cossacks and the Poles' promotion of a Greek Catholic or Uniate Church, subordinated to the pope in Rome, as a means of undermining Orthodoxy in Ukraine. A big revolt, in 1637–8, was brutally suppressed by Polish troops. The Poles clamped down on the rebellious Ukrainian and Cossack lands. Polish officials were brought in. They rode roughshod over Cossack freedoms and elected representatives. Predictably, this campaign of subjugation merely fanned the flames of the rebellion. The elite Cossacks, who might have been co-opted into Polish service, were turned into enemies. Bohdan Khmelnytsky is a case in point. A prosperous landowner and Cossack official, he had shown no sign of joining the rebellion until 1647, when his estate was confiscated, his manor burned, his wife abducted and his son badly beaten on the orders of the local Polish chief. The next year, Khmelnytsky was elected hetman of the Zaporozhian Host.

Under his command the Cossack rebels marched towards Kiev. On their way they easily defeated the Polish troops and attracted more Cossacks as well as peasant fighters wherever they appeared. For many of the rebels this was a war to defend the Orthodox against the Polish king, who had outlawed the Eastern Church and confiscated its buildings. As they advanced, Khmelnytsky's army murdered Poles and Jews. Around 60,000 Jews were killed in 1648 alone – a level of killing that would not be equalled until the pogroms of the Russian Civil War.[18]

Khmelnytsky appealed to the tsar for military help against the Poles. Alexei was at first reluctant to become involved in a war against Poland. Although he wanted to regain the western borderlands (Smolensk, Seversk, Chernigov) previously ceded to the Poles, he also needed an alliance with the Polish king to beat the Crimean Muslims threatening Russia's southern frontier. For five years he delayed his decision. But the patriarch Nikon persuaded him to intervene. This was, he argued, a religious war to liberate the Orthodox from infidels, not just in Polish-ruled Ukraine but in Moldavia and Wallachia, at that time under Ottoman control. Here was a golden opportunity for the Russians to make real gains in the west by fighting in the name of God.

Moscow's backing for Khmelnytsky's war came in the form of a 1654 treaty signed at Pereyaslav in Ukraine. As part of the treaty the Cossack hetman swore a unilateral oath of allegiance to the tsar, who promised to respect the autonomy of the hetmanate. What it meant for the Russian Empire and Ukraine is a subject of controversy. The treaty is regarded by Ukrainians as the founding of an independent 'hetman state', which many of them see as the basis of their modern nationhood. The Russians, by contrast, view the treaty as an act of union between Russia and Ukraine – the moment when these two groups of their race (the Great Russians and the Little Russians) became one nation and one state as a natural outcome of events. There are problems with both views. The hetmanate was a Cossack, not Ukrainian, state. It lacked the potential to become a nation state because the Cossacks' links to the Ukrainian peasantry and other social classes were extremely weak. But contrary to the Russian view, the union between Russia and Ukraine was far from being preordained. In fact it was only one of several possible outcomes of the Cossack war against Poland. Ukraine might have become part of Poland, or have lost its southwest corner to the Turks.

The tsar's commitment to Khmelnytsky involved thirteen years of costly war between Russia, Poland and Sweden. Between 1654 and 1656, the Russian troops made gains against the Poles – they captured Smolensk, Vilnius and Riga – not least because the Swedes attacked the Poles at the same time. Having taken Warsaw, the Swedes then marched on Lithuania, drawing Russia into war with Sweden between 1656 and 1661. The Poles took advantage of their struggle to recapture many of the territories they had lost to the Russians. By 1667, the three northern powers were exhausted from these wars. The Treaty of Andrusovo, in that year, divided Ukraine between Russia and Poland, the former gaining east (left-bank) Ukraine, along with Kiev, and the latter west (right-bank) Ukraine.

The treaty marked a fundamental shift in Russia's foreign policy. By this time the Russians and the Poles had been brought together by their common enemy, the Turks, who were making inroads into west Ukraine with the help of Cossack forces under the command of Petro Doroshenko, hetman of the Zaporozhian Host. For a while the Poles were able to repel the Turkish raids on west Ukraine. But the long war against Russia had weakened Poland, and by the 1670s it was no longer strong enough to prevent the Turkish occupation of Ukraine. It took 100,000 Russian troops to drive the Turkish forces from Ukraine in 1681.

With this victory Russia had at last attracted the attention of the West, which had never seen it as a major power on the continent. Now the Europeans needed Russia to protect them from the Turks. In 1683 they had only just been able to repel the Turkish forces from the walls of Vienna. The Russians' victory against the Turkish forces in Ukraine convinced the European powers of their need to get them on their side against the Turks in Europe. In 1686, Russia signed a Treaty of Eternal Peace with the Polish–Lithuanian Commonwealth. In doing so, the Russians were committing to the Holy League, the anti-Turkish coalition made up of the Commonwealth of Poland–Lithuania, the Holy Roman Empire and Venice. The four powers agreed to coordinate their campaigns against the Turks: the Russians pledged to fight them in Crimea, the Poles in Moldavia, the Austrians in Transylvania and the Venetians in Dalmatia. Russia, for the first time in its history, had entered an alliance as an equal power with Europe. It had entered the European scene.

Europe's first ambassadors to Russia arrived from Sweden, Holland, Poland, Denmark and the Holy Roman Empire in the 1680s and 1690s. At that time Russia was regarded as a backward and barbaric country, mainly on account of its lack of European civilisation. The dominant position of the Church had impeded the development of a secular culture. There were no universities, no academies of science or the arts, and no independent professions. The arts were frozen in the spirit of medieval times. Icons were the main form of painting. Secular portraits had only just begun to appear (Tsar Alexei is the first Russian ruler for whom we have a likeness). Known as *parsuny*, they had a flat iconic style. Landscapes, history and genre painting remained unknown in Russia. Instrumental music (as opposed to sacred singing) was stamped out by the Church wherever it appeared, mostly courtesy of wandering folk musicians and minstrels. Publishing was also controlled by the Church. Russia was the only country in Europe without private publishers, printed news sheets or journals, printed plays or poetry. When Peter the Great came to the throne, in 1682, no more than three books of a non-religious nature had been published by the Moscow press since its establishment in the 1560s.[19]

The growing influence of Europe began to be felt in Tsar Alexei's reign. Alexei was a good deal more dynamic and intelligent than his father Mikhail, the founder of the Romanov dynasty. His tutor, Morozov, had educated him in European ideas, sciences and languages. Poland and Ukraine were the main channels for Western ideas, technologies, arts and entertainments to enter Russia at this time. The war with Poland was a turning-point. Alexei and his armies entered towns like Vilnius and Vitebsk, whose Gothic, Renaissance and baroque architecture was unknown to them. 'Since His Majesty has been in Poland and seen the manner of the Princes' houses there,' observed Alexei's English physician Samuel Collins, 'his thoughts are advanc'd and he begins to model his court and edifices more stately, to furnish his rooms with tapestry and to contrive houses of pleasure.'[20]

Every kind of European luxury – from clocks and telescopes to musical boxes, singing birds and carriages – was imported for Alexei's court. His childhood friend and close adviser Artamon Matveev introduced a court theatre, the first of its kind in Russia, where German baroque dramas were performed. Matveev held receptions at his Moscow home, completely furnished in the Western style, where guests came not to drink excessively, as in the old boyar parties, but to socialise in well-mannered company, where women, for the first time, were expected to appear and even act as hostesses. Previously women had been excluded from the court and boyar entertainments, kept apart in private quarters known as the *terem*, similar to an Islamic harem, where they lived, veiled from public view, until their wedding.

These were superficial signs of European influence – the mere borrowing of social customs and luxuries as markers of 'civilisation' without any meaningful change in Russian sensibilities or attitudes. A deeply pious man, Alexei favoured this limited exposure to Western ways. He thought that as long as Russia could import what it needed from Europe (first and foremost military weapons and technologies), it would not need to learn the science that had created them, nor give up its Orthodox beliefs. As Kliuchevsky put it, Alexei hoped that one could 'wear a German coat and even watch a foreign entertainment while keeping intact such feelings and ideas as a pious fear at the very thought of breaking fast on Christmas Eve before the first star appeared in the sky'.[21]

The Church itself was changing, however. The Russian acquisition of Ukraine had opened Russia to Ukrainian ideas and modes of piety. A new type of religious education, derived from Jesuit models, had developed at the Kiev Academy, where priests were trained in Latin as well as Slavonic. Tsar Alexei was a strong supporter of reforms in the Russian Church. In 1649 he brought the first group of Ukrainian monks to Moscow to update the Russian service books and bring them into line with the modern Greek and Ukrainian versions printed in Europe. Three years later, when the old patriarch Iosif died, he backed the election of Nikon, a man of strong will and action determined to carry out reform, which he saw as a first step to the re-creation of a Universal Church, like the Orthodoxy of Byzantium, under his rule from Moscow.

Nikon's reforms of the service books and rituals of the Church included making the sign of the cross in the Greek manner, with three fingers (a symbol of the Trinity), instead of the ancient Russian way with two fingers (symbolising the dual nature of Christ). This was the cause of a major schism in the Russian Church that also split the nation into two. Religious rituals were at the heart of the Russian faith and national consciousness. The liturgy was the content of the faith itself. To change it was to imply that the old belief had been wrong all along. Led by the archpriest Avvakum, a former ally of Nikon, a large number of the faithful refused to accept the liturgical reforms. Known as the Old Believers, they argued that the Russian rituals were holier than the rituals of the Greeks, who had fallen into heresy by allying with the Roman Church and had been punished by God for their sin when they lost Constantinople to the Turks. Nikon's reforms, they feared, would lead the Russian Church to a similar catastrophe by exposing it to Western books and practices. To the modern reader these arguments may seem petty compared with the great doctrinal disputes of the Reformation period. But in Russia, where faith and ritual were so entangled, the schism assumed eschatological proportions. As the Old Believers saw it, the reforms were the work of the Antichrist, a sign that the end of the world was near.

Dozens of communities of Old Believers rose up in rebellion. At the Solovetsky Monastery, in 1668, the monks refused to recognise the tsar's authority, locked themselves into the monastery and, supported by the local peasants, endured an eight-year siege before they were captured and massacred by the tsar's forces. Elsewhere, as the soldiers of the tsar approached, the Old Believers shut themselves inside their wooden churches and burned themselves to death to avoid submitting to the Antichrist. Others fled to the remote lakes and forests of the north, to the Volga lands, to the Don Cossack regions in the south or to the forests of Siberia. They continued to follow the teachings of Avvakum, disseminated from his place of enforced exile in the Arctic fort of Pustozersk, where in 1680 he was burned at the stake.

The Old Believers' struggle was about more than rituals. It was a protest against the burgeoning power of the Church and state, from which they felt a growing alienation as those institutions sought to control the daily lives of the people. It was a social protest in religious form. The Old Belief was most widespread in those regions where the central state was weak and the spirit of rebellion strong. It was the unifying banner for popular revolts from the 1670s to the 1770s. The religious schism was a deep divide running through society from top to bottom. It divided those who identified with the old Russia and those who would make it into something new on more European lines.

Peter the Great would bring this conflict to a head. He was only ten years old when he came to the throne in 1682, following the premature death of his sickly half-brother Fedor III, who had reigned since the death of their father Alexei in 1676. Born to Alexei's second wife, Natalia Naryshkina, Peter had been chosen by the boyars over Ivan, Peter's other half-brother, who was the son of Maria Miloslavskaya, Alexei's first wife. Ivan was five years older than Peter but was considered too weak-minded to become the tsar. His sister Sophia was appointed regent to Peter instead. Supporters of Ivan's claim stirred revolt among the *streltsy* musketeers of Moscow, who had grievances against their officers. They spread rumours that Ivan, whom they saw as the true tsar, had been strangled in the Kremlin by Peter's family, the Naryshkins. It was a repeat of the Boris Godunov conspiracy.

The *streltsy* stormed the Kremlin and murdered all the boyars they suspected of the regicide, adding their commanders to the victim list. Many of the rebels were Old Believers. They wanted to reverse the Nikonian reforms. Convinced that Peter was a boyar puppet, they were motivated by the same belief in a true tsar as the rebels led by Razin and Bolotnikov. They were joined by Moscow's poor, who rioted for several days. In an effort to end the violence a compromise was reached. Ivan and Peter would rule jointly with Sophia as regent.

This resolution of the succession crisis was not enough to satisfy the Old Believer contingent. Led by their commander Ivan Khovansky, they continued to demand the restoration of the old service books and rituals, threatening to put Khovansky on the throne if Sophia did not yield. Sophia fled with her two charges to Zvenigorod, where she rallied enough troops to re-establish control in the capital. Summoning Khovansky for negotiations, she had him executed for treason and heresy. That was the end of the Khovanshchina, as the uprising would be known, not least through Musorgsky's opera of that name.

History on stage has its own rules. Musorgsky based his opera on three different uprisings – this one, in 1682, and two subsequent rebellions in which the *streltsy* were involved. The first took place in 1689, when Sophia tried unsuccessfully to recruit the musketeers against Peter and secure the throne in her own name. The second was in 1698, two years after the death of Ivan, making Peter the sole ruler, when the *streltsy* marched on Moscow in the false belief that Peter had died in Europe, where he had gone on a Grand Embassy, and that a 'German' would replace him on the throne. One of their petitions had ended, 'we have heard that the Germans are going to Moscow and, following their customs of beard-shaving and smoking tobacco, will bring about the total overthrow of the faith'.[22]

Cutting short his tour of Europe, Peter rushed back to Moscow to suppress the uprising. He appeared in Western dress, sporting a moustache, but without a beard, seen as a symbol of holiness in Russia, where beards had been worn by all the previous tsars. In a declaration of his war against the archaic Russian rituals, Peter ordered all the boyars who had arrived to welcome him to shave their beards. Two thousand *streltsy* musketeers were imprisoned. Brutally tortured, some of them revealed a plot to depose Peter and put Sophia back on the throne. A thousand *streltsy* were subsequently hanged or beheaded. Sophia was imprisoned in the Novodevichy Convent on the outskirts of Moscow. To torture her, Peter had a hundred rebels hanged against the walls outside her window and left there to rot. The young Tsar Peter, then aged twenty-six, had asserted his power.

5

RUSSIA FACES WEST

Until the eighteenth century, the Russians followed the Byzantine custom of counting years from the creation of the world, an event which they believed had occurred 5,508 years before the birth of Christ. But in December 1699 Tsar Peter decreed a calendar reform. Henceforth years were to be numbered from Christ's birth, 'in the manner of European Christian nations', beginning on 1 January 1700 (7209 in the old system). To celebrate the start of the new century Peter organised a magnificent ceremony with fireworks, 200 cannon firing salvos simultaneously, and flame-throwers on the square in front of the Dormition Cathedral in the Kremlin. Muscovites were ordered by decree to join in the festivities by decorating the façades of their houses, shaving off their beards and exchanging their traditional kaftans for Western ('German' or 'Hungarian') dress, as modelled by the mannequins displayed for their guidance in the city's squares.[1]

This was more than a calendar reform. It was the start of a cultural revolution in which the sense of time itself would be transformed. From this point Russia was to measure its progression on a European temporal scale. Its mission was to 'catch up' with the West, to speed up its development by casting off its old and 'backward' culture and following the lead of its advanced neighbours in Europe. This 'catching up' was to be the aim of governments in Russia for the next 300 years. But the emulation of the West posed numerous challenges.

Peter was a man in a hurry. Almost seven feet in height, he walked with giant, rapid strides, leaving his advisers far behind as he personally managed every aspect of his state's affairs with boundless energy (an image captured wonderfully by Serov's 1907 painting, *Peter I, the Great*). He was driven by his restless curiosity. As Pushkin wrote, in words once known by every schoolchild in Russia,

Now an academician, now a hero,
Now a seafarer, now a carpenter,
He with an all-encompassing soul,
Was on the throne an eternal worker.[2]

As a young man, Peter had developed a contempt for 'medieval' Muscovy. He despised its archaic and parochial culture, its superstitious fear and mistrust of the West. He was by temperament a revolutionary. Rejecting Orthodox traditions, he dressed in Western clothes, shaved his beard and spent a great deal of his time in the 'German' quarter of Moscow where, under pressure from the Church, the city's foreigners were forced to live. He hosted all-night alcoholic feasts with jesters, giants, dwarfs and courtesans. To mock the Church he called these sessions of debauchery the 'All Drunken Synod'. The carousers, sometimes numbering up to several hundred of his most important men of state, adopted titles such as 'Patriarch Bacchus' and 'Archdeacon Thrust-the-Prick'.[3]

Among his most trusted drinking friends were two senior military men – Franz Lefort, a Swiss mercenary in Russian service since the 1670s, and the Scotsman Patrick Gordon, the Russian army's quartermaster general – who persuaded Peter of the need to modernise his armed forces if Russia was to keep up with the European states. As so often in the country's history, it was Russia's military needs that prompted him to import Europe's new technologies.

From 1696 he travelled incognito across northern Europe to see for himself what Russia needed to become a military power on the continent. He was the first ruling Russian sovereign to go abroad. In Holland Peter Mikhailov (as the tsar called himself) worked as a shipwright. In London he visited the Greenwich observatory, the Woolwich arsenal, the Royal Mint and the Royal Society. In Königsberg he studied the artillery.

On his return to Russia, in 1698, Peter established a new navy, military schools and industries, and rebuilt the army from the ground up. He set up a new system of conscription, unparalleled in Europe, in which units of twenty peasant households were each collectively responsible for sending one man for life into the army every year, and even more at times of war. This sweeping militarisation of society produced the largest standing army in the world – some 300,000 troops by Peter's death, in 1725, and 2 million men by 1801.[4] No other state could mobilise so many men. But size was not a guarantee of military efficiency. A pattern soon emerged in the history of the armed forces, namely Russia's dependence on quantity because it lagged behind in quality. It was the only way the Russians could catch up with the Western powers in the military sphere. This was how Russia from now on would fight its wars – by expending more lives than its more advanced adversaries. It was why it lost so many troops in the two great wars of the twentieth century.

The cost of keeping such a large army placed a heavy burden on the state's finances – perhaps three-quarters of its total spending during Peter's reign. A share of the expenses was defrayed by making soldiers work for their upkeep. Each regiment was expected to make its own boots and uniforms. Soldiers formed artels (collectives) and worked for nearby landowners to earn money for their regiment. But the army's costs were mostly met by taxation – indirectly from the sale of salt and vodka, two essentials of the peasant household, and directly by a poll or 'soul' tax on the peasants introduced from 1718.

If Russia was to be a European power it needed access to the Baltic Sea. The Baltic coast from Finland to Livonia had been ceded to the Swedes in 1617. Peter wanted these lands back. He needed access to the ports to export to Europe the goods that Russia could supply in abundance (timber, tar, grain, hemp, hides, furs and precious stones) – exports that would pay for Western military technologies. The conquest of the Baltic coast would also give to Russia a natural frontier.

Backed by an alliance with Poland and Denmark, Peter declared war on Sweden and led 40,000 men to attack the fortress town of Narva in 1700. They were badly beaten by a Swedish force of just 9,000 men, better trained, better supplied and stronger in artillery, under the command of Charles XII. A quarter of the Russians lost their lives and many more were captured by the Swedes.[5] The defeat taught Peter two lessons, which would be the spur to his reforms: first, he would need a modern navy to conquer the coastline; and secondly, however large his army was, it stood little chance against the Swedes, at that time among the finest armies in Europe, unless it was equipped and organised to a comparable standard.

The Russians launched a new campaign in 1701, a year when the Swedes were distracted by another war against Poland. They captured Nöteborg Fortress (given the German name Shlisselburg by the Russians), strategically located on the Neva River's outlet to Lake Ladoga. They also conquered Kotlin Island (renamed Kronstadt in the German style as well), which, along with Shlisselburg, secured the defences of St Petersburg (pronounced 'Sankt Piterbourg', another German-sounding name), the city Peter founded where the Neva runs into the Baltic Sea. Peter's army also captured Narva and Dorpat (Tartu), conquests he proposed to give back to the Swedes if Charles would let him keep St Petersburg. Peter saw the latter as the most important of the Baltic ports, because from the Neva boats could reach the Volga River and the Caspian Sea, making Russia the main transit route between Asia and Europe. Charles rejected Peter's compromise. He wanted to eliminate the Russians as a threat to Sweden's Baltic lands, on which the Swedes depended for their grain. Once the Poles had been defeated, Charles led his armies against the Russians, who were then in Lithuania.

Charles was planning to attack Moscow, dethrone the tsar and partition Russia into petty fiefdoms shared out among the boyars. But instead of marching east, directly to the Russian capital, he turned his army south into Ukraine. There he was hoping to be joined by 20,000 Cossacks under the command of their hetman Ivan Mazepa, who had lost faith in the Russian pledge to protect the hetmanate and thought the Swedish king might help them gain their independence from Russia (in the end, just 3,000 Cossacks joined the Swedes). The Swedes were also driven south by their desperate need for food supplies. During their retreat through Lithuania the Russians had adopted a scorched-earth policy, destroying all the crops and animals that could be used to feed the enemy. Charles thought the situation would be better in Ukraine, but there too he found the same destruction. By the time they reached Poltava, on 27 June 1709, the invading troops were too weak and exhausted to match the improved Russian army that engaged them there. The Swedes were decisively defeated, with Charles, wounded, fleeing into Turkish territory on the other side of the Dnieper. The Russians seized their opportunity. They turned north-west, captured Riga and pushed on from there to take the rest of Sweden's Baltic possessions. The Great Northern War, as it would be called, dragged on for twelve more years. The Russians attacked the Swedes in Finland and carried out a series of naval raids, pillaging and burning towns along the Swedish coastline, even threatening Stockholm itself. The Swedes were forced to sue for peace and sign the Treaty of Nystad (1721), by which their Baltic lands were ceded to Russia.

Victory over Sweden confirmed Russia's status as a major European power, recognised as such by all the rulers of Europe. 'We have come from darkness out into the light,' Peter wrote to his son Alexei. 'Before no one in the world knew us, but now they must respect us.'[6] The respect of the West was not enough, however, to allay Russia's fears about its western borderlands, Ukraine in particular, which had shown itself to be an open door for the armies of Europe. The Swedes' invasion of Ukraine, aided by Mazepa's treachery, sealed the fate of Ukraine as an independent hetman state, and over the next decades Russia tightened its control of the Ukrainian territories it had gained in 1654.

St Petersburg was conceived as a European capital – Russia's 'window on to Europe', as Pushkin described it in *The Bronze Horseman* (1833). Planned as a series of classical ensembles linked by avenues, canals and squares, it was built to impress European visitors, demanding their respect for Russia as a power and a civilisation.

Peter was involved in every detail of the city's early construction. He borrowed what he liked from other European capitals. Amsterdam (which he had visited) and Venice (which he knew only from pictures) were inspirations for the palace-lined canals and embankments. The classical baroque of the city's churches was a stylistic mixture of St Paul's in London, St Peter's in Rome and the single-spired churches of Riga. From Europe Peter brought in architects and engineers, craftsmen, artists, furniture designers and landscape gardeners. St Petersburg became a home to Scots, Germans, Frenchmen and Italians. No expense was spared for Peter's model capital. To make the Summer Gardens 'better than Versailles' he ordered peonies and citrus trees from Persia, ornamental fish from the Middle East and singing birds from India.[7]

Like the magic city of a Russian fairy tale, St Petersburg grew with such fantastic speed, and everything about it was so brilliant and new, that it soon became enshrined in myth. According to the legend of its foundation, Peter had been riding with a dozen horsemen across the soggy marshlands where the Neva meets the Baltic when he stopped, dismounted from his horse and with his bayonet cut two strips of peat and arranged them in a cross, pronouncing, 'Here shall be a town!'[8] His words echoed the divine command, 'Let there be light!', suggesting that St Petersburg had been created, like the world itself, *ex nihilo*. Eighteenth-century panegyrists elevated Peter to a tsar-creator equal in his powers to a god. In popular mythology, in illustrated ballads, oral tales and legends, the miraculous emergence of the city from the sea assigned to it a supernatural status from the start. It was said that Peter made his city in the sky and then lowered it, like a giant model, to the ground. Here was a new imperial capital without roots in Russian soil.

In his person, Peter sought to recall the emperors of ancient Rome. He gave himself the Latin title 'Imperator' and had his image cast on a new rouble coin, with laurel wreath and armour, in imitation of Caesar. It was a symbolic break from Muscovy, with its Byzantine mythology, in which the tsar had been portrayed as a divine agent and defender of the faith. Now he appeared in armour with a Western crown and cloak and imperial regalia. This was how he was depicted in a set of portraits by Sir Godfrey Kneller for distribution to the sovereigns of Europe during his Grand Embassy.

The victory at Poltava was the point at which this military–imperial persona took firm root. In a famous print by Alexei Zubov, *The Ceremonial Entry of the Russian Troops to Moscow on December 21, 1709 after their Victory in the Battle of Poltava*, the tsar was pictured riding at the head of his triumphant soldiers into Moscow reimagined by the artist in the form of ancient Rome. None of the triumphant arches in the illustration existed. Moscow's many churches with their onion domes were all removed from the cityscape. The soldiers bore their regimental colours, but there were no priests or icons in the procession to symbolise the role of divine intervention in their victory. It was an entirely secular depiction of imperial military power – a stark contrast to the icon painted for the conquest of Kazan by Ivan the Terrible, *The Church Militant*, which had explained that triumph as the work of God.

Peter's adoption of the title 'Imperator' entailed a change in the naming of Russia itself. Previously the country had been known as Rus, a common appellation for the ethnic homeland of Russians (*russkie*). Peter added the Hellenic term Rossiia which over the next century would replace Rus as the name of the Russian state. The noun Rossiia was meant to signify an imperial identity, uniting all the subjects of the Russian Empire regardless of ethnicity or nationality, albeit in a racial hierarchy that privileged those nationalities (Baltic Germans, Russians and so on) closest to the empire's leadership. The empire was Rossiiskaya (the adjective derived from Rossiia), or sometimes Vserossiiskaya (meaning 'All-Russian') but never Russkaya (from Rus), an adjective applied to the Russian people (*russkii narod*), the Russian language (*russkii yazyk*) and the Russian Church (*russkaya tserkov*), but never to the institutions of the state. If Moscow was the ancient capital of Rus, a 'mother to all Russians', as Tolstoy wrote in *War and Peace*, Petersburg was the capital of Rossiia, the administrative centre of a multi-ethnic empire stretching from the Baltic to the Pacific.

At the heart of this imperial government was a new conception of the Russian state. Until the Law Code of 1649, it had been conceived as the personal patrimony of the tsar. The concept of the state (*gosudarstvo*) had been inseparable from the person of the tsar (*gosudar*), who ruled Russia as his own domain. The Law Code had marked a shift away from this personal conception towards a law-governed realm. But Peter was the first tsar to think about the state as an impersonal machinery whose purpose was to the serve the public good or commonwealth. He had picked up this idea from the German cameralist thinkers, the jurists and officials who assigned the state an active and progressive role to serve the common good by imposing order on the people and stimulating the economy through policies developed from rational accounting and a detailed knowledge of society. Peter was attracted to their philosophy, perhaps because its equation of the common good with the interests of the state justified his use of coercion to push through his reforms. The well-being of society demanded a well-ordered police state.

Like other absolutist states, Peter's regulated every aspect of society. He established colleges, or ministries, nine to begin with in 1718, responsible for its main areas of policy (Foreign Affairs, War, the Navy, Justice, Commerce, Manufacturing and so on). In 1721, he extended state control to Church affairs by establishing a Holy Synod, an organ of the clergy under his control, to replace the independent patriarch. This meant eradicating the Byzantine conception of a symphony between Church and state on which the political philosophy of Kievan Rus and Muscovy had been based. The tsar was now the sole authority.

Peter centralised provincial government by giving greater powers to appointed governors of new and enlarged provinces (*guberniia*). He made state service compulsory for the nobility, whose status was defined by the seniority of their office rather than by birth. The Table of Ranks, introduced in 1722, established fourteen ranks or categories of state service, in which hereditary nobility was conferred on office-holders in the top eight ranks. Commoners could enter at the bottom rank and earn noble titles by working up to the eighth rank (collegiate assessor in the government, major in the army or third captain in the navy). This ordering of the nobles by their service to the state lasted until 1917. It had a deep effect on the nobles' way of life, further weakening their attachment to the land. Because promotion was normally by seniority, the system rewarded time-servers and encouraged bureaucratic mediocrity. It was in many ways a precursor of the Soviet Party-state and its *nomenklatura*, its system of appointing the top posts to loyal, long-serving officials.

The Petrine state pursued an active economic policy. It managed its own factories and mines, built roads and canals and conscripted the state peasants (a category created by Peter for those living on crown lands) as the workers on these sites. The state became the country's main producer and the main consumer of industrial goods, a domination that hampered the emergence of an independent manufacturing class, as appeared in Europe at this time. Where private manufacturers did appear, they soon became dependent on the state for capital investment and help in tying workers down. In the Moscow region, for example, wool and linen factories were established in the early eighteenth century by merchants, artisans and even enterprising state peasants. Yet in the absence of investment banks or a labour market they could not operate without state aid. The government depended on these manufacturers to meet its needs for uniforms. So it created a new class of factory serfs for them, allowing the industrialists to buy entire villages whose peasants were then bound as indentured labour to these textile factories. Peter had intended to create a dynamic entrepreneurial society. But his statist methods reinforced the country's backwardness, rooted in the culture of serfdom.[9]

Alongside its policies for industry, the Petrine state set much store by the spread of education and science, especially the learning of technologies for the military economy. In the early decades of his reign Peter paid for promising young men to visit Europe to study shipbuilding, metalwork, architecture, navigation, commerce and so on. Once the St Petersburg Academy of Sciences was founded, however, the training of young specialists could be carried on at home. Peter was inspired by his visit to the French Académie des Sciences in 1717, and by his meeting in 1716 with Gottfried Leibniz, whose ideas influenced the Academy's focus on geography. It was Leibniz who persuaded him that Russia had a leading role to play in the exploration of Asia.

Geography was the first academic science in which Russia made an international mark. The two Kamchatka expeditions led by Vitus Bering between 1725 and 1743 made it known to Europe that there was no land connecting Asia and America – there were the Bering Straits instead. Sixteen scholars from the Academy went along on the second expedition to make a detailed study of the Siberian peoples, fauna, wildlife and geology under the direction of Gerhard Müller, whom we met at the beginning of this book. After ten years in Siberia, Müller returned to St Petersburg with a huge collection of materials on the ethnic history, languages and customs of its native tribes which he later published in his *Description of the Siberian Kingdom* (1750), a founding work in the field of ethnography.

St Petersburg was more than a city. It was Russia's European school, a civilising project of cultural engineering to reconstruct the Russian as a European citizen. Everything in it was intended to encourage a more Western way of life. Peter told his nobles where to live, how to build their palaces, how to school their children, how to dress and conduct themselves, how to eat and entertain in polite society. A manual of etiquette, *The Honourable Mirror of Youth* (1717), compiled from Western sources, appeared in many editions over the next fifty years. It advised its readers, among other things, not to 'spit their food', nor to 'use a knife to clean their teeth', nor 'blow their nose like a trumpet'.[10] Nothing in this dragooned capital was left to chance. It was administered by the police – in the sense of tight controls on public order and safety, public hygiene and housing, as well as crime prevention – a system Peter modelled on the French *lieutenants-généraux*.

The most contentious part of Peter's cultural engineering was his reform of language. He created a civil script, similar to Latin, to use instead of Church Slavonic for printing. His reforms imported a vast range of foreign words in the governmental, military and legal spheres, where there were no Russian words for most of the basic concepts. The use of French became a mark of civilised behaviour. Again, the problem was a lack of Russian words for the sort of thoughts and feelings that made up salon conversation: 'gesture', 'sympathy', 'privacy', 'impulsion' and 'imagination' – none could be expressed without the use of French. While this 'salon style' of literary Russian derived a certain refinement from its Gallicised syntax and phraseology, the excessive use of French expressions, which were really just clichés, made it clumsy and verbose. This was the language of social pretension that Tolstoy satirised in the opening passages of *War and Peace*: 'Anna Pavlovna had had a cough for some days. She was, as she said, suffering from *la grippe*; *grippe* then being a new word in St Petersburg, used only by the *élite*.'[11]

There was resistance to these cultural reforms. It came partly from provincial nobles, who saw them as a threat to their old 'Russian' way of life, and partly from the merchants and Cossacks, many of them Old Believers, who saw Peter as the Antichrist. A Cossack-led revolt in Astrakhan was easily put down in 1708. But the popular dislike of Western customs, habits and ideas continued long afterwards. It was reflected in folklore, in satirical songs and in stories reproduced in woodcut prints (in Russian they are known as *lubok* prints). The most famous of these *lubok* prints, *The Mice Are Burying the Cat*, appeared in numerous editions and circulated widely throughout Russia in the eighteenth century. It shows the people (in the form of mice) celebrating the death of the Tsar Peter (the cat), whose godless reign had seen the introduction of shaving, smoking, drinking, dancing, even music at his funeral.[12]

From the middle of the eighteenth century we can see the emergence of a new national consciousness which found its first expression in an anti-Western ideology. It was based on the defence of Russian customs and morals against the corrupting impact of the West – a trope of the later Slavophiles. 'When we began to send our youth abroad and entrusted their education to foreigners,

our values changed entirely,' wrote Ivan Boltin, a historian, in the
1780s.

> There came into our hearts new prejudices, new passions,
> weaknesses, and desires that had remained unknown to our
> ancestors. These extinguished our love for our fatherland,
> destroyed our attachment to our ancestral faith and ways. We
> forgot the old before mastering the new, and while losing our
> identity, we did not become what we wished to be. All this
> arose out of hastiness and impatience. We wanted to achieve
> in a few years what required centuries, and began to build the
> house of our enlightenment on sand without having laid firm
> foundations.[13]

Alongside such highbrow treatises, there was a thriving industry of
comic satires to drive home the same point to a broader audience.
The gallomanic Petersburg dandy was the butt of these satires. His
decadent and artificial manners were contrasted with the simple,
natural virtues of the serfs, the material seductions of the European
city with the spiritual values of the Russian countryside. Their
moral lesson was simple: through their slavish imitation of the
West, the Petrine elites had lost all sense of their own nationality.
Striving to make themselves at home with foreigners, they had
become foreigners at home.

Peter the Great divides the Russians like no other figure in their
history. The Slavophiles maintained that he put Russia on to a false
path: following the West and importing its materialist culture could
be achieved only at the expense of national character, the spiritual
values and traditions that distinguished Russia from Europe. But for
the Westernist intelligentsia, who looked to Europe for their values
and ideals, he established a new motherland, Petrine Russia, the
only one in which they could believe. Their position was expressed
by the nineteenth-century philosopher Vladimir Soloviev, who
claimed that Peter had saved Russia from becoming 'purely Asiatic'
in its character: 'All the good and original that we have had in
the sphere of thought and creativity emerged only as a result of

the Petrine reforms; without them we would have neither Pushkin nor Glinka, neither Gogol nor Dostoevsky, neither Turgenev nor Tolstoy.'[14]

One thing can be said with certainty: the reforms created a deep cultural rift between the urban civilisation of the Westernised elites and the village world of the peasants, uneducated and unfree, worn down by serfdom, poverty, clinging to their time-worn communal traditions and interpreting the universe through pagan superstitions and Orthodox beliefs. This divide remained unbridged until 1917. It was the fault line along which the revolution would be fought.

The Bolsheviks took inspiration from Peter (the poet Max Voloshin called him 'the first Bolshevik'). By grabbing hold of backward Russia and forcing it to catch up with the West he had set the example for their own forced programme of hyper-modernisation. But Peter's methods of compulsion had in many ways the opposite effect to those he had intended. Rather than modernising the country, they reinforced the statist tyranny and servile customs of serfdom that had kept Russia – and would go on keeping Russia – in a relatively backward state compared to the West, where societies had more freedom. Here was the paradox of not only his but all the later reform projects led by Westernising Russian governments. Without a free society or active public sphere for enterprise, the state itself became the only motor of reform. And forcing changes from above could only drive a deeper wedge between the state and the people, reinforcing state coercion as the primary mechanism of reform.

In 1722, just three years before his death, Peter announced a new Law of Succession. He had no male heir. His first son Alexei had been executed on his orders for treason four years previously, after he had fled his bullying father and taken refuge in Vienna, while his younger son had died in 1719. Peter left it to himself to name his heir (a clear statement that he stood above the law). His choice fell on his second wife, a woman of lowly Polish origins, whom he crowned as Empress Catherine I in the Dormition Cathedral in

1724. In the coronation ceremony Peter stood in for the patriarch as the agent of divine blessing – another symbolic shift from the old Byzantine symphony of Church and state, which had appeared as equal partners in previous coronation rituals. Now the tsar's will was enough to decide the fate of Russia and give sacred status to his successor.

Given how divisive Peter's reign had been, it is perhaps surprising that his death did not give rise to a civil war, as there had been after Ivan the Terrible had died.[15] The fact that Russia would be ruled by women for most of the remainder of the century – Catherine I (1725–7), Anna (1730–40), Elizabeth I (1741–62) and Catherine the Great (1762–96) between them occupied the throne for all but three of the seventy-one years between Peter's death and Paul's accession in 1796 – may be part of the answer. Female rulers were regarded as 'humane' and 'wise', softer and more yielding than the domineering Peter, which allowed for more court politics, stabilising the system. The leading families at court formed themselves into factions, which provided opportunities for the ruler to assert her domination through divide and rule, a strategy perfected by Elizabeth and Catherine the Great.[16]

The problem of establishing monarchical authority had less to do with gender than with nationality. With the exception of Elizabeth, Peter's daughter, all the eighteenth-century rulers following his death were either foreign-born (Catherine I, Peter III and Catherine the Great), born to German parents (Peter II and Ivan VI) or married into German families (Anna, Paul). On the two occasions when the throne was seized in a palace coup, the plotters would be motivated by hostility to foreign rulers or to foreign powers being served at the expense of Russia's interests.

The first came after Anna's death in October 1740. Anna was the daughter of Ivan, Peter the Great's half-brother. Before becoming empress, she had been the Duchess of Courland, Courland being part of today's Latvia. In Russia she had filled her government and elite regiments with Germans (Ostermanns, Münnichs and Lievens) whose barely concealed contempt for the Russians inflamed nationalist sentiments. The main hate-figure was her lover Ernst-Johann Bühren (Biron to the Russians), a German from Courland, who appeared to wield enormous power without occupying an official post. Discontent with Biron was limited at first to tiny groups of officers united by their desire for a Russian government. But it became more widespread when he forcibly imposed the collection of back-taxes that had been annulled by Russia's previous rulers. When Anna died and Biron was appointed as regent to her heir, Ivan VI, the infant son of the Duke of Braunschweig-Mecklenburg, the Russian opposition, now with a stronghold in the Preobrazhensky Regiment, seized power, arrested Biron and put Elizabeth on to the throne. Biron and the other Germans in his circle were sent to Siberia, while the Russian soldiers killed their German officers.

The second anti-foreign coup was carried out by Catherine the Great (herself a foreigner) against Peter III, her own husband, in 1762. Born Princess Sophie of Anhalt-Zerbst, a minor German state, Catherine came to Russia at the age of seventeen as the intended bride of her second cousin, Charles Peter Ulrich of Schleswig-Holstein-Gottorp, a grandson of Peter the Great and heir to the empress Elizabeth. For their wedding, in 1745, Catherine converted from her Lutheran faith to Orthodoxy and took the name chosen for her by Elizabeth, whose mother had been Catherine I.

The marriage was a disaster. Catherine hated her husband. In her memoirs she described him as stupid, cruel and mean, a view challenged by historians, and claimed that he was impotent. The unhappy couple soon led separate lives. Catherine started an affair with Sergei Saltykov, a handsome chamberlain, and had two miscarriages before giving birth to a son, Paul, the heir to the throne, in 1754. Whether Saltykov was Paul's father remains unknown, but Catherine's memoirs hinted that he was, much to the horror of her nineteenth-century descendants, who censored any mention of his name.

Peter III was an admirer of Frederick the Great, the king of Prussia. He told Frederick he would rather be a general in the Prussian army than the Russian emperor. On his accession to the throne, in December 1761, he appointed Germans to the highest offices.

He abandoned the alliance with Austria and France, on whose side Russia had been fighting since the start of the Seven Years' War, and switched over to the Prussian side. His domestic policies offended Russian national feeling, especially his seizures of Church lands, his military conscription of priests' sons and his order for the removal of all icons except those of the Saviour and the Mother of God from Orthodox churches – measures that displayed his contempt for the faith and raised fears of his intention to put Lutheranism in its place. Catherine justified her coup on the grounds of defending Orthodoxy from the 'destruction of its traditions'.[17] She knew her Russian history well enough to realise the power of religion to unite the Russians against foreign rule.

With the help of Count Orlov, her new favourite, who rallied the elite guards to her side, Catherine donned the green Preobrazhensky uniform and rode out from St Petersburg at the head of her troops to arrest her husband at his palace in Oranienbaum on 28 June. Peter meekly surrendered (on hearing of his overthrow, Frederick the Great said that he had 'let himself be driven from the throne as a child is sent to bed'). Peter was exiled to one of his estates near St Petersburg, where he was murdered three weeks later by Orlov. It was announced that he had died of 'haemorrhoidal colic' – prompting one French wit to note that haemorrhoids must be very dangerous in Russia.[18]

The new empress faced an uphill task to establish her legitimacy. It wasn't easy as a female *and* a foreigner – however much she tried to Russify herself by adopting Russian customs, studying Russian history and folklore and scrupulously observing the Orthodox rituals. Her son Paul, although only eight years old, was seen by many as the rightful heir, while Ivan VI, aged twenty-two, had a strong claim too, despite having been in custody since his deposition by Elizabeth in 1741. Secretly imprisoned in the Shlisselburg fortress, where he was known as 'nameless prisoner no. 1', Ivan had received little schooling, but he was aware of his imperial identity. When his jailers discovered who he was, in 1764, a plan was hatched to free him and proclaim him emperor. The plot was quickly thwarted and, on Catherine's orders, Ivan was killed in his bed. News of his murder circulated widely, giving rise to the customary rumours that he was alive – most of them advanced by Cossack chancers and pretenders claiming to be him.

From the start of her reign, Catherine portrayed herself as Peter the Great's political successor, the ruler who would carry on his transformation of Russia. That was the aim of her monument to Peter, Étienne-Maurice Falconet's equestrian statue, unveiled in St Petersburg in 1782, and later known as the Bronze Horseman, which carried on its massive granite pedestal the inscription 'To Peter I from Catherine II'. In the time that had elapsed since Peter's death, his reforms had lost their controversial character, emerging even as a source of national consensus, which enabled Catherine to invoke them to legitimise her rule. She, like Peter, pledged to serve the common good. The medal issued on her accession depicted her as Minerva, the Roman goddess of wisdom, promising a reign of peace and progress through science and learning. Unlike Peter, however, Catherine rejected state coercion to impose reforms. A follower of the Enlightenment, she emphasised the need to educate the nobles as agents of enlightened government. She wanted to create a noble class that would serve the public good, not by compulsion but from a sense of obligation to society (*noblesse oblige*).

That was Catherine's thinking behind her first major act – the emancipation of the nobles from compulsory service to the state. The decree had been announced by Peter III in 1762. It was a concession to the landowners, who had been lobbying for it for years. They complained that their service obligations were distracting them from the management of their estates. That was not the only reason for their liberation, however. The truth was that the state no longer needed as many noblemen in its service. A new class of permanent officials had been created since the introduction of compulsory service by Peter the Great. Catherine's reform was as much about the state's emancipation from its obligation to employ the nobles as it was about the freeing of the nobles from their service obligations to the state. The idea was to let those stay in service who had chosen to do so, and to let those leave who preferred to dedicate themselves to their estates, improving their economy. Catherine hoped that, like the English gentry or the Prussian Junkers, they would take up leading roles in their own communities, corporate bodies and provincial government. Released from their obligations to the state, the nobles would create the local institutions needed for effective government.

The idea did not work. The high nobility was too dependent on state service as a marker of status. Its young men liked the glamour of St Petersburg and the comradeship of regimental life, and delayed retiring to their estates until middle or retirement age, by which time they had little appetite for agricultural improvements or work in local government. They treated their estates as country homes, palaces of pleasure and culture, filling them with European artworks and employing vast staffs of household serfs – liveried chamberlains, maids, cooks, waiters, gardeners, coachmen, even musicians and artists – in numbers that astonished foreign visitors. Lower down the social scale, among the smaller landowners, the emancipation was welcomed, and they settled down on their estates. But they were unwilling, or too poor, to take up roles in the administration of the provinces.

The weakness of local government was made clear by the Pugachev revolt (1773–4), the last and largest of the Cossack-led rebellions that had rocked the state since the beginning of the seventeenth century. Like them it was carried out in the name of the true and holy tsar sent by God to liberate the people from the landowners. Emelian Pugachev, a Don Cossack and deserter from the army, had appeared in the Yaik Host, on the steppes between the southern Urals and the Caspian Sea. He claimed to be the true tsar, Peter III, who had not been killed by his whorish wife's assassins but had escaped to reappear as the people's saviour. The Yaik Cossacks were unhappy with a recruiting order from the government, issued on the outbreak of the war with Turkey in 1768, which had made them a regular unit of the Russian army, effectively reducing them to ordinary serfs. As Old Believers, they were outraged by the army's order to remove their beards. Their revolt quickly spread to the Volga area, attracting the support of the Bashkirs, opposed to Russian domination, the urban poor and the peasants, who believed that the 'Amperator Peter' (as they called this 'God-sent' emperor) would abolish serfdom and transfer to them the gentry's land. The popular belief in the tsar-liberator was reinforced by Pugachev's commanders, who assumed the names and titles of the leading courtiers (there was a Cossack 'Count Panin', 'Prince Potemkin' and so on). Such was the enduring power of the myth of the holy tsar-protector who would deliver justice and freedom that even now, a century and a half since the appearance of the first pretender rebels in the Time of Troubles, the only way to garner mass support for a rebellion was in the name of that imagined tsar.

It took a large-scale military campaign to defeat the rebel army and capture Pugachev, who was brought back for his execution in Moscow (Catherine ordered the executioners to cut off his head before disembowelling him, rather than, as was usual, the other way around, so as not to offend her 'love of humanity').[19] The memory of Pugachev remained in the popular imagination, inspiring future revolutionaries. Among the propertied classes, the term 'Pugachevshchina' became synonymous with peasant anarchy and violence, 'cruel and merciless' as Pushkin termed it in *The History of Pugachev* (1833).

An inquest into the revolt blamed the incompetence of local officials, who had allowed it to spread without hindrance. General P. I. Panin, who had led the punitive repressions, wrote to the governors of Kazan, Nizhny Novgorod and Orenburg, the areas overwhelmed by the revolt, denouncing their provincial governments: 'It is doubtful if the civil authorities know anything at all about the greater part of their duties or care very much … They carry out Her Majesty's work complaining of red tape, taking bribes, quarrelling among themselves, and not knowing what to do.'[20]

The problem was that the administration was too thinly spread over this vast area – as it was over Russia generally. In the aftermath of the rebellion, in 1775, Catherine tried to remedy the situation by creating more but smaller provinces, divided equally by population size, and increasing the number of officials, mainly through election by the landowners and propertied townsmen. Around 15,000 new officials (two-thirds of them elected) joined the provincial administrations during the last quarter of the century. It was a start. But the fundamental problem of Russia's under-government could only be resolved by creating genuine self-government, and that initiative would have to wait until the abolition of serfdom.

'Russia is a European state.' Thus Catherine wrote in the opening sentence of her most important treatise, the *Nakaz* or 'Instruction to the Legislative Commission', tasked by her with writing a new law code in 1767.[21] What she meant by this simple statement was that, on account of its European character, Russia had a natural mastery over all the peoples of Asia.

It was Peter who had first conceived of Russia as a European empire with a civilising mission in Asia. Previously, the empire had been driven by profit. The Russians had moved east in search of fur and other precious raw materials. They had plundered the Siberian tribes. But they had not been much bothered with converting them to Orthodoxy or integrating them as subjects of the tsar. In this conquest for commercial gain the demarcation between 'Russia' and 'Asia' had not appeared important. But as Russia became conscious of itself as a European empire in Asia, its imperial identity required clearer ideological and cultural boundaries to demarcate the colonisers from the colonised.[22]

The first detailed maps of the Russian Empire were made in the 1720s, mostly by the Geography Department of the St Petersburg Academy of Sciences, which published a general atlas in 1745. The line dividing Europe from Asia was drawn from this point at the Urals – a good deal further east than it had been on earlier maps – with 'European Russia' on the western side of the Urals and its 'Asian' empire to the east of them. The importance of the Urals for Russia's European self-identity has persisted to this day (readers may recall the now utopian notion of a Europe 'from the Atlantic to the Urals' advanced by Gorbachev). Yet, as we have seen, the Urals are not a real barrier between Europe and Asia. They are not like the oceans separating England, Spain or France from their overseas colonies. The Russian Empire was contiguous, a single territorial space, in which the Urals served not so much as a physical divide but rather as a cultural or conceptual marker separating 'Europe' from 'Asia'. To root this division in geography, the Russians embarked on a whole range of scientific studies in a fruitless effort to prove that the flora, fauna and tribes on the Asiatic side of the Urals differed from their equivalents over on the European side. They called Siberia 'our India', or 'our Peru', to equate the Russian Empire with the European overseas empires.[23]

The European part of Russia grew in size in the eighteenth century. If in the east it stretched out to the Urals, in the west it was enlarged by the annexation of Polish territory. The three partitions of Poland (in 1772, 1793 and 1795) were agreed in alliance with the Habsburg Empire and Prussia. Catherine's aim was not to conquer the ailing Polish–Lithuanian Commonwealth but to keep it weak and divided as a buffer state she could control – a foreign policy since pursued by all Russian governments towards neighbouring states. When the Polish king August III died, in 1763, she installed her own man on the throne, in fact her former lover, Stanisław Poniatowski. Backed by the pro-Russian party led by Prince Adam Kazimierz Czartoryski, Poniatowski forced the Sejm (the Polish parliament) to legislate against the persecution of minorities, the Orthodox and Protestants, by the Catholic majority. When, in protest, the Polish Catholic magnates raised an army and declared war against Russia, the Commonwealth descended into civil war between the pro- and anti-Russian groups. This allowed the Russians, Austrians and Prussians to occupy the Polish borderlands and impose a prearranged partition of Poland between themselves. Almost two-thirds of the Commonwealth was swallowed up by Russia between 1772 and 1795.

One of Catherine's hopes of the partitions was to open Russia to the influence of her new subjects – Poles, Baltic Germans and Uniate Ukrainians – from the former Commonwealth. The only ethnic group that was not welcomed was the Jews. Around 100,000 Jews became subjects of the Russian Empire as a result of the first partition of Poland.[24] The influx of skilled Jewish artisans and merchants gave rise to complaints from their competitors, who accused them of all sorts of evil practices, even blaming them for the pestilence that killed tens of thousands every year in Moscow in the first decade of Catherine's reign. To prevent a pogrom Catherine banned the Jews from Moscow, denied them many rights and, in 1791, established a Pale of Settlement in the western part of the empire, where the Jews were forced to live. Aside from the Jews, however, Catherine was a firm believer in the progressive influence of European immigrants. She encouraged them to come from central Europe, where many farmers and traders had been ruined by the Seven Years' War. German immigrants were given generous amounts of land in the Volga provinces, the location of a Volga German Autonomous Republic after 1917.

In the south, meanwhile, European Russia was expanding into Turkish lands, where Greeks and other immigrants were resettled by Catherine. Russia's defeat of Turkey in the war of 1768–74 resulted in the Treaty of Kuchuk Kainarji, which gave the Russians their first Black Sea port (Kherson) as well as the Crimean port of Kerch on the Azov Sea. Through this treaty the Russians also gained substantial rights (or so they believed) to interfere in Ottoman affairs to protect the sultan's Orthodox subjects, the Greeks, Serbs, Bulgarians, Moldavians and Wallachians. Catherine was anticipating the demise of the Ottoman Empire in Europe. She believed that Russia could and should become the beneficiary by championing the Orthodox. She trained Greek officers in her military schools, invited Greeks to settle in her new towns on the Black Sea coast and encouraged Greeks in their belief that Russia would support their national liberation from the Turks. Her greatest dream was to reclaim Constantinople from the Ottomans, establishing a new Byzantine Empire under Russian protection. The French philosopher Voltaire, with whom she corresponded, addressed her as 'votre majesté impériale de l'église grecque', while Baron Friedrich Grimm, her favourite German correspondent, referred to her as 'l'impératrice des Grecs'.[25]

It is unclear how serious she was about this 'Greek project'. She had no concrete plan to expel the Turks from Europe. But there was a desire in her entourage to establish Russia as a major Black Sea power linked through trade and religion to the Orthodox world of the eastern Mediterranean, including Jerusalem.[26]

Catherine believed that Russia had to turn towards the south if it was to be a great power. It was not enough to export furs and timber through the Baltic ports, as in the days of Muscovy. To compete with the European powers it needed to develop trading outlets for the agricultural produce of its southern lands, to build its naval power in the Black Sea and so secure access to the Mediterranean for its military and merchant ships. The Black Sea was crucial, not just for the defence of the Russian Empire on its open southern frontier with the Muslim world, but also for its viability as a power on the European continent. Without the Black Sea, Russia had no sea access to Europe, except via the Baltic, which could easily be blocked by the other northern powers in the event of a European war.

The plan to develop Russia as a southern power had begun in the mid-1760s, when the Ukrainian territories once ruled by the Cossack hetmanate were turned into provinces of the Russian Empire ruled by military governors. But the southern project took off ten years later, when Catherine placed her close friend and former lover Prince Grigory Potemkin in charge of New Russia, the sparsely populated territories newly conquered from the Ottomans on the Black Sea's northern coastline, and ordered him to colonise the area. Germans, Poles, Italians, Greeks, Bulgarians and Serbs were settled on these lands. New cities were established there – Ekaterinoslav, Kherson, Nikolaev and Odessa – many of them built in the French and Italian rococo style. Potemkin personally oversaw the construction of Ekaterinoslav (meaning 'Catherine's glory') as a Graeco-Roman fantasy to symbolise the classical inheritance that he and the supporters of the Greek project had envisaged for Russia. Shops were built in a semicircle like the Propylaeum of Athens; the governor's house resembled a Greek temple, and the law courts a basilica.[27]

The climax of this Black Sea policy was the annexation of Crimea in 1783. As part of the Treaty of Kuchuk Kainarji, the Crimean khanate had been made independent of the Ottomans. Three years later, a new khan, Şahin Giray, was elected with the backing of Russia. Although he had the support of the Crimea's sizeable Christian population, Şahin was opposed by the Ottomans. The Turks encouraged the Crimean Tatars to rise up against Şahin as an 'infidel', and sent a fleet with their own khan to replace him. The Christians and the Tatars soon became embroiled in a religious war. There were terrible atrocities on either side, prompting Russia to evacuate some 30,000 Christians to its Black Sea coastal towns. The departure of the Christians seriously weakened the Crimean economy. Şahin became dependent on the Russians, who persuaded him to abdicate, and then launched a quick invasion to secure the peninsula against the Turks. Forced to submit to Russian rule, the Crimean Tatars gathered with the mullahs in their mosques to swear an oath on the Koran to their new empress, 2,500 kilometres away.

From her teenage years, Catherine had been drawn to the ideas of the Enlightenment. On her accession to the throne she played the role of a philosopher-sovereign. Voltaire, Diderot and Baron Grimm were her long-time guides by mail. For her 'Instruction to the Legislative Commission' she drew upon the work of Adam Smith, Denis Diderot, Cesare Beccaria and William Blackstone, and incorporated almost word for word entire sections of *The Spirit of the Laws* by Montesquieu. Although she disputed Montesquieu's conception of Russia as an oriental despotism, she accepted his idea that laws should be consistent with the spirit of a nation shaped by climate and geography. She applied that principle to the empire, envisaging a legal code to bring the customs and in time the laws of all its subject peoples into line with those of the Russians. The sheer size and diversity of the empire necessitated 'autocratic rulership', Catherine argued, but the rule of law would protect the welfare of society.

Catherine's attraction to the Enlightenment was based on education and science, which she saw as progressive forces for Russia, rather than on its political ideas. She patronised the arts, allowed private publishing, promoted agricultural improvement and broadened access to schooling. In St Petersburg she founded the Smolny Institute for noble girls, the first girls' school in Russia (and in October 1917 the headquarters of the Soviet). She was not so liberal in her political philosophy. She rejected the doctrine of popular sovereignty adopted by thinkers such as Diderot, whose advice she sought on buying art for her collection at the Hermitage in the Winter Palace rather than on government. She paid lip-service to the idea of liberty, but did not believe that everybody should have it.

She had no intention of granting freedom to the millions of serfs. Although she believed that freely hired labour was better than bondage, and perceived the serfs as human beings worthy of their liberty, she ruled out any thought of reforming serfdom, let alone of ending it, for fear of the reaction that it would provoke from the aristocracy. In the wake of the Pugachev revolt she increased the powers of the landowners to exploit their serfs, who were left in their control, beyond the legal reach of the state and its officials. Without restraints on their treatment of the serfs, the worst landowners burdened them with higher labour and cash dues, sold them off like slaves to work in factories and had them flogged or even banished to Siberia (a punishment encouraged by Catherine to promote its settlement) for minor misdemeanours and infractions of the rules. Young serf women were always at the mercy of their master's whims and appetites, many ending up in serf harems, which became fashionable during Catherine's reign, when Turquerie was all the rage across Europe. In short, as Catherine explained to Diderot, the landowners were 'free to do on their estates whatever appeared best to them, except to kill their serfs by the death penalty'.[28]

Catherine's commitment to Enlightenment ideas was broken irrevocably by the French Revolution of 1789. 'You were right in not wanting to be counted among the philosophes,' she wrote to Grimm at the height of the Jacobin terror in 1794, 'for experience has shown that all of that leads to ruin; no matter what they say or do, the world will never cease to need authority. It is better to endure the tyranny of one man than the insanity of the multitude.'[29]

To prevent the 'French madness' from spreading to Russia, she tightened censorship, banning the publication of French works (Voltaire's works were burned), closing down the private presses and imprisoning the radical adherents of the Enlightenment in Russia. Among them was Alexander Radishchev, a nobleman inspired by the Freemasons' humanist ideals, whose *Journey from St Petersburg to Moscow* (1790), an exposure of the country's social evils, was denounced by Catherine as an attempt 'to stir up in the people indignation against their superiors and against their government'.[30] Radishchev was banished to Siberia, where he was sentenced to ten years of hard labour, and all but thirty pre-sold copies of his book destroyed. The ban on it would last until 1905.

Russia's idealisation of Europe was shaken by the violence in France. The once Francophile nobility became Francophobes – 'the French' a byword for inconstancy and godlessness. In St Petersburg, where the aristocracy was totally immersed in French culture, the reaction posed some problems for those liberal noblemen (like Pierre Bezukhov in *War and Peace*) who retained their sympathy for revolutionary France. But even here there was a conscious effort to break free from the intellectual empire of the French. The use of Gallicisms became frowned upon in the salons of St Petersburg (in the streets it was positively dangerous). Nobles gave up Clicquot and Lafite for *kvas* and vodka, *haute cuisine* for cabbage soup. 'Let us Russians be Russians, not copies of the French,' wrote Princess Dashkova, president of the Russian Academy. 'Let us remain patriots and retain the character of our ancestors.'[31]

But what did it mean to 'be Russian'? How could the Russians become Europeans without merely imitating them? Could they be Europeans *and* Russians? These were the questions many Russians asked as their country battled with Napoleon.

6

THE SHADOW OF NAPOLEON

Catherine died in 1796. Contrary to rumours, she was not killed while copulating with a horse – a legend that endured until the twentieth century – but died simply from a stroke. Absurd myths about the 'nymphomaniac empress' had been circulated by her enemies at court. Catherine's love of sex was not exceptional by the promiscuous standards of eighteenth-century kings, but she was judged more harshly for it because of her sex.

On his accession to the throne Paul restored the principle of primogeniture to the law of succession, effectively ensuring that his mother would be the last female ruler of Russia. Determined to reverse her policies, he revoked many of the freedoms she had granted to the aristocracy, reduced the elective element in provincial government, and imposed a military order on society, issuing a series of decrees to stamp out any sign of moral laxity, from French books, music and fashions to socialising after 10 p.m., when a curfew was imposed in St Petersburg. Appalled by his tyranny, a small group of drunken officers broke into the Mikhailovsky Palace and strangled Paul to death on the night of 23–24 March 1801. The officers were acting on the orders of a court conspiracy with close links to Alexander, son of Paul and heir to the throne, who had set the date for the killing. 'In Russia the government is autocracy tempered by assassination,' Madame de Staël remarked.[1]

Handsome, tall and gracious in demeanour, Alexander had been raised by his grandmother, Catherine the Great, in the spirit of the French Enlightenment. His Swiss tutor Frédéric Laharpe was a convinced republican and supporter of the Jacobins. According to his childhood friend the Pole Prince Adam Jerzy Czartoryski (son of Prince Adam Kazimierz Czartoryski), who joined the inner circle of his government, Alexander 'took the liveliest interest in the French Revolution, and while disapproving of its terrible abuses, wished for the success of the Republic'.[2]

In the first years of his reign Alexander enacted a series of political reforms: a new liberal code of censorship was introduced in 1804; the judicial powers of the Senate, Russia's highest court, were strengthened as a counterbalance to the tsar's authority; and government was modernised with the establishment of eight new ministries and an upper chamber (the State Council) modelled on Napoleon's Conseil d'État. In 1809, the emperor instructed his adviser Mikhail Speransky to draw up plans for a constitution based on the Code Napoléon with a national parliament elected on a property franchise. Speransky was a liberal. His analysis of the Russian state – which he described as a despotism based on the enslavement of society – was so devastating that it was not published in Russia until 1961. Had Speransky got his way, Russia might have turned into a constitutional monarchy. But Alexander hesitated to enact his minister's reforms and, once Russia went to war with France, they were condemned by the conservative nobility for being 'French'. Accused of treason by his enemies, Speransky was forced out of office and sent into exile in March 1812.

Three months later, the French imperial army, the Grande Armée, began its invasion of Russia. Napoleon's aim was straightforward – to force the Russians to honour their commitments to France in the Treaty of Tilsit (1807) which had followed the French defeat of Russia's forces at the Battle of Friedland. Alexander had agreed to join Napoleon's Continental System, a Europe-wide embargo against British trade, but all along the Russians had been flouting it. Britain purchased more than half of Russia's exports, especially its primary materials (wood, hemp, linen, wheat, potassium and wax), so the blockade, if implemented fully, would have entailed an economic and financial crisis for Russia. This was not a cause enough for war. Alexander could have backed down over it and avoided a conflict. But he chose to fight instead. He had for a long time been convinced that a showdown with Napoleon was unavoidable. He saw it as an ideological struggle. Napoleon had to be defeated if Europe was to be rebuilt as an international legal order based on constitutional monarchies. One might think there was a contradiction between his support for constitutionalism in Europe and his reluctant opposition to it in Russia. But in his view there was no inconsistency: Russia was not yet mature enough for the freedoms Europe ought to have.[3]

The Grande Armée began its invasion on 24 June. Starting from the Duchy of Warsaw, a Polish client state created by Napoleon in 1807, it crossed the Neman River into Russia's Polish territories. The Grande Armée was the largest army ever assembled, well over 600,000 men, mainly French, but also Germans, Poles and other European nationalities. By mid-August it was in Smolensk. Napoleon had thought that he could bring the Russians to their knees in one devastating victory like the one he had achieved against the Russians and the Austrians at Austerlitz in 1805. But Alexander had since learned that the only way to save his empire was not to fight Napoleon's forces in an open battle but to retreat and draw them into Russia, where they would be beaten by the winter frost and problems of supply created by his scorched-earth policy. Determined to engage the Russian army, Napoleon pushed on to Moscow. The Russians made a bloody stand at Borodino on 7 September, before their commander General Kutuzov gave the order to abandon Moscow to the French. When Napoleon entered Moscow, on 14 September, he found only empty houses, many of them burned in fires started by the Muscovites themselves to rob the French of warm accommodation and supplies. Exhausted and demoralised, the French had thought the fighting would be over when they took Moscow, but now that they had got there they could not even find the enemy.

Had Napoleon retreated at this point, he might have reached his base in Poland before the winter took its toll. But he stayed in Moscow for a month, waiting for the tsar to answer his peace terms.

The reply never came. The French attacked Kaluga to the south in a desperate bid to take its warehouses with their supplies. But they were blocked by the Russians. In mid-October they began their return to Poland, now only possible by the same route they had already trodden, across fields and villages stripped bare of food. As the French retreated, the snowfall became heavier. The temperature fell to minus 30 degrees by early December. Thousands died from cold, starvation and disease. The retreating columns were constantly attacked by Cossack cavalry and peasant volunteers, the latter often stirred up by their priests into believing that Napoleon was the Antichrist, while Alexander was the holy tsar, their saviour. Barely 10 per cent of the invasion force would make it back alive.

Alexander might have let Napoleon run away and lick his wounds, but he pursued him back to France. He committed a large force to the coalition army that defeated the Grande Armée at the crucial Battle of Leipzig, in 1813, from which the French limped back across the Rhine. The tsar saw himself as the liberator of the continent. The Patriotic War, as it was already being called, had displayed the glory of Russia, whose military might had 'saved' Europe. At the Congress of Vienna, convened in November 1814 to secure a long-term peace through the Concert of Europe, Alexander thought he could dictate the new continental balance of power. He had half a million troops on European soil; his Cossacks were the masters of Paris.

Alexander demanded an enlarged Poland – with a liberal constitution under his authority – as 'just' compensation for the sacrifices Russia had made in the war. He wanted Poland as a buffer state, a sphere of influence where he could intervene to prevent the Poles from ever again joining with the French or any other power to invade Russia. The Polish alliance with Napoleon was connected in his mind to the 1612 invasion of Russia by the Poles – an event commemorated by his promotion of the Minin and Pozharsky cult, which served to remind the Russians of their patriotic duty to defend their western frontier. He also saw the longer-term advantages of a Russian-oriented Polish state, which could serve as a cultural and economic intermediary between Russia and Europe. Without Poland, Alexander thought, Russia would become an Asiatic power, excluded from the European continent, as Napoleon had intended it to be by giving independence to the Poles. Alexander's demands for Poland were rejected by the British and the Austrians, who feared Russia's expansionist ambitions on the continent. But a compromise was reached by which the Russians kept around two-thirds of the Polish lands, ceding Poznań to the Prussians and Galicia to the Austrians.

Alexander believed that his empire had been saved by God. The victory reinforced his belief in the myth of Holy Russia as the providential saviour of humanity. From 1815, the tsar became increasingly religious, even mystical in his outlook, as he fell under the influence of Baroness de Krüdener, a Baltic German pietist. She helped him draft the founding text of the Holy Alliance, a union of Christian powers to secure the peace in line with the principles of Holy Scripture, which Alexander managed to persuade the Prussians and the Austrians to join, but not the pragmatic British, who saw it as a 'piece of sublime mysticism and nonsense'.[4] At the time of its conception the Holy Alliance was not wholly incompatible with Alexander's liberal principles. Its stress was on the defence of traditional Christian values against the secular materialism of the Jacobins. But it soon became a force of political repression in the name of religion, an ideology for the defence of divinely ordained and 'legitimate' (that is, monarchical) authorities against revolutionary threats.

Religion underpinned the tsar's reactionary politics during the last decade of his reign. It was from this point that Russia first appeared as the champion of Christian principles against secular democracy and nationalist movements in Europe (a role Russia would play on and off until 1917). The tsar's turn to political reaction was a panicky response to the *carbonari* and other revolutionary societies that surfaced across Europe in the post-war years and were behind the uprisings in Italy and Spain during 1820–1. Alexander was convinced that all these groups were connected to a secret international Bonapartist organisation. He urged the Holy Alliance to root them out and destroy them before they spread to Poland and Russia. At home, he silenced any further talk of constitutional reform, tightened censorship and took counsel only from conservatives. One of his main advisers was Karamzin, the historian, whose *Memorandum on Ancient and Modern Russia* (1811) had persuaded him that Russia was best suited to autocracy, its 'traditional' form of government. The liberal influence of Speransky was now replaced by the harsh disciplinarianism of General Arakcheyev, sometime minister of war, who turned entire villages into military colonies in which the peasants, put in uniform, were dragooned into farming and military duties for the state. Alexander hoped the colonies would teach the peasants discipline and self-sufficiency, but they functioned more like prototypes of the corrective-labour camps of the Gulag.

The tsar's reactionary turn was a bitter disappointment for those officers who came back from the war with liberal reformist hopes. Their encounter with the peasant soldiers in the army (who had fought with a patriotic spirit that shamed the noble class) had turned them into democrats, enemies of serfdom and autocracy. They had marched to Paris in the hope that Russia would become a modern European state, with a constitution where every peasant would enjoy the rights of citizens, but had returned to an unchanged country where the peasant was still treated as a slave. As one officer recalled, going back to Russia from Paris 'felt like returning to a prehistoric past'.[5]

The officers began to organise themselves in secret circles of conspirators, like those in Spain and Italy, often building on the networks of the Freemasons, banned by Alexander in 1822, to which most of them belonged. All were in favour of a liberal constitution and the abolition of serfdom, but they were divided over how to bring this end about. Some wanted to wait for the tsar to die, whereupon they would refuse to swear allegiance to his successor unless reforms were introduced. But others thought this wait would be too long. Alexander was just forty years of age, and in good health. They called for revolutionary action.

By 1825, Colonel Pavel Pestel had emerged as the boldest organiser of an army insurrection. A charismatic hero of the wars against Napoleon, he had a small but committed band of followers in the southern army who planned to arrest the tsar during his inspection of the troops in Kiev in 1826. They would then march to Moscow, and with the help of their allies in the north and the Polish nationalists, who agreed to join the movement in exchange for independence, seize power in St Petersburg. Pestel's manifesto *Russian Truth* (1824) was a strange mix of Jacobin ideas and Russian Orthodox fervour. It called for regicide, the establishment of a revolutionary republic (by means of a temporary dictatorship if necessary) and the abolition of serfdom. But it also wanted the creation of a nation state ruling in the interests of the Great Russians: the other national groups (Finns, Ukrainians and so on) would be forced to 'become Russian'. Only the Jews were beyond assimilation. Pestel thought they should be expelled from Russia.

Pestel's plan was hastily brought forward by Alexander's sudden death from typhus on 19 November 1825. Alexander had no sons, so the Grand Duke Konstantin, his first brother, was the natural heir. Konstantin, however, had renounced the throne because of his marriage to a Polish woman not of royal blood. His younger brother Nicholas did not announce his decision to take the crown instead until 12 December. Pestel resolved to seize the moment for revolt and hurried to St Petersburg to organise it with his fellow officers – the Decembrists as they would be known. They conceived of the uprising as a military putsch, instigated by orders issued by the officers, without even thinking whether the soldiers (who showed no inclination for an armed revolt) would go along with them. In the end, the Decembrist leaders rallied the support of 3,000 troops in Petersburg – far fewer than the hoped-for 20,000 men, but still enough perhaps to bring about a change of government if well organised and resolute. But that they were not.

On 14 December, in garrisons throughout the capital, soldiers were assembled for the ceremony of swearing their allegiance to the new tsar, Nicholas I. The 3,000 mutineers refused to swear their oath and marched to Senate Square, where they thronged in front of the Bronze Horseman and called for 'Konstantin and a Constitution'. The grand duke was popular among the soldiers, who had been told by their leaders that he had been usurped by Nicholas, cause enough for them to fight perhaps. But few had any idea what a constitution was (some of the troops thought it was the wife of Konstantin). For several hours the soldiers stood around in freezing temperatures, until Nicholas, assuming command of his loyal troops, ordered them to fire on the mutineers. Sixty soldiers were shot down; the rest ran away. Within hours the leaders of the rising had been arrested and imprisoned in the Peter and Paul Fortress. At their trial, the first show trial in Russian history, 121 conspirators were found guilty of treason, stripped of their noble titles and sent as convict labourers to Siberia. Pestel and four others were hanged in the courtyard of the fortress, even though officially the death penalty had been abolished in Russia. When the five were strung up on the gallows and the floor traps were released, three of the condemned proved too heavy for their ropes and, still alive, fell into the ditch. 'What a wretched country!' cried one of them. 'They don't even know how to hang properly.'[6]

Nicholas was twenty-nine when he ascended to the throne. Tall and imposing, with a large balding head, long sideburns and an officer's moustache, he was every inch a military man. From an early age he had developed an obsessive interest in military affairs. He learned by heart the names of all his brother's generals, designed uniforms and watched army parades and manoeuvres with a childlike excitement. Having missed out on his boyhood dream of fighting in the war against Napoleon, he prepared for a soldier's life, and in 1817 received his first appointment, inspector-general of engineers. He loved the routines of army life: they appealed to his strict and pedantic character as well as to his spartan tastes (throughout his life he insisted on sleeping on a military camp-bed). He saw the army as the ideal model for his state – ordered, disciplined, based on dutiful obedience and subordination to a single goal set by the autocracy. He filled his government with military men (all but one of his ministers of the interior had held the rank of general) and treated his officials as soldiers. Nobles in state service were forced to wear a uniform.

To strangers he seemed cold and stern, the personification of autocratic strength, but to the empress Alexandra and those at court who knew him well his firmness and insistence on strong action were based, not on confidence, but on insecurity. Throughout his reign he lived in fear of a revolution in Russia. The Decembrist uprising would long continue to haunt him. Coming as it did from the army he had so revered, it left him with a mistrust of society, especially those elements in it that took their ideas from Europe. He was never sure how many more Decembrists there were ready to rise up, should he loosen his police controls. For years he ordered regular reports on the activities of the Decembrists in Siberia. He kept tabs on their relatives and friends, always looking for signs of a new revolt. Any questioning of autocracy was in his view subversive.

To hunt down potential revolutionaries, Nicholas established a new political police. Generally known as the Third Department (its official designation was the Third Department of His Imperial Majesty's Own Chancellery), it was set up in 1826 under the direction of Count Alexander Benckendorff, a general of Baltic German origin who had played a leading role in the suppression of the Decembrists. Although it had a small central staff, the Third Department had at its disposal an investigative force in the Corps of Gendarmes, which had around 2,000 officers, along with powers to spy on every aspect of people's lives (opening their mail, following their movements, acting on denunciations by informers, and so on). It was the start of a long policing tradition in Russia.

Mistrustful of his own bureaucracy, Nicholas surrounded himself with his security forces, who fed his fears by giving him reports of 'Jacobin' societies and secret groups in Russia, mainly among noble youths, with links to foreign revolutionaries. The Poles were often singled out as the main intermediaries between Paris and St Petersburg.[7]

No wonder, then, that Nicholas reacted with such panic to the 1830 revolutions that broke out in Paris, Belgium and Warsaw. He feared that they would spread to Russia, unless checked by his forces. On the outbreak of the Belgian revolution against the Dutch, Nicholas had mobilised the Russian army and, in the face of British opposition, would probably have used it to restore the Dutch king to the throne, had it not been for the Polish uprising, which came to a head at the same time, demanding his attention first.

The uprising had begun in November, after the viceroy of Poland, Grand Duke Konstantin, conscripted Polish troops for the suppression of the revolution in Belgium. A group of Polish officers rebelled against the order, took the Belvedere Palace and with the help of Polish soldiers and civilians forced the Russian troops to leave Warsaw. Prince Adam Jerzy Czartoryski, now turned rebel against the reactionary tsar, was appointed at the head of a Provisional Government, a national parliament was called and Polish independence was proclaimed in January 1831. Within days, the Russian army crossed the Polish border and advanced towards Warsaw, which fell after eight months of fierce fighting. The Russians carried out a number of atrocities against civilians – retribution for the Poles' participation in Napoleon's invasion of Russia.

Nicholas continued punishing the Poles, whom he saw as the main revolutionary threat to his regime. Their liberal 1815 constitution was replaced by the Organic Statute of 1832, which made Poland 'an indivisible part' of the Russian Empire. The statute promised civil liberties, separate legal systems, local government and Polish-language rights. But these were seldom honoured by the new viceroy, Field Marshal Paskevich, the leader of the Russian war against Warsaw, who ruled Poland with an iron fist, closing universities, confiscating the estates of the rebels and imposing Russian as the sole permitted language in high schools and offices. Nicholas was obsessed by the Polish rebels who had fled abroad. At Münchengrätz in 1833, he secured an agreement with the Austrians and Prussians to exchange intelligence and combine their police efforts against these 'Bonapartists', as Benckendorff described them in his frequent correspondence with Count Metternich, the Austrian chancellor, over the next fifteen years.[8]

The uprising had made it clear that the empire needed an ideology to counteract the subversive influence of Western revolutionary and nationalist ideas. In 1833, the minister of education, Sergei Uvarov, defined that ideology in a circular to schools instructing them to teach the people 'in the spirit of Orthodoxy, Autocracy and Nationality'.[9] This trinity of national principles – Uvarov's answer to 'Liberté, égalité, fraternité' – would, he claimed, save Russia from the 'crisis' of the West, by which he meant the democratic challenge to monarchical authority and the erosion of Christian values by secular ideas. Known as 'official nationality', this new ideology was based on the old myth that the Russians were distinguished from the Europeans by the strength of their devotion to the Church and tsar and by their capacity for sacrifice in the service of a higher patriotic goal.

Similar ideas about the Russian character and mission in the world were developed by the Slavophiles, who emerged as an intellectual circle in Moscow at this time. If Uvarov's national ideology was rooted in the institutions of the Church and state, the Slavophiles' conception of the national identity was based in the peasants' folk culture. They had a romantic notion of the village commune as a uniquely Russian institution, beyond which the country need not look for guiding moral principles. 'A commune', declared Konstantin Aksakov, one of the leading Slavophiles, 'is a union of the people who have renounced their egoism, their individuality, and who express their common accord; this is an act of love, a noble Christian act.'[10]

The key to this communal harmony, the Slavophiles maintained, was the principle of *sobornost*, a spiritual union (from *sobor*, the Russian for 'cathedral' and 'assembly') in which the individual found a moral purpose in the collective – a concept foreign to the individualistic West. Because *sobornost* had to be a voluntary communion, the peasants needed to be free to join it in the right spirit, and on this basis the Slavophiles were committed to the abolition of serfdom.

The Slavophiles were opposed to the Westernising reforms begun by Peter the Great. They feared that these changes, imposed by a state that was 'foreign' to the peasants, would result in the loss of Russia's national character, its native customs and traditions. The latter, they believed, were based on higher principles – on the Christian harmony, humility and willingness to sacrifice which, in their imagination, had animated Muscovite society before Peter's reign. The Slavophiles were building on the myth of Russia as the defender of Christian principles against Western secular materialism, the same myth developed by 'official nationality'. If Russia lagged behind the West in its material development, it was superior to it in its spiritual principles. The simple, peasant 'Russian soul' was more truly Christian than the egoistic spirit of the Western bourgeois citizen.

In the fictions of Nikolai Gogol (and the later Dostoevsky) Slavophile ideas gave rise to a mystical conception of the Russian soul – a universal spirit of Christian love and brotherhood innate only in the Russian people, whose providential mission was to save the world from egotism, greed and all the other Western sins. Here, in this myth of the Russian soul, was a messianic concept of Russia as an empire of the Orthodox without territorial boundaries, a spiritual empire linking Moscow, the Third Rome, with Constantinople and Jerusalem. For Slavophiles like Fedor Tiutchev, a diplomat and poet, it was Russia's soul that made it different from the West – unknowable by any Western measure, as he put it in this famous quatrain, known by almost every Russian:

Russia cannot be grasped by the mind,
No yardstick will measure her,
She is of a special kind –
In Russia you can only believe.

Gogol tried to develop this conception in a three-part novel called *Dead Souls*, in which the providential plan for Russia was at last to be revealed. The grotesque imperfections of provincial Russia exposed in the first and only finished (1842) volume of the novel – where the adventurer Chichikov travels through the countryside swindling a series of moribund squires out of the legal title to their deceased serfs – would be transcended by Gogol's lofty portrait of the Russian soul, living in a realm of Christian brotherhood, which he was intending to reveal in the second and third parts. The trouble was that Gogol could not picture this idealised Russia in a living human form. He, the most pictorial of all the Russian writers, could not conjure up an image of the actual Russia that satisfied his Slavophile ideals. His observations of reality were such that he could not help but burden all his characters with the faults and imperfections derived from their natural habitat. As he himself wrote despairingly, 'this is all a dream and it vanishes as soon as one shifts to what life is really like in Russia'.[11] Sensing he had failed in his fictional endeavour, he sought instead to drive his message home in *Selected Passages from Correspondence with Friends* (1846), a moral sermon on the divine nature of Russia in which he preached that salvation lay in the spiritual reform of every individual citizen. He said nothing about reforming serfdom or the autocratic state, claiming that both were morally acceptable if combined with Christian principles. The intelligentsia was outraged.

'Intelligentsia' is in origin a Russian word. In Russia it refers to an educated stratum of society sharing certain principles – namely, opposition to autocracy and commitment to the 'people's cause'. The Russian intelligentsia had its roots in the institutions and ideas of the nobility in the eighteenth century. But its politics were rooted in the uprising of 1825. After the suppression of the Decembrists, entering the military or civil service became unthinkable for those noble sons who shared their democratic principles. Where state service had defined their fathers' class, they themselves would be defined by their service to society. Acutely conscious that their wealth and privilege had been achieved by the exploitation of their fathers' serfs, they sought to redeem their guilt by becoming doctors, teachers, statisticians or agronomists to improve the people's lives, or else by becoming writers, journalists and critics, whose mission was to the raise the educated public's awareness of Russia's social ills. The task of literature was not to entertain but to portray Russia as it really was, so that its readers might change it. Realism was the creed that united all the writers, among them Dostoevsky and Turgenev, who emerged on the literary scene in the 1840s – the 'extraordinary decade', as Pavel Annenkov, the critic, described it.[12]

Their intellectual guide and inspiration was the literary critic Vissarion Belinsky, who did more than anyone to define the moral principles of Russian literature. In his 'Letter to Gogol' (1847), a passionate rejection of *Selected Passages*, Belinsky wrote what could serve as a manifesto of the Westernist intelligentsia. In the absence of a parliament, Belinsky wrote, the public looked to writers for moral leadership against the autocracy, and they judged their writing on this principle: 'That explains why every so-called liberal tendency, however poor in talent, is rewarded with universal attention, and why the popularity of great talents that sincerely or insincerely give themselves to the service of orthodoxy, autocracy and nationality declines so quickly.' Gogol had betrayed the moral duty of the writer by siding with the Church and state against reform. This explained his literary failure:

> you failed to realise that Russia sees her salvation not in mysticism or asceticism or pietism, but in the successes of civilisation, enlightenment and humanity. What she needs is not sermons (she has heard enough of them!) or prayers (she has repeated them too often!), but the awakening in the people of a sense of their human dignity lost for so many centuries amid dirt and refuse; she needs rights and laws conforming not to the preaching of the Church but to common sense and justice, and their strictest possible observance. Instead of which she presents the dire spectacle of a country where men traffic in men, without even having the excuse so insidiously exploited by the American plantation owners who claim that the Negro is not a man; a country where people call themselves not by names but by nicknames such as Vanka, Vaska, Steshka, Palashka; a country where there are not only no guarantees for individuality, honour and property, but even no police order, and where there is nothing but vast corporations of official thieves and robbers of various descriptions.[13]

Words still relevant today.

The tsar's fear of revolution reached new heights in 1848, another year of revolutions across Europe. They began in Paris, where the monarchy was replaced by a republic towards the end of February, followed by revolts in Vienna, Berlin, Dresden, Leipzig, Milan, Venice, Prague, Budapest and Bucharest. Everywhere the crowds demanded civil freedoms, democratic parliaments, national liberation from empires.

The French Republic was a direct challenge to the legitimist principles established at the Congress of Vienna and upheld by the Holy Alliance. The main republican leaders at once declared their support for an independent Poland and the liberation of northern Italy from Habsburg rule. Nicholas was in no doubt that the revolution of 1789 had 'arisen from the ashes', as he put it to the Prussian king, and that military measures would be needed to prevent it spreading east.[14] Within two weeks of receiving news of the events in Paris, he had mobilised 400,000 troops. They occupied the empire's western borderlands, the most susceptible to revolution, where martial law was soon declared. Together with the army, the gendarmes of the Third Department raided homes in a frantic hunt for weapons, illegal literature and any other signs of revolutionary activity.[15]

Nicholas did not intend to send his troops to France or Italy. But he was prepared to use them against revolutions in Austria or Prussia, if asked to by their rulers, because they bordered on Russia. Where he was the quickest to intervene, however, was in Moldavia and Wallachia, where he barely recognised the sovereignty of the Ottoman Empire. The principalities had gained their autonomy in 1829, but had since fallen under Russian domination, against which their revolutions broke out in the spring of 1848. In Bucharest, a Wallachian republic was declared by the revolutionary government, whose leaders called for the union of the principalities as an independent national state (Romania). Alarmed by these developments, Nicholas sent 14,000 troops to occupy Moldavia, and then 30,000 more to conquer Bucharest and crush the revolution there. 'A system of espionage has been established here,' the British consul in Bucharest reported. 'No person is allowed to converse on politics. German and French newspapers are prohibited.'[16]

The intervention in Romania encouraged Nicholas to do the same in Hungary. The Hungarian revolution had begun in Budapest in March 1848. Inspired by events in France and Germany, its leaders formed a democratic parliament and government, declared their independence from Austria and passed a series of reforms in which serfdom was abolished, freedom of the press was established and the Hungarians assumed control of their own units in the Habsburg army. The Austrian imperial government declared war on the Hungarians, who, with the Slovaks, Ruthenians and other minorities opposed to Habsburg rule, proved more than a match for the Austrian forces. The newly installed eighteen-year-old emperor Franz Joseph appealed to the tsar to intervene.

Defending 'legitimate authorities' was sufficient cause for intervention according to the principles of the Holy Alliance. But for Nicholas there was more at stake than that. He could not afford to stand aside and watch the spread of revolutionary movements in central Europe that might lead to a new uprising in Poland. The Hungarian army had many Polish exiles in its ranks. Some of its best generals were Poles, including General Jozef Bem, one of the main military leaders of the 1830 Polish uprising and in 1848–9 the commander of the victorious Hungarian forces in Transylvania. Unless the Hungarian revolution was defeated, there was every danger of it spreading to Galicia, a largely Polish territory controlled by Austria, which might reignite the Polish problem in Russia. Galicia also had a sizeable Ukrainian minority, the 'Ruthenians' as they were called by the Austrians, with a thriving centre of Ukrainian culture in its capital Lemberg (called Lviv by the Ukrainians), so Nicholas had reason to be fearful that a revolution in Galicia might provide the springboard for a broader nationalist movement in tsarist Ukraine. In June 1849, some 190,000 Russian troops crossed the Hungarian frontier under the command of Paskevich, the leader of the punitive campaign against the Poles in 1831. Vastly outnumbered by the Russians, most of the Hungarian army surrendered in August, but around 5,000 soldiers fled to the Ottoman Empire, where under pressure from the British and the French the sultan gave them sanctuary. In London and Paris, the Hungarian rebels were hailed as freedom-fighters against Russian tyranny. Among their champions was one Karl Marx, then in exile in London, who in a series of articles attacked Russia as the enemy of liberty.

Nicholas, meanwhile, began an all-out war against any sign of potential opposition, real or phantom, in Russia. Foreign citizens were watched by the police; the universities were barred from teaching philosophy or constitutional law; and while the regime did not stop the press reporting on events abroad, it ordered the arrest of anyone discussing them, even in their homes, lest such conversations should give the wrong ideas to their servants, as Nicholas explained to the Petersburg nobility. The Gendarme Corps of the Third Department was massively increased. Its agents donned civilian dress instead of their sky-blue uniforms to infiltrate the circles of suspected revolutionaries.

The one 'plot' they uncovered was a weekly gathering of students, teachers and minor civil servants hosted by a young official in the Foreign Ministry, Mikhail Petrashevsky, in St Petersburg. The writers Dostoevsky and Saltykov-Shchedrin were regulars at these Friday evenings, begun in 1846, where the works of foreign socialists were earnestly discussed alongside other ideas of reform. In April 1849, the group was arrested and imprisoned in the Peter and Paul Fortress on false charges that it was preparing for a revolution in cities across the empire. Twenty-one of the accused, including Petrashevsky and Dostoevsky, were condemned to death; fifty others were sent into exile or conscripted by the army as privates. Just before their execution on Semenevsky Square the men were spared by Nicholas, who had planned this cruel torture. Some were sent to prison, others to hard labour in Siberia. Dostoevsky spent four years in the Omsk prison camp, where he came face to face with the most brutal criminals. It was an experience that formed his vision of the human psyche in *The House of the Dead* (1862), a fictionalised memoir of his prison years.

Dostoevsky's crime had been to read aloud Belinsky's letter to Gogol which by then had become famous, in part because it had been banned. The revolutions in Europe led to even tighter laws of censorship. The monthly list of books forbidden by the Third Department grew from 150 titles before 1848 to 600 in that year.

A new board of censors, the Buturlin Committee, was appointed by the tsar with extensive powers of preventive censorship. Its vast army of censors pored over every manuscript submitted to the board for approval. They were now told to flag up any work that could potentially be deemed subversive, even if that had not been the author's intention. The results were often farcical. One censor banned a new edition of Shakespeare's *Richard III* because it dealt with themes that were 'dangerous in a moral sense'. Another disallowed a reprint of Catherine the Great's letters to Voltaire. On this basis, as a censor noted, 'even the Lord's Prayer could be interpreted as a Jacobin speech'.[17]

One book that slipped through the censors was to have a powerful effect in changing attitudes towards serfdom, the most crucial and explosive issue of the day. Turgenev's *Sketches from a Hunter's Album* (1852) had been passed for publication. Most of the stories had already been published in the journal *The Contemporary* so the censor no doubt thought there was no harm in passing them. None of them contained a single sentence that could be read as an overt attack on the tsarist system or serfdom – although the whole book was suffused with a subtle condemnation of both. For the first time the peasants were portrayed not as simple 'rustic types' but as thinking, feeling, complicated individuals. By simple observation of the way that serfdom shaped their lives, Turgenev had aroused the moral indignation of his readers more effectively than any socialist manifesto could have done. Published in the same year as *Uncle Tom's Cabin*, the *Sketches* had as big an impact in swaying Russian views against serfdom as Harriet Beecher Stowe's book had on the anti-slavery movement in America. Infuriated by the publication of the *Sketches*, Nicholas had Turgenev arrested, not for the book, but for an obituary of Gogol he had since published in the *Moscow Herald*. Turgenev was imprisoned and then placed under house arrest. One night in prison he was visited by the chief of police, who was curious to meet the famous writer. The police official brought champagne. After a few glasses and some amiable talk, the visitor proposed to drink a toast: 'To Robespierre!'[18]

*

The shadow of Napoleon returned in the form of his nephew, Louis Napoleon, elected president of France in December 1848. Four years later, a national referendum made him emperor of the French, Napoleon III. Nicholas was the only European sovereign not to recognise the new Napoleon. Emperors, he claimed, were made by God, not elected in a plebiscite. To show his contempt for him, he addressed Napoleon as 'mon ami' rather than 'mon frère', the customary greeting to another sovereign. Some of his advisers wanted the French emperor to seize on the insult and force a break with Russia, but Napoleon passed it off with the remark, 'God gives us brothers, but we choose our friends.'[19]

Napoleon III aimed to restore France to a position of respect and influence abroad, if not to the glory of his uncle's reign, by revising the 1815 settlement and reshaping Europe as a family of liberal nation states along the lines envisaged by Napoleon I. Russia was the biggest obstacle to this ambition. Its defeat would be revenge for 1812.

A long-running dispute in the Holy Lands brought that conflict to a head. The dispute involved the Church of the Nativity in Bethlehem and the Church of the Holy Sepulchre in Jerusalem, then ruled by the Ottomans. It turned on which side should control them – the Orthodox, who were backed by Russia, or the Catholics, defended by the French? The Ottomans, who did not really care, could be swayed one way or another by French or Russian bullying. The Russians had maintained the upper hand since the Treaty of Kuchuk Kainarji (1774), which they claimed had given them the right to represent the interests of the Orthodox in the Ottoman Empire. But all that changed in 1851, when the Marquis de La Valette, a zealous Catholic, was appointed by Napoleon, keen to curry favour with the Church, as the French ambassador in Constantinople. La Valette declared that the Latin claims had been 'clearly established' and threatened war against the Turks if they refused to enforce them.[20] The Turks gave in to the French demands in November 1852.

Nicholas was furious. More than any recent tsar he placed the defence of the Orthodox at the centre of his foreign policy. He was devoted to the Russian Church, which sent more pilgrims to the Holy Lands than any other church, and shared their intense passion for the sacred shrines. Like many Russians, he saw the Holy Lands as an extension of Holy Russia, a mystical idea that had never been defined by territorial boundaries, and he was prepared to go to war, against the whole of Europe if need be, to protect Orthodox interests. He mobilised his forces for a lightning strike on Constantinople to force the Turks to reverse their ruling for the Catholics, and sent ahead Prince Menshikov, a veteran of the wars against the French, to impose a treaty on the sultan. Encouraged by the British, who feared Russia's expansion, the Turks held firm, rejecting Menshikov's bellicose threats. Large and angry crowds in the Turkish capital called for holy war against Russia.

The failure of the Menshikov mission convinced the tsar to send his troops into Ottoman Moldavia and Wallachia once again. The invasion started in June 1853. Nicholas was counting on uprisings by the sultan's Slavs to help the advance of Russian troops. He thought the Slavs would welcome the Russians, their co-religionists, as their liberators from the Turks. 'There is no other way for us to move ahead,' the tsar wrote in November, 'except through a popular uprising for independence on the widest and most general scale.'[21]

His thinking had come a long way from the defence of legitimate authorities. He was now calling for a Balkan revolution to promote his aims against the Turks. In his mind the call was justified by the religious nature of the war. It was his sacred duty to free the Orthodox from Muslim rule. In any case the sultan could not count as a legitimate ruler because he was not Christian. Pan-Slav ideas also influenced the tsar's thinking. Of particular importance was a memorandum written by the leading Pan-Slav ideologist, Mikhail Pogodin, in December 1853. The memorandum clearly struck a chord with Nicholas, who shared Pogodin's sense that Russia's role as the protector of the Orthodox had not been recognised or understood by the French or the British and that Russia was unfairly treated by the West. Nicholas especially approved of the following passage, in which Pogodin railed against the double standards of the Western powers, which conquered distant colonies but forbade the Russians to intervene in neighbouring countries to protect their co-religionists. It is worth quoting at length, because it says a lot about Russia's grievances against the West.

> France takes Algeria from Turkey, and almost every year England annexes another Indian principality: none of this disturbs the balance of power; but when Russia occupies Moldavia and Wallachia, albeit only temporarily, that disturbs the balance of power … The English declare war on the Chinese [the Opium Wars] who have, it seems, offended them: no one has a right to intervene; but Russia is obliged to ask Europe for permission if it quarrels with its neighbour. England threatens Greece to support the false claims of a miserable Jew and burns its fleet [a reference to the Don Pacifico affair]: that is a lawful action; but Russia demands a treaty to protect millions of Christians, and that is deemed to strengthen its position in the East at the expense of the balance of power. We can expect nothing from the West but blind hatred and malice, which does not understand and does not want to understand (*comment in the margin by Nicholas I*: 'This is the whole point').
>
> Who are our allies in Europe? (*comment by Nicholas*: 'No one, and we don't need them, if we put our trust in God, unconditionally and willingly'). Our only true allies in Europe are the Slavs, our brothers in blood, language, history and faith …
>
> If we do not liberate the Slavs and bring them under our protection, then our enemies, the English and the French … will do so instead (*comment by Nicholas*: 'Absolutely right') … Then we will have ranged against us not one lunatic Poland but ten of them (*comment by Nicholas*: 'That is right').[22]

As the Russian troops advanced towards Constantinople there was no uprising by the Balkan Slavs. Their love for Russia was a Pan-Slav myth. But the invasion stirred the British to action. The impetus for intervention came from the home secretary, Lord Palmerston, an outspoken advocate of an aggressive offensive to bring Russia to its knees, who was loudly supported by the Russophobic British press. For years the press had presented Russia as a threat to 'British principles' – liberty, free trade and civilisation – and to the empire's interests in India. Once the British had decided on a war, Napoleon concluded that his best bet was to join them so as not to lose out on the spoils.

This was the start of the Crimean War. The allies planned to destroy the Russian naval base at Sevastopol to force the Russians to withdraw from the principalities, although Palmerston had more ambitious plans to break up the Russian Empire by giving independence to the lands which it had conquered during the past century and a half. The allied forces landed on the Crimean peninsula on 8 September 1854. Heavily defeating the Russian forces at the Alma Heights, they began the siege of Sevastopol, a year-long industrial bombardment of the city's defences which in its intensity would not be matched until the First World War. In September 1855, the allied forces stormed the Malakhov Redoubt, the key to the defence of the city, forcing the exhausted Russians to evacuate Sevastopol and sue for peace. Palmerston proposed continuing the war in the Baltic and the Caucasus to liberate these territories from the Russians. But the French had had enough.

Under the terms of the Paris Treaty (1856), the Russians renounced any claims to Moldavia or Wallachia, now placed under the protection of the European powers, and agreed to dismantle their Black Sea Fleet, a humiliation for Russia. No compulsory disarmament had ever been imposed on a defeated great power. Not even France had been disarmed after the Napoleonic Wars. The way Russia was treated was unprecedented for the Concert of Europe, which was supposed to be guided by the principle that no great power should be humbled by others. But the allies did not really think that they were dealing with a European power in Russia. They equated it with China, on which they had imposed similar humiliating conditions after the First Opium War.[23]

The humiliation was to leave a deep and lasting sense of resentment towards the West. It continues to this day. All Putin's talk of Western 'double standards' and 'hypocrisy', of Western 'Russophobia' and 'disrespect' for Russia, goes back to this history. In the 1860s, these complaints were amplified by writers such as Tyutchev, Danilevsky and Leontiev, who twisted earlier Slavophile ideas about Russia's role as the protector of Christian principles against the materialism of the West to argue that the latter was an existential threat to it. 'Europe', Danilevsky argued in *Russia and Europe* (1869), 'is not only alien to us but even hostile; its interests cannot be the same as ours, and in most cases they will be opposed to ours.'[24] Putin would develop these and other similar ideas about Russia's conflict with the liberal West in the wake of his war in Crimea.

The defenders of Sevastopol had fought with courage and tenacity, as Tolstoy had revealed in *Sevastopol Sketches* (1854–5), written when he was an army officer. These stories made his name as a writer. A quarter of a million Russians gave their lives, their bodies buried in mass graves all around Sevastopol. Their heroism would allow Russian nationalists to claim a moral victory in the Crimea by retelling the story of the war as a tale of Russia fighting on its own, against all the powers of Europe, for its Orthodox beliefs. The city's spirit of defiance became central to the myth of Russia as the last defender of truly Christian values against the materialism of the West.

The war had brutally exposed the country's many weaknesses: the corruption and incompetence of the command; the technological backwardness of the army and navy; the poor roads and lack of railways that accounted for the chronic problems of supply; the poverty of the army's serf conscripts; the inability of the economy to sustain a state of war against the industrial powers; the weakness of the country's finances; and the failures of autocracy. Critics focused on the tsar, whose arrogant and wilful policies, as they now seemed, had led the country to defeat and sacrificed so many lives. Even within the governing elite the bankruptcy of the Nicholaevan system was coming to be recognised. 'My God, so many victims,' wrote the tsarist censor Alexander Nikitenko in his diary. 'All at the behest of a mad will, drunk with absolute power ... We have been waging war not for two years, but for thirty, maintaining an army of a million men and constantly threatening Europe. What was the point of it all?'[25]

Nicholas died on 2 March 1855. He had been in bed with influenza but had gone out in freezing temperatures to inspect his troops without a coat. He died from pneumonia. Rumours circulated that the tsar had killed himself. Probably untrue, they were believed by his enemies, who saw it as a recognition of his sins. Whether true or not, Nicholas was broken morally, filled with remorse for the military disaster he had brought about. All his reign he had been fighting with the shadows of Napoleon, waging war against the liberal Western forces which he saw as a threat to his beloved Holy Russia, only to discover that it was a fight he could not win. Holy Russia was a myth.

The new tsar Alexander II was no less committed to autocracy, but, unlike his father Nicholas, he understood that reforms were needed to save it. Defeat in the Crimea had persuaded him that Russia could not compete with the Western powers until it abolished serfdom. The economic case was irrefutable. The gentry had never learned to make a profit from their own estates. They were heavily indebted to the state, itself bankrupted by the war, which knew that abolition was essential for a market-based agrarian economy. The moral argument for abolition was also indisputable. No one had the will to defend serfdom any longer, least of all the noble service class, immersed as it was in the cultural and moral values of Europe.

On top of all these arguments there was an urgent need to prevent another Pugachevshchina – a serf war against the state. The soldiers who had fought in the Crimean War had been led to expect their freedom; when it did not come they organised rebellions – some 500 of them in the first five years of Alexander's reign.[26] In March 1856, not long after signing the Treaty of Paris, the new tsar warned the Moscow nobles: 'You know yourselves that the existing order of ruling over living souls cannot remain unchanged. It is better to abolish serfdom from above than to await the day when it will begin to abolish itself from below.'[27] But would the end of serfdom solve the problems of the peasantry?

7

AN EMPIRE IN CRISIS

The Emancipation Decree was proclaimed on 19 February 1861. It was not read to the peasants until 7 March, the first day of Lent, when, it was assumed, they could be counted on to listen to their priests, charged with its communication, in a sober and submissive mood. Expectations had been running high. The peasantry believed that they would gain their freedom from the landowners: they would no longer have to work for them or pay them dues because they would be given all their land. As the authorities were well aware, the decree fell a long way short of such utopian hopes. The gentry had battled to limit the reform at every stage of its legislative journey from the Editing Commission of 1859 to its final passage through the State Council in January 1861. The result was a compromise, which satisfied no one, least of all the peasantry.

The decree removed the peasants from bondage to the landowners, but tied them legally to the commune, which received a share of the gentry's land in communal ownership. The land did not come free, as the peasants had expected, but for a sum the commune had to pay through a sort of mortgage with the state. The commune's household members were collectively responsible for these redemption payments, as they were for all taxes. For the next nine years, while the land to be transferred to the communes was determined by the local gentry committees, the status quo was not to change.

When the statutes were read out by the priests, the peasants scratched their heads in disbelief. Where was their land and freedom? In the village of Bezdna, near Kazan, the peasants reasoned, as they did in many villages, that the failure of the priest to mention them must mean either that he could not read correctly or that he had been instructed by the gentry to leave those provisions out. The peasants went in search of more reliable readers. They found one, a semi-literate peasant and Old Believer called Andrei Petrov. After studying the proclamation for three days, he managed to interpret the statutes in a way that told the peasants what they had wanted to hear all along. News of his discovery spread rapidly. Peasants came from all around to hear the long-awaited 'golden charters' in which their land and freedom were awarded to them by the *tsar-batiushka*, who in the popular imagination was still the same divine and paternal figure, the embodiment of their ideals of justice, invoked and impersonated by the Cossack rebel leaders of the past. The landowners were alarmed. Troops were sent to Bezdna, where they found 5,000 peasants, six times the population of the village, defending Petrov's house to prevent his arrest. The peasants would not listen to the officer's demands to give Petrov up. Chanting '*volia, volia*' (freedom, freedom), they said they would rather die. After several warnings, the soldiers opened fire on the crowd: sixty-one people were killed and hundreds more were wounded before Petrov surrendered.[1]

There were similar disturbances in other provinces. Troops were sent to put down peasant protests in 718 villages between March and May.[2] The threat of revolution quickly passed. But the peasants' disappointment dealt a mortal blow to the *tsar-batiushka* myth, which died a slow death over the next fifty years, the period we are covering in this chapter. After the Emancipation, moreover, the peasants never fully recognised the gentry's landed property. They fell so far behind in their mortgage payments – a sign of their rejection of the settlement as much as a marker of their poverty – that the debt was cancelled by the government in the revolutionary year of 1905.

The commune emerged from the Emancipation as the basic unit of administration in the countryside. The *mir*, as it was called, a word that also means 'world' and 'universe', regulated every aspect of the peasants' lives: it decided the rotation of the crops (the open-field system of strip farming necessitated uniformity); took care of the woods and pasture lands; saw to the repair of roads and bridges; established welfare schemes for widows and the poor; organised the payment of redemption dues and taxes; fulfilled the conscription of soldiers; maintained public order; and enforced justice through customary law.

In the central agricultural zone, where the land was overpopulated, the commune tried to share it equally by repartitioning the strips of arable between the peasant households every few years according to their size (usually determined by the number of 'eaters' but sometimes by the number of male adult labourers). The origins of this egalitarian practice are probably related to the collective payment of taxes, most likely starting with the poll tax introduced in 1718.[3] It made sense for the commune to give more land to the bigger families, which had to pay a larger share of the collective tax burden, and which also had more mouths to feed. Changes over time in the households' size necessitated changes in the distribution of the strips to optimise the village's ability to pay its tax and feed itself. If its origins were practical, the repartitioning was also a reflection of the peasant ideology, a form of primitive socialism, which would guide the agrarian revolutions of 1905 and 1917.

Three ideas were at the centre of this peasant ideology. They can be seen in customary law, which was codified by jurists after 1861. The first was the concept of family ownership – that all the household assets (livestock, tools, crops and buildings but not the women's dowries) remained in common ownership, inherited by all the sons with provisions made for unmarried daughters and widows. Membership of the peasant household was defined by participation in its economic life ('eating from the common pot') rather than by blood or kinship ties. Second was the labour principle – basically a peasant version of the labour theory of value. The peasants attached rights to labour on the land. They believed in a sacred link between the two. The land belonged to God. It could not be owned by anyone. But every peasant family should have the right to feed itself from its own labour on the land. On this principle the landowners did not fairly own their land, and the hungry peasants were fully justified in claiming their right to farm it. A constant battle was thus fought between the state's written law, framed to defend property, and the peasants' customary law, which they used to defend their transgressions of the landowners' property.

The third idea was articulated in the way the peasants applied customary law. They judged the merits of a case according to the position of the parties concerned. In this way of thinking stealing from a rich man was less serious than stealing from a man who could barely feed his family. Swindling a neighbour was immoral, but cheating on a landlord or government official was not subject to any moral censure under customary law. The peasantry rejected the state and its laws. Centuries of serfdom had bred in them a deep mistrust of all authority outside their *mir*.[4]

The Emancipation failed to resolve the fundamental question: how could the peasants' growing need for land be reconciled with the landowners' rights of property? The problem was most acute in the central agricultural zone, where the landowners' estates were historically located. The practice of communal repartitioning encouraged the peasants to have bigger families – the main criterion for receiving land. The birth rate in Russia was nearly twice the European average in the latter nineteenth century. The rapid growth of the peasant population (from 50 to 79 millions between 1861 and 1897) resulted in a worsening land shortage. By the turn of the century 7 per cent of the peasant households in the central zone had no land at all, while one in five had less than one hectare. Although the average peasant allotment (at 2.9 hectares in 1900) was comparable in size to the typical smallholding in France or Germany, Russian peasant farming was much less intensive, with grain yields at barely half the level reached by farmers in Europe. The light wooden scratch plough used by Russian peasants with a single horse, or pair of oxen, was vastly inferior to the heavy iron ploughs used in western Europe with a four- or six-horse team.[5]

Lacking the capital to modernise their farms, the easiest way the peasants had to feed themselves was by ploughing more land at the expense of fallow and other pasture lands. But this made the situation worse. It meant reducing livestock herds (the main source of fertiliser) and the exhaustion of the soil. By 1900, one in three peasant households did not have a horse.[6] To cultivate the land they dragged their ploughs themselves.

Such was the peasants' demand for land that many were prepared to pay excessive rates to rent it from the landowners. Land rents increased seven-fold between 1861 and 1900.[7] The easy profits the landowners made from renting out their land reduced their interest in farming it themselves. World grain prices were depressed in any case. But that changed in the 1890s, when prices rose sharply, encouraging the gentry to take the land back into cultivation by themselves. Large commercial farms employing new machines instead of peasant labour began to appear in the fertile steppelands of the south, where the railways and steamships opened up the channels for export through the Black Sea. The impact on the peasantry was disastrous. It hit them hardest in a band of provinces, running from Saratov to Voronezh, Kursk and Poltava, between the overpopulated centre and the new commercial farms of south Russia – areas, in other words, where the peasants suffered from both shortages of land and the loss of jobs to the machines. These were the regions where the peasant revolution was most violent in 1905 and 1917.

The Emancipation was the first in a series of reforms in the 1860s, the so-called Great Reforms. Their main aim was to energise society by granting freedoms within the framework of autocracy. One of the problems of the tsarist system was the absence of provincial institutions it could entrust to extend its influence and run local government. We have already reviewed this problem, most recently in Catherine the Great's reign when the weaknesses of the provincial government were exposed by the Pugachev rebellion. The Great Reforms were meant to prevent that from happening again.

A law of 1864 established a new system of self-government, the rural councils or zemstvos, in most Russian provinces. Elected on a property franchise, the zemstvos (whose name derived from the word for land, *zemlia*) were dominated by the landowners. They were set up only at the provincial and district levels (below that the peasant communes ruled themselves under the loose supervision of gentry magistrates and police constables). The judicial reforms of the same year set up an independent legal system with public jury trials. There were new laws granting more autonomy to universities (1863), expanding primary schooling (1864), relaxing censorship (1865) and introducing universal military conscription (for up to seven years) in place of the old system of conscripting only serfs (1874). The aim of these reforms, in the words of a progressive jurist, was 'to put a repressed and humiliated society on its feet and let it flex its muscles'.[8]

Had the spirit of the 1860s continued to pervade the work of government, Russia might have become a more liberal society. During Alexander's reign (1855–81) there was also a growing 'public sphere' (to adopt the concept of Jürgen Habermas).[9] Civil society began to organise and represent itself through institutions of its own making – professional organisations, voluntary societies and charities, zemstvo bodies, universities and a proliferating press, including the 'thick journals', the intelligentsia's literary parliament, through which public opinion appeared as a force the state could not ignore. Russia was at last developing the civic institutions that any country needs to build a political democracy.

The zemstvos had the most potential for this liberal development. Run by squires of the sort who fill the pages of Tolstoy and Chekhov – well-meaning men who dreamed of bringing civilisation to the countryside – they founded schools and hospitals, provided veterinary and agronomic services, built roads and bridges, aided local trades and industries, financed rural credit and carried out statistical surveys into every aspect of the agricultural economy with a mission to improve the welfare of the peasantry.

The 'small deeds liberalism' of the provincial zemstvos was not a challenge to the central state. Indeed, in so far as the crucial weakness of the tsarist system was the *under-government* of the localities, they were a vital supplement to it. The presence of the state stopped at the eighty-nine provincial capitals. Neither the district towns nor the *volost* rural townships had any standing tsarist officials. There was only a series of magistrates who appeared from time to time on some specific mission, usually to sort out local conflicts and then disappear again. The common image of the tsarist regime as omnipresent and all-powerful was largely an invention of the revolutionaries, who spent their lives in fear of it, living in the underground. The reality was different. For every 1,000 inhabitants of the Russian Empire there were only four state officials at the turn of the twentieth century, compared with 7.3 in England and Wales, 12.6 in Germany and 17.6 in France. For a rural population of 100 million people, Russia in 1900 had no more than 1,852 police sergeants and 6,874 police constables. The average constable was responsible for policing 50,000 people in dozens of settlements scattered across 5,000 square kilometres.[10]

In this space the zemstvos had a huge amount of work to do. They were limited, however, by the taxes they could raise from the local landowners, whose more reactionary members were opposed to paying for the welfare of the peasantry. They also faced increasing opposition from the Ministry of the Interior, which came to see them as a breeding ground for revolutionaries. The main concern was the zemstvo employees (teachers, doctors, statisticians, engineers and agronomists) known as the Third Element. In contrast to the first two elements, the administrators and elected officials, who were mostly landowners, these employees were predominantly from the towns. Many had indeed been exiled to the countryside because of their involvement in student demonstrations and other radical activities. Through their work in the zemstvos they hoped to serve the people's cause.

This was the environment in which Populism emerged as an ideology. It entailed a belief in the peasantry and its egalitarian customs as the model for a socialist society, which could be reached in Russia, the Populists believed, without going through the negative effects of industrial capitalism experienced in the West.

At its heart was a new myth to reshape the country's history: the simple Russian people as the carrier of socialist ideals. The Populist intelligentsia idolised the peasantry. They filled their libraries with books about folklore, studied Russian peasant myths, proverbs, songs and customary laws. Riddled with the guilt of privilege, they dedicated their lives to the service of the people's cause.

From this loosely defined ideology Populism evolved into a political movement, the first real socialist movement in Russia. Students took the lead. During the 'mad summer' of 1874, thousands of students left their lecture halls and arrived in the countryside hoping to convert the peasants to their revolutionary struggle. Dressed like peasants, they learned rural trades to make themselves more useful to the peasantry, and brought books to help teach them how to read. The students were met with suspicion by the villagers. 'Socialism', one of the Populists later wrote, 'bounced off the peasants like peas from a wall. They listened to our people as they do to the priest – respectfully but without the slightest effect on their thinking or actions.'[11] Most of the activists were rounded up by the police, sometimes tipped off by the villagers themselves.

These sobering encounters led to a split in the movement. Some remained committed to the task of winning over the peasants through propaganda and 'small deeds'. It was, they said, the only way to build a democratic social movement, the only guarantee against the use of violence. Others feared that this process was too slow – the police would always have the upper hand. They argued for a tighter party structure to organise political revolt, acts of terror and a coup against the state. Only when the police state had been paralysed would the peasants join their cause.

One of the most important theorists of this putschist strategy, Petr Tkachev, was to have a major influence on Lenin, who owed as much to him as he did to Marx. After the failure of the 'Going to the people', as the events of 1874 were known, Tkachev argued that such methods were too slow. Before a social revolution could be organised a class of richer peasants, whose interests lay in the status quo, would appear as a result of capitalist development and assert its domination in the countryside. Tkachev argued for a putsch by a disciplined vanguard, which would set up a dictatorship *before* engineering the creation of a socialist society by waging civil war against the rich. He claimed the time was ripe to carry out this coup, since as yet there was no major social force, just a weak landowning class, prepared to defend the monarchy. Delay would be fatal, Tkachev argued, because soon there would be such a force, a bourgeoisie, supported by the 'petty-bourgeois' peasantry, which would be formed by the new market forces in Russia.

The immediate consequence of this turn to putschist methods was a wave of terrorist attacks on government officials, many by a group, the People's Will (Narodnaya Volia), which killed the tsar in 1881. It had made a number of attempts on Alexander's life before one of its agents threw a bomb into his carriage in St Petersburg, killing one of the Cossack riders flanking it. When the emperor emerged unhurt, a second bomb was hurled by another agent which blew away his legs and ripped open his stomach. Taken in a sleigh to the nearby Winter Palace, he died shortly afterwards from his wounds.

It is hard to think of a more momentous turning-point in Russian history. On the day the tsar was killed, 1 March, he had agreed to a reform that would include elected representatives from the zemstvos and town councils in a new consultative assembly. Although it was a limited reform, by no means implying the creation of a constitutional monarchy, it showed that Alexander was prepared to involve the public in the work of government. On 8 March, the proposal was rejected by his son and heir, Alexander III, in a meeting of grand dukes and ministers. The most reactionary and influential critic, Konstantin Pobedonostsev, procurator of the Holy Synod, warned that accepting the reform would represent a first decisive step on the road to constitutional government. At this time of crisis, he maintained, Russia was in need not of a 'talking shop' but of firm actions by the government. From that point, the new tsar, who would rule from 1881 to 1894, pursued an unbending course of political reaction to restore the autocratic principle.

Alexander was a giant of a man, who liked to entertain his drinking friends by crashing through locked doors and bending spoons in his fingers. He looked like a Russian tsar should look, stern and fierce with a thick beard framing his square head. He openly despised not only the zemstvos but all levels of bureaucracy, which he saw as a wall between the tsar and his people. He introduced a series of reactionary 'counter-reforms' to strengthen forms of personal rule ('power verticals', as Putin would call them) and weaken representative bodies. The provincial governors received new powers over the zemstvos and town councils. They capped their budgets and obstructed their activities by subjecting them to frequent police raids and arrests of their employees as suspected revolutionaries. The governors appointed gentry land captains, who ruled the countryside like 'little tsars'. Among their many powers were the rights to overturn the communes' decisions, to discharge elected peasant officials and to act as judges in communal disputes. Until 1904, they could even have the peasants flogged for minor crimes. The impact of such corporal punishments – decades after the Emancipation – cannot be overstressed. It made it clear to the peasantry that violence was the basis of state power – and that violence was the only way to remove it. One peasant wrote that his fellow villagers had seen the appointment of the land captains as a 'return to the days of serfdom, when the master squire had lorded it over the village'. There could not have been a less effective way of asserting the tsar's power in the countryside.

The same could be said of the regime's policies towards the national minorities. Before 1881, the government pursued a varied policy towards the nationalities. It ranged from loose controls to full-scale Russification. Finland, for example, enjoyed more self-rule and cultural autonomy than any other part of the empire (more indeed than the Irish enjoyed under British rule) because on its capture from Sweden, in 1808–9, the Russians had confirmed its substantial rights and privileges granted under Swedish rule. In the Baltic provinces the loyalty of the German elites was rewarded by the tsars, who upheld their rights against the nascent nationalist movements in Estonia and Latvia. In Central Asia, conquered by the Russians in the 1860s, the imperial government was likewise careful to avoid offending local Muslim sensibilities. It ruled through Islamic institutions, mosques and madrasas, and incorporated tribal customs into law, enabling it to govern relatively peacefully.[12] In the Caucasus, by contrast, the Muslim population was never pacified, following the region's gradual conquest by the Russians from the reign of Catherine the Great. The Russians fought a constant war against the mountain tribes. Poland too was a battleground, particularly after the Polish uprising of 1863, when Alexander II intensified the Russification of the empire's western provinces, areas where the Polish landowners remained strongly nationalist. Russian was made compulsory in schools and public offices. Polish students at Warsaw University had to suffer the indignity of studying their national literature in Russian translation. There were even signs forbidding the use of Polish in railway stations, restaurants and shops.

The assassination of the tsar led to more repressive policies. Now, more than ever, certain nationalities (Poles, Armenians, Jews) were branded as disloyal, identified with the revolutionary movement and subjected to further language bans and prohibitions that became ever more absurd. In Stalin's church school in Gori, which he began attending at the age of nine, in 1888, the boys were forced to speak in Russian at all times and were beaten by their masters when they lapsed into Georgian. During the 1907 cholera epidemic in the Kiev area, doctors were forbidden to publish warnings not to drink the water in Ukrainian. But the peasants could not read the Russian signs, and many died as a result.

Of all the empire's national minorities, the Jews suffered most. They were at the bottom of the empire's racial hierarchy. Since their incorporation into Russia during the partitions of Poland, the Jews had been subjected to a comprehensive range of legal disabilities and discriminations which by the end of the nineteenth century embraced some 1,400 different statutes and regulations. They were forbidden to own land, to hold civil service posts or to serve as officers in the army; there were strict quotas on Jewish admissions into higher schools and universities; and they were forced by law to live within the empire's fifteen western provinces, which made up the Pale of Settlement. Blamed by Russian 'patriots' for the assassination of Alexander II, the Jews were victims of hundreds of pogroms in 1881. There would be many more pogroms, especially in 1905–6 and 1917–21, as anti-Jewish violence became a major part of counter-revolutionary activity. The last two tsars encouraged this. Nicholas II, in particular, saw the pogroms as an act of loyalty by the 'good and simple Russian folk'. He became a patron of the Union of the Russian People, formed in 1905, which instigated more than one pogrom.

Little wonder, then, that Jews were prominent in the revolutionary underground. The Marxist movement, in particular, was attractive to the Jews. The Jewish Labour Bund was the first mass-based Marxist party in Russia. Formed in 1897, it had 35,000 members by 1905. Jews occupied a visible position in the leadership of the Mensheviks and Bolsheviks, the two main factions of the Russian Social Democratic Labour Party (the SDs). The Jews were drawn to the Marxist cause above all by its European character. Whereas Populism had proposed to build a socialism based on peasant Russia, the land of pogroms, Marxism was based on a modern Western vision of Russia. It promised to assimilate the Jews into a movement of universal human liberation based on internationalism.

It was not just the Jews who were radicalised after 1881. Throughout the empire the Russification campaign was to drive non-Russians into nationalist parties: the Social Democrats in Finland and the Baltic lands; the Socialists in Poland; the Revolutionary Ukrainian Party; the Georgian Social Democrats (the young Stalin among them); and the Dashnaks in Armenia. In all these societies national divisions were reinforced by class divides: the native labouring class and peasantry were ready to be set against the foreign landowners, businessmen and officials. The most successful nationalist movements combined the peasants' struggle for the land, especially where it was owned by foreigners, with the demand for native language rights, enabling the peasants to gain full access to schools, the courts and government. This combination was the key to the success of the Ukrainian nationalist movement, which organised the peasants against foreign (mainly Polish and Russian) landowners. It is no coincidence that the peasant uprisings of 1905 erupted first in those regions of Ukraine where the nationalist movement was also most advanced.

A revealing survey was carried out in Russia's village schools in 1903. The researchers asked the children what they wanted to become when they grew up. Less than 2 per cent said they wanted to be peasant farmers, as most of their parents were. Almost half had set their hearts on a city job. 'I want to be a shop assistant,' said one boy, 'because I do not like to walk in the mud. I want to be like those city people who are cleanly dressed.'[13] Their desire for social betterment was synonymous with employment in the town. Virtually any urban job seemed desirable compared with the hardships and routines of peasant life.

Millions of peasants came into the towns, some drawn by ambition, others forced to leave the countryside because of overpopulation on the land. Between 1861 and 1914 the empire's urban population grew from 7 to 28 million people. First came the young men, then the married men, then unmarried girls, who worked mainly in domestic service, and finally the married women with children. The rural migrants tried to keep their farms alive for as long as possible by waged labour in the towns. They sent their earnings to their villages, where they themselves returned at harvest time. As in all developing societies, there was a constant to and fro between the city and the countryside.[14]

Factory conditions were atrocious. According to Count Witte, the finance minister who oversaw the growth of industries in the 1890s, the worker 'raised on the frugal habits of rural life' was 'much more easily satisfied' than his counterpart in Europe or North America, so that 'low wages appeared as a fortunate gift to Russian enterprise'.[15] There was little regulation of the factories. The gains made by British workers in the 1840s, and by the Germans in the 1880s, remained out of reach of Russian workers at the turn of the century. The two most important factory laws – one in 1885 prohibiting the night-time employment of women and children, the other in 1897 restricting the workday to eleven and a half hours – had to be wrenched from the government. Small workshops were excluded from the legislation, although they employed the majority of the country's workforce, especially its female contingent. Unventilated working areas were filled with noxious fumes, shopfloors crammed with dangerous machinery. Strikes were illegal. Trade unions banned. Yet there were more strikes in Russia than in any other country of Europe.

Many of these strikes were led by workers with links to Marxist propaganda circles, mostly organised by intellectuals. This was the context in which Lenin, or Ulianov as he was then known, entered revolutionary politics.

Contrary to the Soviet myth, in which Lenin was a Marxist theorist from his infancy, he came late to politics. He was born in 1870 into a respectable and prosperous family in Simbirsk, a typical provincial town on the Volga. His father was inspector of the Simbirsk district's primary schools. In Lenin's final year at secondary school, a middle-class gymnasium, he was highly praised by his headmaster, who by one of those strange historical ironies was the father of Alexander Kerensky, the prime minister Lenin would overthrow in October 1917. Kerensky *père* described Lenin as a 'model student ... never giving cause for dissatisfaction, by word or by deed, to the school authorities', and put this down to his 'moral and religious upbringing'. The young man was accepted to read law at Kazan University. All the indications were that he would follow in his father's footsteps, making a distinguished career for himself in the imperial bureaucracy.[16]

The charmed life of the Ulianovs came to an abrupt halt in 1887 when Lenin's elder brother, Alexander, was executed for his involvement in an abortive plot to kill the tsar. The conspiracy was hatched by a group of seventy-two students at St Petersburg University, where Alexander had been studying sciences since 1883. He had made the bombs they were meant to throw at the tsar's carriage on 1 March, the sixth anniversary of Alexander II's assassination by the People's Will, an organisation he had idolised. The plot ended Lenin's hope of graduating with a law degree (he was expelled from Kazan University) and catapulted him into the revolutionary movement in St Petersburg.

His first inclination was, like his brother's, to adopt the violent methods of the People's Will. They were suited to his personality, which was angry, fiery and dogmatic, hardened by a hatred for the tsarist system and anyone who went along with it (this was a man who once admitted after a performance of Beethoven's Appassionata Sonata that he could not listen to music too often because 'it makes me want to say kind, stupid things, and pat the heads of people. But now you have to beat them on the head, beat them without mercy').[17] Lenin came to Marx already armed with set ideas. All the main components of his ideology – his stress on the need for a disciplined 'vanguard'; his belief that action (the 'subjective factor') could alter the objective course of history; his defence of terror and dictatorship; his contempt for democrats (and for socialists who compromised with them) – stemmed not just from Marx but from Tkachev and the People's Will. He injected a distinctly Russian dose of conspiratorial politics into a Marxist dialectic that might have remained passive otherwise, tied down by a willingness to wait for the revolution to develop socially rather than bringing it about through political action. It was not Marxism that made Lenin a revolutionary but Lenin who made Marxism revolutionary.

Marxist groups had been in operation for at least a dozen years when the Russian Social Democratic Labour Party, the SDs, was formed in 1898. It was a party led by intellectuals, and the focus of its efforts was to educate a politically conscious vanguard of the working class which would organise their factory comrades for the revolutionary struggle. The problem was that literate workers tended to be focused more on bargaining for better pay and conditions than on political activity and were represented by a group of Marxists known as the Economists. Lenin attacked them with the sort of violence that would become the trademark of his rhetoric. He argued that their peaceful tactics would undermine the revolutionary movement, which depended on a workers' party that was ready for the fight.

The type of party Lenin had in mind was revealed in his 1902 pamphlet *What Is to Be Done?* He wanted followers who would devote their whole lives to the Party's cause. It had to be a small but secret party made up of committed revolutionaries (be they workers or, more likely, intellectuals) who understood 'the fine art of not getting arrested'.[18] At that time no one fully realised the implications of this principle. They became clear only at the Second SD Party Congress, which met in London in 1903. The Party was divided on the obligations of its membership. Lenin wanted all its members to be activists, whereas Yuli Martov, his ally in the fight against the Economists, thought that anyone should be allowed to join the Party if they subscribed to its policies. Here were two opposing views of what the Party ought to be: a conspiratorial organisation or a broad-based parliamentary party like the labour parties of the West. Lenin won by a small majority, enabling his faction to call themselves the Bolsheviks (Majoritarians). Their opponents became known as Mensheviks (Minoritarians). It was a mistake by the Mensheviks to accept these names. It made them look like losers from the start.

Other parties were appearing by this time. A major famine in 1891 had politicised society, which was angered by the failure of the government to deal with the crisis, blamed by many on its over-taxing of the peasantry. The zemstvos expanded their activities to deal with the catastrophe. Effectively becoming a shadow government, they called for a national assembly to be involved in framing policies. The professions, for their part, set up unions, Russia's first trade unions (hence they were known as *profsoiuzy*, professional unions), and demanded greater influence over public policy. The universities were rocked by student demonstrations between 1899 and 1901. Students and professors joined the Union of Liberation, formed in 1903 to campaign for a constitution, from which the Kadet Party (Constitutional Democrats) would be formed in 1905. Others joined the Socialist Revolutionary Party (SRs), established in 1901. The SRs carried on the Populist tradition but sought to lead the 'labouring poor', meaning both workers and peasants.

Nicholas II was not inclined to compromise with these demands for political reform. On his accession to the throne, in 1894, he had sworn to uphold his father's autocratic principles. He was a firm believer in the medieval myth of the tsar as an instrument of God, divinely sanctioned to rule over Russia as his personal domain. From his tutor, the arch-reactionary Pobedonostsev, Nicholas had learned to see his sovereignty as absolute, unlimited by bureaucracy, parliaments or public opinion, and guided only by his conscience before God. He did not see the need to adapt his rule to the demands of the modern world.

Here were the roots of the revolutionary crisis – in the growing conflict between a dynamic public culture and society, on the one hand, and, on the other, a reactionary monarchy, fossilised in its medieval concept of autocracy, which resisted, until it was too late, the demands of this emerging public sphere for a greater role in government.

On Sunday, 9 January 1905, a large crowd of workers marched towards the Winter Palace to hand in a petition to the tsar – a custom of the Russian people going back for centuries, as we have seen. They were led by a priest, Father Gapon, who had made a name for himself as a preacher in the factory districts of St Petersburg. He had told his followers in simple terms, with quotations drawn from the Bible, that the *tsar-batiushka*, the little-father tsar, would answer their demands if they went to him in supplication: that was his obligation before God. The petition humbly asked for an improvement in their working conditions, which had become intolerable. 'SIRE,' it began: 'We, the workers and inhabitants of St Petersburg, of various estates, our wives, our children, and our aged, helpless parents, come to THEE, O SIRE, to seek justice and protection. We are impoverished, we are oppressed, overburdened with excessive toil, contemptuously treated [by our employers].'[19]

The tsar was absent from the capital. He had gone to his palace at Tsarskoe Selo for his usual weekend break of country walks and family games of dominoes. On his orders soldiers blocked the main approaches to the city centre and fired at the crowds to turn them back. On Palace Square a huge body of cavalry and several cannon were placed in front of the Winter Palace to stop those who had managed to get through, some 60,000 protesters. The guards tried to clear the crowds by using whips. When this failed, they took up firing positions. The demonstrators fell to their knees, took off their caps and crossed themselves. A bugle sounded and the firing began. Around a thousand people were killed or wounded on Bloody Sunday, as these events became known.

When the firing finally stopped and the survivors looked around at the dead and wounded bodies on the ground, there was a decisive moment of truth, the starting-point of any revolution, when their mood changed from disbelief to anger and hatred. In that moment, the folk myth of the *tsar-batiushka* – an idea that had underpinned the monarchy for centuries – was finally destroyed.[20] The people had discovered that there was no holy tsar.

Society was outraged by the massacre. Students turned the universities into bastions of opposition to the government, which closed them down. The professional unions organised a national Union of Unions, joined by the first workers' unions. Strikes and protests took place everywhere. Barricades went up in Warsaw and Łódź, where nationalists seized their opportunity to organise a revolt against Russian rule. The peasants also took their chance. They attacked the estates, seizing property, burning manor houses, forcing landowners to flee. Nearly 3,000 manors were destroyed, most of them in the central agricultural zone, during the peasant jacquerie of 1905.

The army was deployed to put down the rebellions, but the best troops were in Manchuria, fighting a disastrous war against Japan which had begun in 1904 over the two powers' rival claims in Manchuria and Korea. The reservists left behind were inexperienced. Most of them were peasant sons. They resented being used against their fellow peasants, and refused to carry out orders. Mutinies spread through the army, and then broke out in the Black Sea Fleet, where famously the sailors of the battleship *Potemkin* rebelled in June.

The strikes became more organised and militant, as socialists became involved. In September there was a general strike, begun by the printers of Moscow but soon joined by the railway workers and millions of others – shop workers, bank and office clerks, teachers, lecturers, even the actors of the Imperial Theatre of St Petersburg. It was a national strike against the government. In St Petersburg the strike was directed by a Soviet of Workers' Deputies – an ad hoc council of socialists and workers dominated by the Mensheviks and led by Leon Trotsky (at that time a Menshevik) which published its own newspaper, *Izvestiia*.

So far the regime had responded to the crisis with incompetence and blindness to reality. Nicholas refused to recognise the danger he was in. He thought the protests had been organised by foreign revolutionaries and were not supported by the Russian people, who were of course loyal to him. But the general strike at last forced him to listen to his ministers, who warned him he would lose his throne unless he made political reforms. On 17 October he reluctantly agreed to sign a Manifesto, drawn up by Count Witte, the prime minister, granting freedoms of speech, assembly and religion, and establishing a legislative parliament, or Duma. The electoral law for the Duma, passed in December, gave the vote to most men (but not women) over the age of twenty-five but set up six electoral colleges to weight the votes in favour of the landowners.

The Manifesto's proclamation was received with jubilation in the streets. There was a sense of national unity, a feeling that all social classes would be brought together by this 'people's victory'. It was expressed by Repin's painting, *Manifesto of 17 October*. But this feeling was illusory. The people's unity was one more myth. For the propertied elites, whose interests were political, the Manifesto was a real breakthrough, perhaps an end to their struggle. But for the workers and peasants political reforms were no solution to their social grievances. Where was the workers' eight-hour day, the better treatment they deserved? Where was the land for the peasants? Their struggle, surely, had only just begun.

Russia's parliamentary era started with a ceremony celebrating the creation of the Duma in the Coronation Hall of the Winter Palace on 27 April 1906. On one side of the hall stood the great and good of autocratic Russia: ministers, state councillors, old and grey court dignitaries, all turned out in their brilliant dress uniforms.

Confronting them were the Duma deputies, a motley collection of professionals, peasants dressed in cotton shirts and tunics, but almost no workers. The two sides faced each other with hostility.

The confrontation was a taste of things to come. The so-called Duma period between 1906 and 1917 should be understood as a battle between the competing principles of autocracy and parliamentary control. Much depended on the willingness of Nicholas II to allow the Duma more powers, and on the Duma's willingness to work with the government in shaping the reforms needed to stabilise the country. It was a test that both sides failed.

Nicholas refused to accept the October Manifesto as a limitation of autocracy. He had granted it reluctantly to save his throne, but had not recognised it as a constitution which conferred any rights on the Duma. No mention of a constitution had been made in the Manifesto or the Fundamental Laws of April 1906 which formalised the new relationship between the crown and parliament. The omission ruled out any hope of the Kadets working with the government. They preferred to stay in opposition rather than compromise their constitutional principles. The Fundamental Laws left full power with the tsar. He appointed the prime minister and Council of Ministers. Under Article 87, he could dissolve the Duma and rule by emergency decree. Although it was a legislative parliament, the Duma could not pass its own laws without the endorsement of the tsar and the State Council, dominated by the court's officials and the aristocracy.

The Duma was more radical than the government had bargained for when it drew up the electoral law. From its opening session in the Tauride Palace in St Petersburg, it became a revolutionary tribune, demanding radical political reforms, including the appointment of a government responsible to the Duma, the abolition of the State Council and universal adult male suffrage. The two largest parties, the Kadets and Trudoviks, a Populist grouping formed to compete in the 1906 elections when these were boycotted by the SRs and SDs, agreed on the need for land reform in which the estates would be expropriated by the state for the needs of the peasantry (unlike the Trudoviks, the Kadets proposed compensation for the landowners). Unwilling to consider such demands, the tsar dissolved the Duma on 8 July.

Two weeks later, Nicholas appointed Petr Stolypin as his new prime minister. Stolypin was one of the finest statesmen Russia ever had. His five years in office were the regime's best chance to avert catastrophe. Tall, imposing and intelligent, fearless in authority, he had come to the attention of the tsar as the provincial governor of Saratov, whose peasants were the most rebellious in the whole of Russia during 1905. Stolypin restored order through repressive measures (hangings and mass exile to Siberia) that made him a hate-figure of the left. But he also realised that the land question could be resolved only by a profound reform. His model came from Kovno, a Polish–Lithuanian province where he had served for thirteen years. Like the empire's other western provinces, Kovno did not have the peasant commune. The peasants owned their land, and as a result they farmed it more efficiently than the peasants did in central Russia where the commune gave them no incentive to improve their landholdings. Stolypin's solution to the land question was to help the peasants break away from the commune and consolidate their landholding as private property.

By a law of 9 November 1906, the male head of a peasant family received the right to convert his land into an enclosed private farm (*khutor*) or privatise it inside the village (*otrub*). The state put its full weight behind the reform, employing thousands of agronomists and providing loans through a Peasant Bank to help the separators purchase and consolidate communal land. Stolypin called it a 'wager on the strong'. Only by creating a new class of peasant landowners could the state prevent another revolution on the land.

A second Duma convened in February 1907. Stolypin had been hoping that the Octobrists, a 'party of state order' based on the political principles of the October Manifesto, would win a majority. His government relied on their support. But the fifty-four Octobrist deputies, even if supported by the ninety-eight Kadets, were outnumbered by the socialists, with 222 seats, now reinforced by the SRs and SDs, who had a clear majority for land reform based on expropriating gentry land without compensation. On 3 June, the tsar again closed down the Duma. This time he used his emergency powers to pass a new electoral law so that when the next assembly convened it would be dominated by conservatives. The electoral weight of the peasants, workers and national minorities was reduced, while the representation of the gentry was even more exaggerated than before. The Kadets and socialists denounced it as a coup. When the Third Duma assembled, in November 1907, the pro-government parties controlled 287 of the 443 seats. The opposition called it the 'Duma of Lords and Lackeys'.

Even with this parliamentary backing, Stolypin failed to make much headway with his wide-ranging programme of reforms. His proposal to create a *volost* zemstvo was blocked by the United Nobility, a landowners' organisation with powerful supporters in the court and State Council, which feared that the zemstvos would be swamped by the peasants. His attempt to expand the state system of primary schools was defeated by the Church, which had its own parish schools. His land reform lost momentum. Only 15 per cent of the peasants consolidated private plots – mostly in the face of bitter opposition by the rest of the commune.

There were good reasons for the peasants to oppose the break-up of the commune, which had been the focus of their lives for centuries. They feared that giving some the right to privatise their plots would deprive others of their customary rights of access to the land as their basic means of livelihood. What would happen if the household head bequeathed the land to his eldest son or sold it altogether? The younger sons and daughters would be forced to leave farming. The peasants were afraid that the government surveyors would give separators more than their share of the land. They had never learned to calculate the area of a piece of land. They divided it by pacing out the strips, making rough adjustments for their quality. They were suspicious of the modern methods employed by the surveyors. How would they make the necessary adjustments? How would they divide the meadows, woods and rivers, which were common property? Stolypin had misunderstood the peasantry's attachment to the *mir*. He had assumed that they were poor because of it. But in fact it was the other way around: the commune served to share the burden of their poverty, and as long as they were poor they had no reason to leave it.

Stolypin was assassinated on 1 September 1911. A student revolutionary shot him at close range in the Kiev Opera. On hearing of his death, the tsar is alleged to have said, 'Now there will be no more talk about reform.' The empress was relieved to see the end of Stolypin, a principled opponent of the 'holy man' Rasputin, in whom she had placed her faith as a healer for her haemophiliac son, the tsarevich Alexei, a faith unshaken by the mounting evidence of Rasputin's debauched lifestyle. It is not known if Stolypin's killing was approved, facilitated or even organised by the police.

By the time of his assassination, Stolypin's reforms had run aground and could not have gone much further. He had antagonised the old elites by challenging their vested interests, as well as the liberals by his high-handed tactics in the Duma. Like all reforming statesmen in Russia (Alexander II and Gorbachev are obvious parallels), he was too dependent on a small reformist segment of the state bureaucracy. He failed to mobilise a broader social base. There was a Stolypin but no Stolypinites.

After him no prime minister was able to prevent the empire's drift towards catastrophe. All thoughts of reform were abandoned. Vladimir Kokovtsov, the prime minister until 1914, took his instructions from the court and sidelined the Duma. There were calls from right-wing groups to reduce the powers of the parliament – some even wanted to abolish it – and it was only Western pressure that restrained the tsar from doing so.

Nicholas was increasingly removed from political reality. He was retreating into a fantasy of popular autocracy, a communion of God, tsar and people, such as he imagined had existed in medieval Muscovy. That was why he tolerated Rasputin, despite the rumours of his sexual escapades. He saw in him 'a good, religious, simple-minded Russian', who could guide his conscience before God.

The fantasy was on display for the tercentenary celebrations of the Romanov dynasty in 1913. The imperial family appeared before their subjects and opened churches on the sites connected with the founding of the dynasty. At the Ipatiev Monastery in Kostroma, where Mikhail Romanov had taken refuge from the Polish invaders in 1612, they received a peasant delegation that bowed down to the ground before Nicholas and posed for a photograph with the descendants of the boyars who had travelled from Moscow to offer the crown to the Romanovs in 1613. In Moscow they attended a grand costume ball where all the guests appeared in replicas of court dress from the seventeenth century. To symbolise the union between tsar and people the jubilee gave centre stage to the cult of Ivan Susanin, a peasant on the Romanov estate in Kostroma who, according to legend, had sacrificed his life to save Mikhail from capture by the Poles. The Susanin myth was endlessly retold, most famously in Glinka's opera, *A Life for the Tsar*, which was performed in theatres throughout Russia in the tercentenary. Military newspapers published features on Susanin, whose story, it was said, 'should inspire every soldier how to serve his tsar and fatherland'.[21]

The threat of war in Europe was meanwhile increasing. The rise of nationalist movements in the Balkans, especially the Serbs', destabilised the Austrian–Hungarian Empire, creating tensions between Russia and the German powers, as Berlin backed Vienna's policies against the Slavs. For most of the nineteenth century, Russia had pursued its interests in Europe through an alliance with Germany and Austria. But the growing strength of Germany had pushed Russia into an alliance with the French in 1894. Thirteen years later, a Triple Entente was formed with Britain as a deterrent against German expansion.

It was no longer possible to limit the discussion of foreign policy to the narrow circles of the court, the tsar's ministers and diplomats. Public opinion was growing in importance through the Duma and the press. Pan-Slav sentiment was particularly powerful. It had the support of senior members of the court, and a mouthpiece in *Novoe Vremia* (*New Times*), the country's leading conservative newspaper. Calls for Russia to take a harder pro-Slav line grew in volume after 1908, when the Austrians annexed Bosnia, part of the Ottoman Empire, to prevent the Serbs from making territorial gains. The Pan-Slavs were outraged by Russia's failure to oppose the Austrians, and equally determined not to let it fail the Serbs again. They believed that Europe was heading unavoidably towards a final struggle between the Teutons and the Slavs. They saw the *Drang nach Osten*, the Drive to the East, as part of a broader German plan to undermine Slavic civilisation, concluding that, unless it made a firm stand to defend its Balkan allies, Russia would suffer a long period of imperial decline and subjugation to Germany. 'In the past twenty years,' declared a 1914 editorial in *Novoe Vremia*, 'our Western neighbour has held firmly in its teeth the vital sources of our well-being and like a vampire has sucked the blood of the Russian peasant.'[22] The wealth of the Germans in Russia, their prominence in government and the growing presence of their exports in Russia's foreign markets added to this sense of an existential threat from Germany.

Whether Russia's interests were best served by coming to the aid of the Balkan Slavs was not clear at all. Despite the Pan-Slav myth, the Slavs had never shown much interest in Russian protection (if anything, they looked for inspiration to the West). To be sure, if Austria extended its power in the Balkans, it would pose a challenge to Russia, if that meant the growth of Ukrainian nationalism, not just in Galicia, where the Austrians encouraged it, but across the border in Russia, where the eight Ukrainian provinces produced one-third of the Russian Empire's wheat, two-thirds of its coal and more than half its steel. If Russia lost Ukraine, it would no longer be a great power. But Russia also had a growing empire in Siberia, which it could develop without conflict in Europe, and it had substantial interests in the Black Sea area which could be defended without war with Germany. The Dardanelles were arguably more important than the Balkans for Russia's security. The tsar certainly thought so, particularly after news leaked out that the Turks were buying dreadnought battleships from the Germans – ships the Russian navy could not match. The prospect of Turkey becoming a German military protectorate was alarming for Russia, fuelling the belief that the Germans were encircling Russia's empire from the south.

Nicholas did not want war. Nor did his military chiefs. They told him that his forces needed time to rebuild after their defeat by Japan. The tsar was hoping that the Triple Entente would act as a deterrent against Austria and Germany – at least until Russia recovered its military strength. But everything was altered by the assassination of the Archduke Ferdinand by Serbian nationalists on 28 June 1914. The murder of the heir to the Habsburg throne prompted Austria to declare war on Serbia. Under pressure Nicholas agreed to the partial mobilisation of his troops. He appealed to his cousin, the Kaiser, to restrain the Austrians. But Germany was backing Austria. It was preparing for a war with Russia which it needed to fight quickly, if at all. The Germans were hoping to knock out France in a lightning war (*Blitzkrieg*) before the Russian army could be mobilised – a process that took weeks longer because of Russia's size and weak transport.

News of the German preparations forced the tsar to agree to a general mobilisation on 31 July – an order that was bound to trigger war with Germany. Nicholas was under intense pressure from his generals and ministers, Duma leaders and the press to go to war. Sergei Sazonov, his foreign minister, told him that 'unless he yielded to the popular demand for war and unsheathed the sword on Serbia's behalf, he would run the risk of a revolution and perhaps the loss of his throne'. Nicholas went pale. 'Just think of the responsibility you're advising me to assume,' he said to Sazonov. But he was too weak to argue against him.[23]

Nicholas and his advisers were anticipating a short war. The tsar believed in the loyalty of his forces. 'You see,' he told his children's tutor after appearing on the balcony of the Winter Palace to survey the cheering and flag-waving crowd that had assembled on the square to greet his declaration of war, 'there will now be a national movement in Russia like that which took place in the great war of 1812.'[24] It was an unrealistic hope. Nicholas had become a victim of his regime's propaganda about the 'simple' people's devotion to him. But that myth had been destroyed, not least by the actions of his troops on the same square on Bloody Sunday 1905. There was no national unity, no love of Russia that was strong enough

Above: Putin opens the monument to Grand Prince Vladimir – in his words the 'founder of the modern Russian state' – near the Moscow Kremlin on November 4, 2016. It is a metre taller than the nineteenth-century statue of Volodymyr in Kiev where the grand prince is seen as the founder of 'the European state of Rus-Ukraine'. *Below*: Viktor Vasnetsov, *The Invitation of the Varangians: Rurik and his Brothers Arrive at Old Ladoga* (1912), a fanciful depiction of the Normanist foundation myth in which the Viking leader was invited by the Slavs to establish order in their lands.

The Church of St Sophia, Kiev, built in the reign of Grand Prince Yaroslav (1019–54). It is closely modelled on the Hagia Sophia in Constantinople, the source of Russia's Orthodox Christianity.

Above: The Iconostasis, or wall of icons, separates the altar from the main part of the church – in this case the Kremlin's Dormition Cathedral, where Russia's tsars were crowned. The placement of the icons is symbolically significant. The Mother of God and Christ Pantokrator, the most sacred icons, are on the left and right, respectively, of the 'royal doors', a symbol of the gates of Jerusalem, in the middle of the screen. *Below*: An example of the birch-bark writing found by archaeologists in Novgorod.

Andrei Rublev's *Trinity* (between 1408 and 1425), a supreme example of the Russian icon-painting tradition. Seeing is believing for the Orthodox. Russians pray with their eyes open, their gaze fixed on an icon, which serves as a window onto the divine sphere.

Above: The Solovetsky Monastery. Founded on an island in the White Sea in 1463, the monastery was used as a prison camp after 1917. *Below*: Part of the Kremlin complex. The Dormition Cathedral (centre) and the Hall of Facets (left) were built by Italian architects in the late fifteenth century but were later Russified.

The Blessed Host of the Heavenly Tsar was painted in the 1550s to commemorate the conquest of Kazan by Ivan the Terrible. Known as the *Church Militant*, it is almost four metres in length. The icon shows the mounted figure of Ivan following the Archangel Michael in a procession of Russian troops from the hell-like burning city of Kazan to Moscow, depicted here to resemble Jerusalem, where they are welcomed by the Mother of God with the infant Jesus. It was a statement of Moscow's mythic status as the Third Rome, the last true seat of Christianity, and of Ivan's claim of descent from the Byzantine emperors.

Above: Vasily Surikov, *Ermak's Conquest of Siberia* (1895). Armed with muskets, Ermak's Cossacks are too strong for the Tatars with their bows and arrows in this reimagination of the Russian capture of Qashliq, the capital of the Siberian khanate. *Below*: Ilya Repin, *Ivan the Terrible and his Son Ivan on 16 November 1581* (1885). The remorseful tsar, haunted by his own destructive terror, captured the imagination of many artists from the nineteenth century.

Left: Viktor Vasnetsov, *Tsar Ivan IV the Terrible* (1897), an iconic image of the 'Russian tsar', terrible and fierce with an all-seeing eye. *Above*: *Tsar Alexei* (unknown artist, 1670s), one of the first portraits of a tsar known to bear a likeness to the subject. *Below*: Putin at the Minin and Pozharsky monument, a symbol of the people's sacrifice united by religion and devotion to the motherland.

Above: Valentin Serov, *Peter I the Great* (1907). Peter was a man in a hurry. Almost seven feet in height, he walked with giant, rapid strides, leaving his advisers far behind.
Right: Godfrey Kneller, *Peter the Great, Tsar of Russia* (1698), a portrait presented by the tsar to the King of England William III during his Grand Embassy. The European image of the tsar, dressed in armour with a Western crown and cloak and imperial regalia, represents a stark contrast to the portrait of Alexei, Peter's father, painted only twenty years earlier.

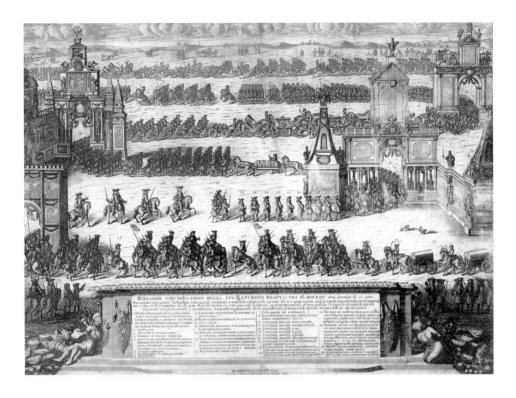

Above: Alexei Zubov, *The Ceremonial Entry of the Russian Troops to Moscow on December 21, 1709 after their Victory in the Battle of Poltava* (1711). Moscow here is reimagined in the form of ancient Rome. None of the triumphant arches in the illustration existed. *Below*: *The Mice are Burying the Cat* (Lubok print, *c.*1760), a popular satire on the foreign manners of the deceased Tsar Peter.

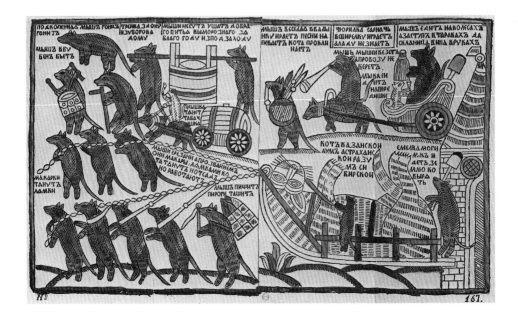

Above left: Vigilius Eriksen, *Equestrian Portrait of Catherine II (1729–96) the Great of Russia* (18th century). Catherine's love of horses gave rise to the absurd myth that she was killed by one in the act of copulation. *Above right*: *The Bronze Horseman*, Étienne-Maurice Falconet's equestrian statue of Peter the Great (1782), a source of many myths about St Petersburg and the nature of imperial power in Russia. *Below*: Ilya Repin, *17 October 1905* (1907), an idealistic image of the people's revolutionary unity.

Above: Peasants of a northern Russian village, 1890s. Note the lack of shoes and the uniformity of their clothing and their houses. This was the 'communal harmony' imagined by the Slavophiles and Populists. *Below*: Ivanovo textile mill, 1905. Women and children were heavily employed in the textile industry.

Right: Nicholas II and the Empress Alexandra with their haemophiliac son, the tsarevich Alexei, during the Romanov tercentenary celebrations of 1913 in Moscow. The jubilee cemented the Romanov myth of a mystical union between tsar and people. *Below*: That myth collapsed in the revolution of February 1917, when Romanov symbols and statues were destroyed. The head here belonged to a statue of Alexander III in Moscow.

Above: Fedor Shurpin, *Morning of our Motherland* (1948), a classic example of socialist realist portraiture in the service of the leader cult. Stalin's gaze is fixed ahead, beyond the frame, to a future only he can see. *Left*: Irakli Toidze, *Mother Russia Calls* (1941). The mother shows a military oath and calls on Russia's sons to defend her from the enemy.

Above: A United Russia party electoral poster (2003). The map of Russia is filled with portraits of historic Russian figures, including Stalin – the first time he appeared in Putin's historical mythology. *Below*: Part of Alexander Nevsky's exhibit in the St Petersburg 'My History' park. The panels on the left emphasise the role of Nevsky in defending Russia from 'the aggression of the West', while those on the right show his statesmanship in forging new alliances with the Mongols and Asia.

to cross the deep divide between the social classes exposed in that revolutionary year. The cheering crowd on Palace Square was made up of well-dressed men and women of the middle classes, clerks, shopkeepers, artisans, not the peasants who would fight the war.

The soldiers, for the most part, were strangers to the sentiment of patriotism. With little direct knowledge of the world outside their villages, they had only a weak sense of their identity as Russians. They thought of themselves as natives of their village or region. 'We are from here and Orthodox,' they would say in response to questions about their nationality. As long as the Germans did not threaten to invade their area, they saw no reason to fight them. 'We are Tambov men,' the recruits would complain. 'The Germans will not get to our village.' A farm agent heard such comments from the peasant conscripts in Smolensk:

> 'What the devil has brought this war on us? We are butting into other people's business.'
>
> 'We have talked it over among ourselves; if the Germans want payment, it would be better to pay ten roubles a head than to kill people.'
>
> 'Is it not all the same what Tsar we live under? It cannot be worse under the German one.'
>
> 'Let them go and fight themselves. Later we will settle our accounts with them.'[25]

Wiser men had tried to alert the tsar to the dangers of a war – among them Petr Durnovo, the interior minister, who in February 1914 had pleaded with him not to drag the country into a needless clash with Germany. This would be a long conflict, he had warned, a war of attrition, in which the main burden would be placed on Russia to break through the German defences. Economically the country was too weak to fight for long. The government would lose authority, and social revolution would follow:

> The trouble will start with the blaming of the government for all disasters ... The defeated army, having lost its most

dependable men, and carried away by the tide of the primitive
peasant desire for land, will find itself too demoralized to serve
as a bulwark of law and order. The legislative institutions and
the intellectual opposition parties, lacking real authority in the
eyes of the people, will be powerless to stem the popular tide
aroused by themselves, and Russia will be flung into hopeless
anarchy, the issue of which cannot be foreseen.[26]

No one paid attention to the prophecy.

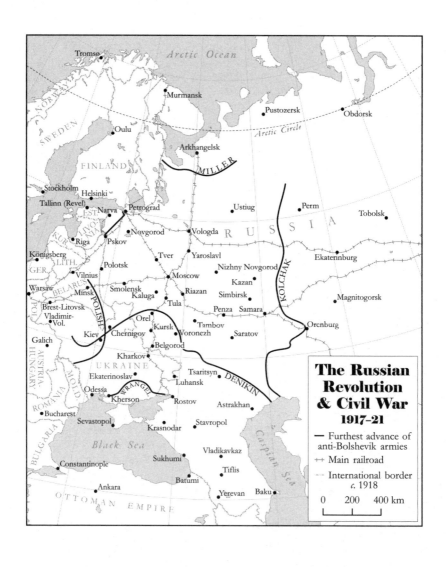

Tromso

Arctic Ocean

Murmansk

Pustozersk

Obdorsk

Oulu

Arctic Circle

Arkhangelsk

FINLAND

MILLER

Stockholm

Helsinki

Tallinn (Revel)

Narva

Petrograd

Ustiug

Perm

Tobolsk

EST.

Novgorod

Vologda

R U S S I A

Riga

Pskov

Königsberg

Tver

Yaroslavl

Ekaterinburg

LITH.

Polotsk

Nizhny Novgorod

Vilnius

Moscow

Kazan

Magnitogorsk

Warsaw

Smolensk

Riazan

Simbirsk

Minsk

Kaluga

Tula

KOLCHAK

Brest-Litovsk

POLISH

Penza

Samara

Vladimir-Vol.

Orel

Kursk

Tambov

Orenburg

Galich

Kiev

Chernigov

Voronezh

Saratov

Belgorod

Kharkov

DENIKIN

UKRAINE

Tsaritsyn

Ekaterinoslav

Luhansk

Odessa

WRANGEL

Kherson

Rostov

Astrakhan

ROMANIA

MOLD.

Bucharest

Sevastopol

Stavropol

BULGARIA

Krasnodar

Black Sea

Vladikavkaz

Caspian Sea

Constantinople

Sukhumi

Tiflis

Ankara

Batumi

Yerevan

Baku

O T T O M A N   E M P I R E

The Russian Revolution & Civil War 1917–21

— Furthest advance of anti-Bolshevik armies

⊹ Main railroad

‑‑ International border *c.* 1918

0   200   400 km

8

REVOLUTIONARY RUSSIA

Durnovo's warning soon proved justified. Under pressure from the British and the French, the Russians attacked the Germans in East Prussia to force them to withdraw troops from the Western Front. Heavily defeated by the Germans at the battles of Tannenberg and the Masurian Lakes in August and September 1914, they fell back and dug in for the long defensive war of entrenched artillery positions in which Russia's weaknesses began to show.

The country was not prepared for a war of attrition. Its single greatest asset, its seemingly inexhaustible supply of peasant soldiers, was not such an advantage as its allies had assumed when they had talked of the 'Russian steamroller' moving unstoppably towards Berlin. A large proportion of the population was younger than the minimum draft age. Where 12 per cent of the German population was mobilised for military service, Russia was able to call up only 5 per cent. More serious still was the weakness of the Russian reserves. To save money the army had provided little training for the Second Levy, which were soon called up to the front. By October, recalled General Brusilov, then commanding the Eighth Army in Galicia, the men sent to replace the casualties of the first disastrous battles 'knew nothing except how to march … many could not even load their rifles, and, as for their shooting, the less said about it the better. Such people could not really be considered soldiers at all.'[1]

As the war dragged on through the winter the army began to experience terrible shortages of materiel. The transport system could not cope with the deliveries of munitions, food and medical supplies to the fronts. The War Ministry had reduced spending on the arms industries before the war, and now had to order shells and guns abroad which took ages to arrive. By 1915, new recruits were being trained without rifles. Thrown into battle, they were ordered to retrieve the guns dropped by men shot down in the line in front of them.

The army's morale and discipline began to fall apart. In the summer of 1915, when the Germans and the Austrians broke through the Russian lines across the front, a million men surrendered to the enemy. Part of the problem was the loss of officers. Huge numbers were killed in the first months of the war. The NCOs who took their place were young peasants and workers: their sympathies lay firmly with the troops, who were reluctant to fight for a regime in which they did not believe. These NCOs would become the leaders of the army revolution during 1917.

The collapse of discipline was related to the spread of rumours about treason at the court. It was said that the empress and Rasputin were working for the Germans, that they were pushing for a separate peace (a myth encouraged by the German press which printed fake news of negotiations with the Russian government). The court had no idea how to counteract these damaging rumours. It had never attached any importance to public opinion and had not learned to manage it. To propagandise their patriotic credentials the imperial family arranged a photo opportunity for the empress and her daughters dressed in Red Cross uniforms. They had visited the wounded at military hospitals in Petrograd, as St Petersburg had been renamed to make it sound less German at the beginning of the war. What they did not realise was that a consignment of nurses' uniforms had fallen into the hands of the city's prostitutes, who dressed in them to work the streets.[2]

Anti-German sentiment could turn violent easily. In response to the German breakthrough at the front, angry crowds in Moscow burned and looted German shops and offices. In Red Square they shouted insults at the 'German woman', as they called the empress, and called for her to be locked up in a convent. It was hard to tell how much of this anger was patriotically motivated and how much based on hatred of the wealthy urban class in which the Germans were so prominent. The revolutionary mood was nationalist in character.

In September 1915, in a desperate attempt to restore morale, Nicholas took over supreme command from the Grand Duke Nikolai. He thought that his presence at the front would inspire the soldiers, that if they would not fight for Russia they would surely do so for their holy tsar. It was a terrible mistake. From this point, Nicholas was blamed for every defeat, prompting further rumours not only of his incompetence (he had no military experience) but also of his treacherous conduct of the war. To explain the unending sequence of defeats, it was said that he was informing the Kaiser about the movement of his troops, that the empress, left in control in the capital, was working for the Germans, and so on.

There was no truth in these rumours. But that was not the point. The fact that people were prepared to believe them made them politically dangerous. In a revolutionary crisis it is perceptions and beliefs, not realities, that count. Without trusted information from official sources and the press, the rumours gained wide credence in society. They were believed by politicians and even foreign diplomats. Through their ability to mobilise an opposition and give its protests meaning as a patriotic act against the 'German' court they contributed to the revolutionary mood.

The public, like the soldiers, blamed the government for the reverses at the front. It had responded to the supply crisis by springing into action with its own initiatives through the Duma and Zemgor, a national network of public bodies formed by the Zemstvo Union and the Union of Towns. Led by Prince Lvov, a veteran zemstvo activist, Zemgor was allied to the Duma's Progressive Bloc, formed in 1915 by two-thirds of its deputies to demand a 'ministry of national confidence' (a government appointed by the tsar but approved by the Duma). The Bloc was supported by several generals and some members of the government who understood the need to involve the public in the war campaign. But it was opposed by the more reactionary ministers, urged on by the empress, who accused the Bloc of pushing for a Duma government. Bullied by his wife ('Show your fist. You are the Autocrat'),[3] the tsar closed the Duma and sacked his ministers if they showed any signs of working with the Bloc.

By the autumn of 1916 confidence in Nicholas had sunk so low that there were a number of conspiracies in the army's high command, in Duma circles and in the court, to replace him with his younger brother, the Grand Duke Mikhail, or some other Romanov capable of working with a Duma government. The only action to succeed was the murder of Rasputin, on 16 December, by a circle of conspirators, including two grand dukes and one of Russia's grandest princes, Felix Yusupov. Luring Rasputin to the cellar of the Yusupov Palace, the killers shot him in the heart, and, apparently, when he refused to die, fired at him four more times, the last from close range into his forehead, whereupon they wrapped his body in a coat and dumped it into the river. They had hoped that his removal would save the monarchy from imminent catastrophe. But it changed nothing.

Food shortages brought catastrophe closer. In freezing temperatures the transport system failed to deliver fuel and flour to the capital. Long queues appeared outside bakeries. Prices soared. Workers' strikes became common. The call for higher pay soon gave way to political demands. The strikes became more violent as factories closed. At the New Lessner machine-building plant in Petrograd strikers fought with the police. The soldiers in the nearby barracks were ordered to suppress the strike, but instead they joined the workers' side, throwing rocks and bricks at the police.

On 23 February 1917, International Women's Day, a large crowd of women, mostly shop and office workers, marched through the centre of the capital to demand better rations for the soldiers' families. Joined by workers, they clashed with the police before dispersing in the evening. More protesters came out the next day. There was a monster rally on Znamenskaya Square. In full view of the police, orators addressed the crowd from the equestrian statue of Alexander III, which they decorated with red banners and daubed with the graffito 'Hippopotamus', the people's nickname for this obese monument to the immovable autocracy. People called for the downfall of the monarchy. The protest movement grew. By 26 February, the centre of Petrograd had been turned into a militarised camp. Soldiers and police were everywhere. Around midday, crowds of workers once again assembled in the factory districts and marched to the centre. On Nevsky Prospekt they were met by the police and soldiers who shot at them with live bullets. The bloodiest incident took place on Znamenskaya Square, where more than fifty people were killed by a training detachment of the Volynsky Regiment.

The regiment's mainly teenage soldiers were shaken by the incident. One said he had seen his mother in the crowd of people they had fired at. The next morning, when ordered to disperse the crowds again, the soldiers killed their officer and came out on the people's side. The mutiny was soon joined by other regiments. The soldiers gave a military strength and organisation to the crowds. They fought the police, the last defenders of the monarchy, and led the capture of the arsenal, the telephone exchange, the railway stations, the police headquarters and the prisons, which they burned. Their actions turned the demonstrations into a full-scale revolution.

In the Tauride Palace the Duma leaders formed a Temporary Committee for the Restoration of Order and proclaimed themselves in charge. A Petrograd Soviet of Workers' and Soldiers' Deputies was meanwhile formed in the same building. It could have taken power, but agreed instead to the formation of a Provisional Government led by Prince Lvov with all its members drawn from the Duma. The Soviet leaders, mostly Mensheviks, believed in line with Marxist doctrine that Russia was too backward to proceed at once to a socialist government. Marx had taught them that what was needed now was a 'bourgeois democratic' period of development with freedom for the masses to organise themselves through trade unions, political parties and so on. These were the democratic principles on which they gave their support to the Provisional Government. As socialists, the Soviet leaders were, moreover, fearful of a counter-revolution if they formed a government. Russia would be plunged into a civil war. They thought the Duma leaders would be better able to persuade the generals not to send in troops against the revolutionary capital.

Nicholas had ordered forces to be sent from the Northern Front. But the intervention of the Duma leaders did indeed persuade the generals to revoke his command and urge the tsar to abdicate. It was the only way to restore order, save the army and continue fighting in the war, his senior commanders advised him. Nicholas agreed to abdicate in favour of his son. But he was then warned that Alexei would not live long because of his haemophilia. If Nicholas renounced the throne for him, he would have to go abroad. He would be separated from his family. Determined to remain with them, whatever happened to Russia, he resolved to hand the crown instead to his younger brother, the Grand Duke Mikhail.

A shy and modest man, even less intelligent than Nicholas, Mikhail was reluctant to accept the crown. There had been violent protests when it was announced to the crowds outside the Tauride Palace that the tsar would abdicate in his favour. Mikhail was not inclined to risk his life. Bunkered in the mansion of Princess Putiatina, not far from the Winter Palace, he met with the Duma leaders on 3 March. The Kadet leader Pavel Miliukov, who was still concerned with questions of legality, tried to persuade him to accept the crown on the grounds that a monarchy was needed as a symbol of authority giving legal sanction to the transfer of power to the Duma Committee. Without it, he argued, the Provisional Government would be 'an unseaworthy vessel liable to sink in the ocean of popular unrest'.[4] But nobody could guarantee the grand duke's personal safety if he became tsar – and that made up Mikhail's mind. The abdication manifesto, which brought to an end 300 years of Romanov rule, was drawn up by two jurists at a school desk in the study of Putiatina's daughter and then copied out in one of her school notebooks.

The end of the monarchy was marked by scenes of rejoicing throughout the empire. Rapturous crowds assembled in the streets of Petrograd and Moscow. Red flags were hung from the buildings. In Helsingfors, Kiev, Tiflis and other capitals, national flags were also hung. Symbols of the monarchy – Romanov emblems, coats of arms, double-headed eagles – were torn down from buildings by the crowds.

The monarchy was dead. All its institutions of support had collapsed virtually overnight. No one tried to revive it. None of the counter-revolutionary armies of the Civil War – the fight to remove the Bolsheviks from power after 1917 – embraced monarchism as a cause, although many of their officers were monarchists. Doing so would be a guarantee of their defeat. So much for the myth that Russia needs a tsar. As Trotsky put it in his history of the revolution, 'the country had so radically vomited up the monarchy that it could never ever crawl down the people's throat again'.[5]

But if politically the monarchy was dead, it was still alive in a broader sense, in the psychology that made the people so receptive to later Soviet cults of the Leader. 'Oh yes, we must have a Republic,' a soldier said to George Buchanan, the British ambassador, 'but we must have a good Tsar at the head.'[6] Soldiers' letters expressed a similar misconception: 'We want a democratic republic and a *tsar-batiushka* for three years.'[7] The idea of the state was too confused with the person of the tsar in the minds of ordinary Russians for them to imagine a new state without a monarch at its head. A member of the Moscow Workers' Soviet went to agitate at a regimental meeting near Vladimir in March:

> A platform stood in the middle of the field. Two or three
> soldiers were on it, and a crowd of thousands stood around.
> It was black with people. I talked, of course, about the war
> and about peace, about the land – 'land to the people' – and
> about the advantages of a republic over a monarchy. But when
> I finished and the endless 'hurrahs' and applause were over,
> a loud voice cried out: 'We want to elect you as our Tsar,'
> whereupon the other soldiers burst into applause. I refused the
> Romanov crown and went away with a heavy feeling of how
> easy it would be for any adventurer or demagogue to become
> the master of this simple and naive people.[8]

Kept under house arrest at Tsarskoe Selo, in August 1917 the imperial family was evacuated to Siberia out of fears for their personal safety. It had been intended to send them to England, but George V withdrew his invitation, for fear of sparking an uprising against the British monarchy, so the Romanovs were sent instead to the provincial backwater of Tobolsk, far from the revolutionary crowds. There they lived in comfortable conditions until the spring, when, after rumours of a plot to rescue them, they were sent on Lenin's orders to Ekaterinburg. The entire family were executed on the night of 16–17 July 1918. Informed of the murder in the press, 'the population ... received the news with astonishing indifference', according to Robert Bruce Lockhart, the British agent in Moscow.[9]

The leaders of the Provisional Government saw themselves as a wartime government of national salvation, above class or party interests. No one had elected them. They had come to power through a parliamentary coup backed by the Soviet on condition of their adherence to democratic principles. As they saw it, their purpose was to see the country through to the ending of the war and the election of a Constituent Assembly, which alone could legally resolve the fundamental issues of the revolution, such as who the land should belong to, the constitution of the state and the nationalities question, whether they should keep the empire's lands together or allow its peoples to leave it. Their position was understandable. But it could hardly satisfy the urgent expectations unleashed by the February Revolution. It was not long before the peasants, factory workers and soldiers took matters into their own hands.

In the countryside the peasants formed their own ad hoc committees (they sometimes called them Soviets) and seized the gentry's property, first the tools and livestock and then their fields, which the commune divided in line with its customary principles (usually according to the number of 'eaters' in each household). These land seizures were 'legalised' by district and provincial peasant assemblies, and then endorsed by the First All-Russian Peasant Assembly which sat from 4 to 25 May.

Meanwhile the workers imposed their demands on the factory management. Their organisations spread quickly. The trade unions and Soviets resumed from where they had left off in 1905. But they were joined by two new organs dominated by the Bolsheviks: the factory committees, which supervised the management (they called it 'workers' control') to prevent factory closures and lay-offs; and the Red Guards, formed by workers to defend the factories.

Soldiers' committees supervised relations with the officers and discussed their military commands. In some units they refused to fight for more than eight hours a day, claiming the same rights as the workers. Throughout the army they demanded to be treated as equals by their officers when they were not engaged in fighting. This assertion of 'soldier power' was essential to the spirit of 'trench Bolshevism' – a term used by the officers to describe the troops' refusal to obey their orders – which swept through the forces during 1917.

The war was the most divisive issue for the Provisional Government. The politics of 1917 were a battle between those on the left who saw the revolution as a means of ending the war and those on the right who saw the war as a way to stop the revolution and restore order. When Miliukov, the foreign minister, announced that Russia would honour its imperial commitments to the allies, despite the Soviet's peace campaign, tens of thousands of armed workers and soldiers came out to demonstrate on the streets of Petrograd, where they clashed with 'patriotic' groups calling for the war campaign to continue until final victory.

To reinforce the government's authority and prevent the country sliding into civil war, six Menshevik and SR leaders joined it during May. The coalition was based on a policy known as Revolutionary Defencism. It meant continuing with the war, not for imperial gains, but solely for the defence of the revolution and Russia. Defeat by Germany would mean, they believed, the restoration of the Romanov ('German') dynasty, but fighting to defend the revolution would restore national unity. On this assumption they bowed to allied pressure to launch a summer offensive.

Kerensky, now the minister of war, toured the front to raise the troops' morale. He dressed in military uniform and wore his right arm in a sling, although no one knew of any injury. Kerensky was an actor-politician, made for the revolutionary stage, where his fiery speeches, filled with theatrical gestures and even fainting fits, genuine but timed to coincide with the dramatic climax of his speech, captured the emotions of the crowd. Standing in his open-top Renault, Kerensky called on the assembled troops to place their 'civic duty' above class interests. Like 'every citizen', they had to make a sacrifice for the nation. The soldiers had fulfilled this obligation to the old regime, so they should do the same for the defence of Russia's liberty. 'Or is it', he now asked in a phrase charged with meaning and emotion for the peasant soldiers, 'is it that the first free Russian state is in fact a state of rebellious slaves?'[10] It was a question carrying the weight of all the country's history.

Everywhere he went he was hailed as a hero. The soldiers he encountered – carefully hand-picked by their officers – 'kissed his hand, his uniform, his car, the ground on which he walked', according to an English nurse, who compared the cult of Kerensky to the former worship of the tsars. 'Many of the soldiers were on their knees praying; others were weeping.'[11] The adulation he received created the impression that the rank and file were eager for battle. In fact, as the date of the offensive approached, the flood of deserters rose sharply. The attack began on 16 June. For two days the Russians advanced, led by the Women's Battalion of Death, formed by female volunteers in 1917 and chosen now to shame the men into fighting; but when the Germans launched a counter-offensive, the Russians fled to the rear in panic.

The coalition government collapsed. The soldiers of the Petrograd garrison prepared an armed uprising to transfer power to the Soviets – a policy the Bolsheviks had come round to support since Lenin's return from exile in April. The lead was taken by the First Machine Gun Regiment, the most pro-Bolshevik of all its troops, after they were ordered to the front. They were supported by the Kronstadt sailors, strongly Bolshevik, 'maximalist' or anarchist in their outlook, who had declared their own Soviet republic during May. On 3–4 July they occupied the capital. With a clear order from the Bolsheviks they would have staged a coup. But Lenin was unable to make up his mind if the time was ripe 'to try for power'.[12] When the armed sailors and machine-gunners congregated outside the Bolshevik headquarters to receive his instructions, he gave them none. Confused by his vague words of encouragement, they went on to the Tauride Palace, where they called on the Soviet leadership to seize power. Their demand was rejected by the SRs and Mensheviks, who still controlled the Soviet, whereupon the would-be insurrectionists no longer knew what they should do. They were tired and hungry, it was raining heavily, so they dispersed.

The failed uprising sparked a reaction from the right. Leaflets were released by the Ministry of Justice claiming that the Bolsheviks were German agents – an idea based on concrete evidence (the Bolsheviks undoubtedly received German money and logistical support in 1917) but giving rise to the dangerous myth that Soviet power was imposed on Russia by the Germans, Jews and other foreign enemies of the country. In April Lenin had arrived on a 'sealed' or uninspected train from Switzerland supplied by Germany to foment opposition to the war, it was now revealed. The Bolshevik headquarters were raided, hundreds of Party members arrested. Lenin fled to Finland disguised in workers' clothes. He refused to stand trial for treason on the grounds that the government had now become a 'military dictatorship' engaged in a 'civil war' against the proletariat.[13] The only way to fight it was to seize power.

Kerensky formed a new coalition government of SRs, Mensheviks and the Kadets. He introduced restrictions on public gatherings, restored the death penalty at the front, agreed to roll back the influence of the soldiers' committees to restore military discipline and appointed General Kornilov as the supreme commander. A hero of the right, Kornilov pushed for a military dictatorship to close down the Soviets. He thought he had Kerensky on his side. But when Kornilov despatched a Cossack force to occupy the capital and disarm the garrison, Kerensky condemned him and mobilised the Soviet to resist his coup attempt. There was no need for fighting in the end. On their way to Petrograd the Cossacks were met by a Soviet delegation from the northern Caucasus who talked them into laying down their arms.

The Kornilov Affair destroyed all support for Kerensky and his government. The mass of the soldiers suspected that their officers had backed Kornilov. Discipline collapsed. The rate of desertion rose sharply. The soldiers returned to their villages, where it was harvest time, and assumed control of the peasant revolution, which became more violent as the soldiers took the lead in burning manor houses to force the gentry off the land. Workers too were radicalised. Abandoning the Mensheviks, who refused to break with the Kerensky government, they swung towards the Bolsheviks, the only party to stand firmly for 'All power to the Soviets', giving them a clear majority in the Soviets of Moscow, Petrograd and other big industrial cities.

At the Second Soviet Congress in October it was almost certain that the delegates would pass a resolution calling for Soviet power. That would mean a government made up of all the parties in the All-Russian Soviet. The Bolsheviks were likely to be the largest party, but they would have to share the government with the SRs and the Mensheviks. Until 24 October, most of the Bolshevik leaders were prepared for this outcome. But Lenin had different ideas. He did not want to share power. From his hideout in Finland, he had been calling for an armed uprising *before* the Congress met. The Party 'can and *must*' seize power, he had argued in a series of impatient letters to the Bolshevik Central Committee. He said 'can' because the Party had enough support to win a civil war, which was more important than elections at this point. And 'must' because by waiting for a vote in the Congress they would give time to Kerensky to organise a counter-revolutionary force and close down the Soviet.[14]

Under pressure from Lenin, who returned to Petrograd on 10 October, the Central Committee agreed to prepare an uprising, but when it would take place was not yet clear. On 16 October it decided that the time had not arrived. The masses of Petrograd would not come out on the Party's call alone, it was said by local activists, but 'would have to be stung by something, such as the break-up of the garrison, to support an uprising'.[15] Lenin was irate. A coup needed only a small force. He was prepared to carry out the putsch, if necessary, as a military invasion from Finland, where he could count on the support of the Baltic regiments.

Kerensky played into his hands. Confident that he could crush the Bolsheviks, whose plans for an uprising had been revealed, he ordered the soldiers of the Petrograd garrison to be sent to the Northern Front, where the Germans were advancing fast towards the capital. This was the sting that Lenin had been waiting for. It enabled him to rally armed support for an uprising behind the slogan 'The Revolution in Danger!' To prevent their transfer to the front the soldiers formed a Military Revolutionary Committee (MRC) which took command of the garrison on 21 October. Over the next days, as delegates arrived for the Soviet Congress, the MRC organised the defence of the capital by seizing control of the railway stations, the post and telegraph, the telephone exchange and the electricity station, and putting soldiers on the streets.

This was the scene on the night of 24 October when Lenin, in disguise, made his way across the capital to the Smolny Institute, the former noblewomen's school, where the Congress would be held the following day. The building was ablaze with lights and heavily defended by armoured cars and machine guns. In Room 36, the Bolshevik headquarters, Lenin bullied his comrades into ordering the insurrection to begin. He wanted it completed before the Congress voted on the transfer of power. After a day of technical delays, a signal shot was fired by the cruiser *Aurora* and the Bolshevik attackers stormed the Winter Palace to arrest Kerensky's ministers – they were bunkered in a small dining room, where they sat amid the plates of their last meal (borscht, steamed fish and artichokes). Kerensky was not there. He had left that morning for the Northern Front in a desperate search for loyal troops. His government by this time was so helpless that it did not even have a car: he had departed in a Renault seized from the American Embassy.

The arrest of the ministers was announced to the Soviet Congress in the smoke-filled hall of the Smolny Institute. The 670 delegates – mostly workers and soldiers in their tunics and greatcoats – had unanimously passed a resolution proposed by the Menshevik Martov to form a socialist government based on all the parties in the Soviet. When the seizure of power was reported, most of the Menshevik and SR delegates denounced this 'criminal venture' and walked out in protest. Lenin's plan had worked. The seizure of power was a provocation against the SRs and the Mensheviks as much as a coup against the Provisional Government. By walking out of the Congress, the Mensheviks and SRs had surrendered the Soviet to the Bolsheviks. Trotsky pounced on the opportunity. Denouncing Martov's resolution, he gave his verdict on the renegades: 'You are miserable bankrupts, your role is played out; go where you ought to go – into the dustbin of history!' Trotsky then proposed a resolution condemning their 'treacherous' attempts to kill Soviet power at its birth.[16] The Soviet delegates, who did not understand what they were doing, raised their hands to support it. The effect of their action was to give a Soviet stamp of approval for a Bolshevik dictatorship.

Not that anybody gave them long in power at that point. The Bolsheviks had a tenuous hold on the capital – where the civil service, state bank, post and telegraphs all came out on strike in protest against them – but no grip whatsoever on the provinces. They had no means of feeding Petrograd, nor of getting forces to Moscow, where they were engaged in a bitter struggle against troops loyal to Kerensky. They had lost control of the railways because of a strike by the Railway Workers' Union (Vikzhel), which demanded that the Bolsheviks form a coalition government with the other socialist parties, and forced them to open talks with them. Even if they managed to survive these challenges, there were yet to be elections for the Constituent Assembly, the true organ of democracy in so far as every adult citizen would have a vote, and on this the opposition parties pinned their hopes.

Such hopes were naive. The Bolsheviks refused to play by normal rules in consolidating their dictatorship. From their first day in power, they issued orders through the Council of People's Commissars (Sovnarkom), Lenin's preferred means of government, rather than the Soviet, where the Left SRs, the Anarchists and a small number of left-wing Mensheviks remained as a parliamentary brake on their executive power. They banned the opposition press, and had hundreds of Kadets, Right SRs and Mensheviks arrested by the MRC, which was soon replaced by the Cheka (short for Extraordinary Commission for Struggle against Counter-Revolution and Sabotage), Lenin's new political police. The Bolsheviks took over the state bank, arrested striking officials and, once Moscow had been won, walked out of the Vikzhel talks, as they had intended all along. They allowed the elections for the Constituent Assembly to go ahead in November because they thought they would win; but when the SRs emerged as the largest party they declared the result was unfair. Soviet power, Lenin claimed, was a higher democratic principle than 'the formal rights of a bourgeois parliament'. He ordered the Assembly to be closed down by armed guards only hours after it had opened in the Tauride Palace on 6 January 1918.

Meanwhile, at the grass-roots level of society, the Bolsheviks gave free rein to the 'looting of the looters' – mob trials, lynchings, violent robberies and requisitionings of anyone who bore the slightest trace of wealth or privilege. Socialists like the writer Maxim Gorky who had hoped the revolution would fulfil their humanist ideals and bring Russia closer to the West saw these acts of vengeance as a terrible explosion of the Russian people's 'Asiatic savagery'. 'I am', he wrote in his newspaper *Novaya Zhizn* (New Life) on 19 November, 'especially distrustful of a Russian when he gets power into his own hands. Not long ago a slave, he becomes the most unbridled despot as soon as he has the chance to become his neighbour's master.'[17]

But Lenin saw the 'looting of the looters' as a deepening of the 'class struggle', a necessary form of civil war. In 'How to Organize

Competition?', written in December 1917, he suggested that each town should develop its own means of:

> cleansing the Russian land of all vermin, of scoundrel fleas, the bedbug rich and so on. In one place they will put into prison a dozen rich men ... In another they will be put to cleaning latrines. In a third they will be given yellow badges after a term in prison ... In a fourth one out of every ten will be shot. The more variety the better.[18]

Soviet officials, bearing flimsy warrants, went round the houses of the 'bourgeoisie' – the hated *burzhooi* as they were called – confiscating anything of value 'for the revolution'. They levied taxes on the *burzhooi* and imprisoned hostages, threatening to shoot them if they failed to pay the tax. Their terror took a leaf out of the old playbook of *krugovaya poruka*, collective responsibility, applied now to a whole social class. They called this terror the 'internal front' of the Civil War.

Much of this violence was instigated by the soldiers, returning in their millions from the fronts following the Bolshevik Decree on Peace, passed on 26 October 1917. The soldiers took the decree as a licence to demobilise themselves and headed for the nearest railway station. They formed themselves into militias, or Red Guards, to carry out the revolution in their towns and villages.

Without an army to go on with the war, the Bolsheviks were forced to open peace talks with the German high command at Brest-Litovsk. But they were divided over strategy. To those on the left wing of the Party, like Bukharin, a separate peace with 'imperialist' Germany would represent a betrayal of the internationalist cause. It would end all hopes of the revolution spreading to the West, which they saw as crucial to the cause. The Russian Revolution on its own, they thought, could not survive without the support of the more advanced industrial societies. On this reasoning, they favoured spinning out the peace talks with the Germans for as long as possible and, if need be, fighting against them with Red Guards and militias (what they called a 'revolutionary war') in the hope of inspiring the European proletariat. Lenin, by contrast, wanted to conclude a separate peace, and as soon as possible, in order to secure a 'breathing spell' for the revolution in Russia. 'It is now only a question of how to defend the motherland,' he argued as the spokesman for a small minority in the Central Committee on 11 January 1918. There was no point risking the defeat of Russia on the chance that a German revolution might break out, which Lenin doubted would happen. 'Germany is only just pregnant with revolution, but we have already given birth to a completely healthy child.' The Civil War demanded an immediate peace, or as Lenin put it with his usual bluntness, 'The bourgeoisie has to be throttled and for that we need both hands free.'[19]

Because of these divisions, the Bolshevik negotiators, led by Trotsky, played for time at Brest-Litovsk. Trotsky ran rings around the German diplomats and generals, subjecting every sentence in the draft treaty to lengthy abstract discussions. Finally the Germans lost patience and signed a separate treaty with Ukraine, whose nationalist leaders in the parliament in Kiev declared Ukraine's independence on 22 January and sought at once the Germans' help in their war against the Red Guards based in east Ukraine where the ethnic Russians were in the majority. Signed on 9 February, the treaty turned Ukraine into a German protectorate, opening the way for its occupation by the Germans and the Austrians. Having detached the Ukrainians from the Russians, the Germans were in a position to increase their demands at Brest-Litovsk. Yet still Lenin could not get the votes he needed in the Central Committee. It was not until 23 February, with the Germans dropping bombs on Petrograd, that he got his way and the German terms – now much worse than they would have been in January – were accepted by the Bolsheviks. Under the Brest-Litovsk Treaty, Russia was forced to give up most of its former imperial territories on the European continent. Poland, Finland, Estonia and Lithuania gained nominal independence under German protection. Soviet troops were evacuated from Ukraine, which was quickly occupied by half a million Austrian and German troops, mainly bent on plundering as much foodstuffs as they could from the Ukrainian peasantry as they pushed the Red Guards back to east Ukraine. All in all, the Soviet Republic lost 34 per cent of its population (55 million people), 32 per cent of its agricultural land, 54 per cent of its industrial capacity and 89 per cent of its coalmines (peat and wood now became its biggest source of fuel).[20] As a European power, Russia was reduced to a status on a par with seventeenth-century Muscovy. The transfer of the Soviet capital to Moscow on 12 March symbolised this retreat from Europe. St Petersburg had always been a European city, 'Russia's window on the West'; Moscow, by contrast, was a physical reminder of its Asiatic traditions. As an international movement the revolution had been dealt a heavy blow. But the Russian Revolution, in the meantime, had been saved.

The armies of the Civil War were being formed. The anti-Bolshevik forces, known as the 'Whites' (a name derived from the white cockades worn in the hats of the anti-Jacobins during the French revolutionary wars), were a motley bunch without a clear or unifying ideology except to remove the 'Reds' from power and restore the 'old Russia'. But what that Russia should be like – a monarchy or a republic, an empire or a federation, a system based on private property or a socialist society – was a question that divided them.

In south Russia, there was a Volunteer Army. Formed by Kornilov on the Don following the Bolshevik coup, it comprised mainly officers, whose right-wing politics created tensions with the Don Cossacks, on whom they relied to do the fighting, because many of the younger Cossacks wanted their own socialist republic rather than the restoration of the Russian Empire, which the leaders of the Volunteer Army clearly favoured. General Anton Denikin, who assumed command on Kornilov's death in April 1918, failed to specify his policies. The experience of 1917 had taught him to keep the army out of politics and rely on simple slogans, such as 'Russia One and Indivisible', which did nothing to endear the Cossacks or other national minorities to him.

Meanwhile, on the Volga, a Czech Legion was the major force supporting the Komuch, an SR government based in Samara fighting for the restoration of the Constituent Assembly and the resumption of the war. Stranded behind German lines, the Czechs were keen to rejoin the fighting on the Western Front to win their national independence from the Austrian–Hungarian Empire. Politically weak, without much support from the peasants, the Komuch soon became dependent on the Siberian Army based in Omsk, where a group of rightist officers installed Admiral Kolchak, the tsar's commander of the Black Sea Fleet, as supreme ruler in a military dictatorship that set about conscripting peasants for its war against the Bolsheviks. The Western powers supported all these counter-revolutionary armies in the hope of getting Russia to rejoin the war – that at least was how they presented their involvement in the Civil War – and on that basis they provided them with most of their equipment, including tanks and aircraft, and sent troops to help them fight the Reds.

The Red Army was formed on the Volga front. To begin with it consisted of Red Guards, the workers' militias, whose revolutionary zeal was not enough to compensate for their lack of military discipline against the more experienced Czech soldiers. The ease of the first Czech victories made it clear to Trotsky, the commissar of war, that the Red Army had to be reformed on the model of the imperial army, with conscript units instead of the Red Guards, experienced (tsarist-era) officers and a centralised command. Many of the rank and file resented these reforms as a restoration of the old military order. They saw the ex-tsarist officers as an obstacle to their own promotion through the ranks. A Military Opposition crystallised around this lower-class resentment of the professional officers and other 'bourgeois specialists'. Its stronghold was on the Tsaritsyn Front where Stalin, known for his ruthless methods, had been sent to requisition grain, though he soon took over the military command, wreaking havoc with his wholesale arrests of Trotsky's tsarist officers.

Mass conscription was introduced in June. The Red Army mobilised a million men by the spring of 1919, three times that number by 1920 and 5 million by 1921. It was a pattern we have seen before in which quantity was made to substitute for quality because of the country's backwardness. The armed forces grew much faster than the war-torn economy was able to supply them with munitions, transport, food and clothes. The soldiers' morale collapsed and they deserted in their thousands, especially during harvest time when they were needed in their villages. New recruits were thrown into battle without training, making them more likely to desert. A vicious circle thus developed where mass conscription led to supply shortages and mass desertion. It locked the Soviet economy into a system – War Communism, as it became known – whose purpose was to channel all production towards the demands of the army.

War Communism was the first attempt by the Bolsheviks at a command economy. Some believed it would lead directly to a Communist society. The system began with a grain monopoly in May 1918, but broadened to include a comprehensive range of state controls over the economy: the stamping out of private trade; the nationalisation of industries; the militarisation of labour; and at its height, in 1920, universal rationing, which was meant to lead to the abolition of money.

The grain monopoly was a response to the exodus of workers from the cities in the first six months of the regime when there was neither food nor fuel. A million workers moved into the countryside to feed themselves more easily. Factories closed for lack of fuel. The revolution was in danger of being starved out of existence – the fate suffered by the Paris Commune in 1871, whose defeat had long served as a warning to the Bolsheviks. Its failure had taught them that if they were to survive in their urban strongholds they had to fight a war for foodstuffs in the countryside.

The root of the crisis was the peasantry's reluctance to sell their surpluses for worthless paper money – a problem going back to the war years, when manufacturing had declined and there was a steep rise in prices. A barter economy rapidly developed with 'bagmen' from the towns travelling by rail to exchange clothes and household goods for bags of grain. Leather-jacketed Cheka agents went round trying to eradicate this trade, which they called 'speculation', but they could not cope with the enormous numbers of bagmen. So more coercive measures were employed. Under the grain monopoly all the peasants' surplus became the state's property. Armed brigades were organised by the Bolsheviks in factories and sent into the countryside to requisition grain by force. Where they found none, they assumed that it was being hidden by the 'kulaks' – the phantom class of 'capitalist' peasants invented by the Bolsheviks – and an unequal 'battle for grain' began. The brigades beat and tortured villagers; villages were burned, until they handed over what they had, which was often their last stocks of food and seed for the next year. There were hundreds of peasant uprisings – a 'kulak counter-revolution' according to the Bolsheviks – behind the Red fronts in the Civil War.[21]

The Civil War was a formative experience for the Bolshevik regime, whose methods of coercion, of ruling by the gun, became established in these years. The military emergency strengthened its dictatorship. It was used by the Bolsheviks to justify the Red Terror, with its mass arrests and shooting of 'class enemies', and to enlarge the centralising powers of the Party-state, which under War Communism imposed its control on every aspect of the economy and social life. By 1920, some 3 million people were employed in the Soviet bureaucracy. This was not a Dictatorship of the Proletariat but a Dictatorship of the Bureaucracy.

Enrolment in the Party was the surest way to climb the ranks of this bureaucracy. Over a million people joined it during the Civil War. Many were recruited through the Red Army, which taught its conscripts how to read and how to speak and act like Bolsheviks. The leadership was worried that this mass influx would reduce the Party's quality. How could they stop it being swamped by careerists, motivated only by the perks of membership (better jobs, higher food and fuel rations, access to special shops, and so on)? How could they know who they really were if they hid behind a Party mask? They called them 'radishes' (Red on the outside, White inside). Annual purges of the membership were carried out. But this fear remained a source of insecurity until at least the 1930s, when it fuelled the Stalinist purges.

As the Party grew, its members came to dominate the Soviets, transforming them from local revolutionary bodies controlled by an assembly into bureaucratic organs of the Party-state. In the provincial cities and some district towns, the Soviet executives were appointed by Moscow from a central pool of Bolsheviks, who had no connection necessarily with the region under their command. But in the rural areas there were too many *volost* Soviets to fill with appointees. Here the Bolsheviks who took control were young peasant men, many of them soldiers who had returned from the wars, newly skilled in military techniques and organisation, literate and versed in socialist ideas.[22] Like the village children polled in 1903, they did not want to return to a farming life, but saw in Party work a way to obtain office jobs. Throughout the peasant world Communist regimes have been built on the ambition of peasant sons to join the bureaucratic class.

By the spring of 1920, the Bolsheviks had all but won the Civil War. Kolchak's army had been defeated in Siberia. Denikin's had retreated to the Crimea, where under the command of General Wrangel the remnants of the Whites made one last stand. By November they too had been overcome. Thousands of defeated troops scrambled on to allied ships taking them into exile where another 'Russia' would be built in Berlin, Paris and New York.

What was the key to the Bolsheviks' success? They had the Party's discipline and organisation. They also had a unifying goal (the defence of 'the revolution') with clear symbols (the Red Flag and the Red Army's emblem, the Red Star) capable of winning mass support. The Bolsheviks were masters of propaganda, which they deployed in every form – posters, pamphlets, free newspapers, films and agitational dramas – all sent to the fronts on special agit-trains, equipped with printing presses, libraries, theatre troupes (who used open goods wagons as their stage) and even cinemas inside the carriages.

Their propaganda was cleverly adapted to the old religious myths of social justice and freedom which had long inspired popular rebellions. It was communicated in a simple visual and iconic form easily accessible and understood by a population with low rates of literacy and little understanding of political discourse. Pamphlets for the rural poor compared socialism to the work of Christ. The cult of Lenin, which took off from August 1918 after he was wounded in an assassination attempt, carried clear religious overtones. Lenin was depicted as a Christlike figure, ready to die for the people's cause, and, because he had survived, blessed with miraculous powers.

Even the Red Star had religious connotations deeply rooted in folklore. A Red Army leaflet explained to the soldiers why the Red Star appeared on their caps and uniforms. It was a symbol of the goddess Pravda, who had a burning red star on her forehead which lit up the whole world and brought it truth and justice, the dual meaning of her name. One day the red star was stolen by Krivda (meaning falsehood) whose rule brought darkness and evil to the world. At last the people, called upon by Pravda, rose up against Krivda to retrieve the star. The 'brave lads' of the Red Army, the leaflet concluded, were 'fighting against Krivda and her evil supporters so that truth should rule the world'.[23]

The mobilising power of folk myths was not the only reason for the Bolsheviks' success. Geography was also important. They had control of central Russia, where the bulk of the population lived, and held the core of the country's railway network, which converged on Moscow like a spider's web, enabling them to shift their forces and resources from one front to another, wherever the Whites attacked. The Whites, by contrast, had to fight on several fronts. Without a network of communications, they found it hard to coordinate their operations against the Reds. They also had to rely on the allied powers for much of their supplies.

But at the heart of the Whites' defeat was a failure of politics. They were unwilling to put forward policies capable of winning mass support. They failed completely to adapt to the new revolutionary realities. It was not until the last year of the Civil War, and then only on the allies' insistence, that they devoted any real resources to propaganda work, and even then it was directed to the allied powers rather than to the people. The Whites' refusal to recognise the national independence movements was disastrous. It lost them the support of the Poles, Ukrainians, Estonians and Finns – any one of which could have tipped the military balance in their favour – and complicated their relations with the Cossacks, who wanted more autonomy from Russia than the White leaders were prepared to give.

The main cause of the Whites' defeat, however, was their failure to accept the peasant revolution on the land. It alienated them from the rural population in the central agricultural zone, the Civil War's decisive battlefield, where the land gains of the peasants had been greatest during 1917. This fatal shortcoming is illustrated well by the Denikin offensive against Moscow in 1919. The Whites pushed north from their bases in Ukraine and the lower Volga in July. They moved fast in an all-or-nothing gamble to break through to Moscow. In mid-October they took Orel, not far from Tula, the Red Army's main arsenal, then in the midst of workers' strikes, which, if taken, would give the Whites a crucial advantage in the battle for Moscow. For once the Whites had managed to coincide their attack on the Southern Front with another against Petrograd led by General Yudenich coming through Estonia. The Bolsheviks were thrown into panic. They thought that Moscow was about to fall. Many packed their bags to flee abroad. Secret plans were made to evacuate the Soviet capital. But at this vital moment, when the fight for Tula was finely balanced, a quarter of a million peasant soldiers from that area, all deserters from the Red Army, willingly returned to fight the Whites.[24] However much the peasants might have detested the Bolshevik regime, with its food brigades and commissars, they would side with it against the Whites to defend their revolution on the land.

Once the Whites had been defeated the peasants turned against the Bolsheviks, whose requisitionings had brought them to the brink of starvation. By the autumn of 1920, the whole of the country was engulfed in peasant wars. Most were small revolts but there were also larger armies, sometimes called the Greens, such as Makhno's in Ukraine or Antonov's in Tambov, which set up peasant governments. Everywhere their aims were basically the same: to restore the peasant self-rule of 1917. Some expressed this in the slogan 'Soviets without Communists!'

Bolshevik power ceased to exist in much of the countryside. The consignment of grain to the cities was seriously affected. Workers went on strike. It was not just the shortages that angered them. They were protesting against the loss of rights hard won in 1917. They objected to the quasi-military subordination of the trade unions to the Party's industrial bureaucracy, a policy pursued by Trotsky as commissar for transport from 1920, and opposed what they saw as the decline of democracy in the Party, as policies increasingly were pre-decided by the leadership and then imposed on the rank and file. They found a voice in the Workers' Opposition, as it was named by Lenin, a group of Bolsheviks, led by Alexander Shliapnikov and Alexandra Kollontai, who called for more trade union powers and a return to Soviet democracy. The strikes began in Moscow and soon spread to Petrograd where this proclamation appeared on the streets on 27 February, the fourth anniversary of the revolution. It was a new call to arms:

> The workers and peasants need freedom. They do not want
> to live by the decrees of the Bolsheviks. They want to control
> their own destinies. We demand the liberation of all arrested
> socialists and non-party working men; abolition of martial law;
> freedom of speech, press and assembly for all who labour; free
> elections of factory committees, trade unions and soviets.[25]

That day the rebellion spread to the Kronstadt naval base. In 1917, Trotsky had called the Kronstadt sailors the 'pride and glory of the Russian Revolution'. They had played a crucial role in the October seizure of power. But now the sailors were calling for an end to the Bolshevik dictatorship. Electing a new Soviet, they demanded freedom of speech and assembly, 'equal rations for all working people' and no more requisitioning.[26] Trotsky took command of the suppression of the mutiny. The assault began with a bombardment of the naval base on 7 March, just as the Tenth Party Congress was assembling in Moscow.

There Lenin introduced a tax in kind to replace requisitioning. Once the tax was paid, the peasants were allowed to sell their surplus foodstuffs on the free market. This was necessary, he argued, to quell the peasant uprisings, which were 'far more dangerous' than all the Whites together, and to build a new alliance (*smychka*) with the peasantry. It meant abandoning the central plank of War Communism and laying the foundations of a New Economic Policy (NEP) in which private trade and small-scale manufacturing would be allowed within the socialist system. There were many Bolsheviks who feared that this would lead to the return of the capitalist system. But Lenin insisted that as long as the state controlled the 'commanding heights of the economy' (heavy industry, the utilities and natural resources), there was no danger in allowing private farming, retail trade and handicrafts to satisfy consumer needs.

To enforce party unity and suppress the Workers' Opposition, Lenin also introduced a ban on factions inside the Party. It was a fateful decision. Henceforth the Central Committee was to rule the Party on the same tightly dictatorial lines as the Party controlled the country; no group could question its decisions without exposing itself to the charge of 'factionalism', which could mean expulsion from the Party.

The NEP was to be a temporary retreat from the utopian dream of building socialism by decree – the essence of the War Communist model. It meant confronting Russia as it was – a country of small peasant farms – and forging policies to engage them through the market in the socialist sector. 'Only in countries of developed capitalism' was it possible to make 'an immediate transition to socialism', Lenin told the Congress. This was what the Mensheviks had said in 1917. Now he was adopting their approach, calling on the Bolsheviks to set about the task of 'building Communism with bourgeois hands'. There would have to be a new *modus vivendi* with the Church, with private enterprise, with the intelligentsia and its 'bourgeois' culture, all of which had been attacked, condemned as 'class enemies', under War Communism. The Bolsheviks would have to change their ways, if Lenin's vision was to be achieved. They could no longer rule by threatening people with rifles. Now, Lenin warned, they had to 'proceed more slowly'. They needed Western education and culture, to 'learn how to govern' properly.[27] But were they ready to do so?

9

THE WAR ON OLD RUSSIA

The restoration of the market brought back life to the Soviet economy. Private trade responded instantly to the chronic shortages that had built up over seven years of war, revolution and the Civil War. Flea markets boomed. Peasants brought their produce to markets. Private cafés, shops and restaurants sprang up everywhere. Long-forgotten luxuries (butter, cheese and meat, pastries, sweets) were displayed in shop windows, but at prices well beyond the means of ordinary citizens. A new-rich class of private traders, the 'Nepmen', soon appeared. They dressed their wives and mistresses in diamonds and furs, drove around in huge imported cars and boasted loudly in expensive hotel bars of the fortunes they had wasted at the newly opened race tracks and casinos. Was this what the revolution had been for? That was the question many asked. Workers in their thousands threw away their Party cards in disgust at the NEP, which they called the New Exploitation of the Proletariat.

Urban opposition to the NEP was sharpened by shortages of food in the state shops. The root of the problem, as before, was the absence of consumer goods to trade with the peasants. Industry had been badly damaged by the Civil War. It took longer to recover than the peasant farms, which had good harvests in 1922 and 1923. The result was a widening gap (the 'scissors crisis') between deflated agricultural prices and steeply rising prices for consumer goods. As the cost of manufactures rose, the peasantry reduced its grain sales to the state depots. The state's procurement rates were too low for the peasants to earn enough from sales to afford the household items they needed. The Bolsheviks were split about how to deal with the issue. Those on the left wing of the Party, like Trotsky, thought the top priority was to increase the supply of factory goods. They favoured keeping agricultural prices low and taking grain by force if necessary to boost large-scale industrial production with the benefit of planning by the state. Those on the right, like Bukharin, advocated raising the procurement prices, even if this entailed slowing down the rate of capital accumulation for industrialisation. Higher prices would stimulate the peasants' marketing of grain and preserve the *smychka*, the state's alliance with the peasantry, on which the survival of the revolution depended.

There were disagreements too on the international consequences of the NEP. When the Bolsheviks took power they had all assumed that the revolution would soon spread to the more advanced industrial societies. In their view socialism was unsustainable in Russia on its own because it lacked the industries it needed, machine-building and munitions, to defend itself against the hostile capitalist powers. They dreamed of the revolution spreading through the world as a liberating force. That was why they had set up the Comintern, the Communist International, to organise the Communists of other countries under Moscow's leadership. The Comintern's foundation was a fundamental break from the position of the socialist parties in the Second International, which had dissolved in 1916 amid conflicts over whether socialists should support their country's war campaign. To mark their ideological opposition to the Social Democrats, some of whom had backed their national wartime governments, the Bolsheviks in 1918 changed their name from the SDs to the Communist Party. The distinction was reinforced by the Comintern, known as the Third International, whose 'Twenty-One Conditions' (passed in 1920) obliged its member parties to rename themselves as Communist, to fight against the 'social patriots' of the parliamentary socialist parties and give loyal support to the Soviet Republic, which, as the sole existing seat of Communism in the world, was their only true homeland. Through the Comintern, Russia gained a new position on the international stage. Communism gave it a new messianic role. In the medieval myth of the Third Rome, Moscow had been cast as the one true holy saviour of the world. Now, at the head of the Third International, it assumed the mission of its liberation from capitalist oppression. Western Communists who joined the Comintern bowed to Russia's leadership.

By 1924 it had become apparent, however, that a revolution in the West was unlikely. The immediate post-war instability had passed. In Italy the Fascists had come to power. In Germany strikes organised by Communists had failed to develop into larger uprisings. Abandoning the goal of exporting revolution in the immediate future, Stalin and Bukharin advanced the policy of 'socialism in one country'. It was a dramatic turnaround in the Party's revolutionary strategy. Instead of waiting for support to come from the industrialised states, the Soviet Union, formed by the Russian, Transcaucasian, Ukrainian and Belarusian Soviet Republics in 1922, would now have to become self-sufficient and defend itself by building industries with capital extracted from its own economy. It would export grain and raw materials to pay for tools and machines imported from the West.

The debates about the NEP came down to a question about time. How long would it take for the Soviet Union to industrialise through the market mechanisms of the NEP? Would these means be fast enough to build the defence industries the Soviet Union needed before a war with the capitalist states which all agreed was unavoidable? This was the fear that fuelled Stalin's rise to power with the launching of the Five-Year Plan.

In his brilliant chronicle of 1917 the Menshevik memoirist Nikolai Sukhanov famously described Stalin as a 'grey blur, which flickered obscurely and left no trace'.[1] Stalin had appeared in Petrograd that March after many years of underground activity in his native Georgia and the Caucasus, ending in arrest and exile in Siberia. During the Civil War he took on many jobs that others had considered too mundane. He was the commissar for nationalities, the commissar of Rabkrin (Workers' and Peasant Inspectorate), a member of the Politburo and the Orgburo (Organisational Bureau) and the chairman of the Secretariat in charge of the Party's management. As a consequence he had gained a reputation for modest and industrious mediocrity.

Short in size with a deformed arm and pockmarked face, speaking Russian with a Georgian accent, Stalin felt the condescension of the Party's metropolitan leaders. Quick to take offence, but holding on to grudges for ever, he plotted his revenge by building up his power-base in the Party's lower ranks. All the Bolshevik leaders underestimated him. Lenin was as guilty as the rest. For too long he indulged his rudeness, violence and criminality – methods which he saw as useful for the cause. In April 1922, he made him the general secretary of the Party. He thought that Stalin's ruthless discipline would help him to enforce the ban on factions and rid the Party of the Workers' Opposition, which was still attracting the support of workers opposed to the NEP. It was, as Lenin came to realise, a terrible mistake.

The key to Stalin's growing power was his control of the Party apparatus and his secret use of the OGPU police, as the Cheka was renamed, to remove his enemies from it. As the chairman of the Secretariat, and the only Politburo member in the Orgburo, he could promote his supporters to the key regional Party posts, thus securing a majority in the Party Congress and the Central Committee. During 1922 alone, more than a thousand senior Party officials, including forty-two provincial Party bosses, were appointed by the Orgburo.[2] This was the core of the *nomenklatura*, a listing of positions filled by the Central Committee and ranked in a hierarchy of status, privilege and patronage, not unlike the system of *mestnichestvo* by which the princes and the boyar clans were ordered in the closed and minutely graded service class of medieval Muscovy. These appointees became Stalin's loyal supporters in his struggles for the leadership. Like him, they came from humble origins. Most of them had no more than a few years' schooling. They had a feeble grasp of Marxist ideology, which they had learned through primers, and mistrusted intellectuals like Trotsky and Bukharin, whose theorising went over their heads. They preferred to place their trust in Stalin's down-to-earth wisdom which he expressed in simple terms.

Not that Stalin ever felt secure. Naturally suspicious, he was obsessed with the idea that local Party cells were hiding 'oppositionists' (remnants of the Menshevik and SR parties, Workers' Oppositionists and supporters of Trotsky). Through his control of the Secretariat and its Orgburo he put pressure on the regional Party secretaries to expose oppositionist activities (which could mean nothing more than voicing criticisms of the Party leadership). He measured the success of these regional leaders by the quality of information they passed on to the Central Control Commission, responsible for Party discipline, which he headed until 1923, when it was taken over by his ally Valerian Kuibyshev.

Beyond the Party's mechanisms of control and punishment, Stalin also relied on OGPU, which answered to him as the general secretary. He formed a tight alliance with Felix Dzerzhinsky, the OGPU chief, who pushed for more resources and power by providing evidence of 'anti-Soviet' groups in the Party and society. Stalin employed the political police to spy on Party officials and collect or fabricate incriminating evidence (*kompromat*) that could be used against them when needed. Thousands of potential oppositionists were purged from the Party in this way – and once they had been expelled they could be arrested, even killed, without awkward questions being asked. Stalin himself liked to spy on his comrades. He had a 'secret department' in the Secretariat, whose staff compiled an office-full of dossiers on Party leaders detailing their weaknesses and fears learned from intercepted mail and conversations bugged by the police. Hidden in a drawer inside his desk, Stalin had a secret telephone on which he was able to listen to the private conversations of senior government officials in the Kremlin. He knew all his comrades' weaknesses – their mistresses, their cocaine use, their homosexuality – and knew how to exploit them.[3]

As general secretary, Stalin was in charge of Lenin's medical care when the latter suffered from the first of several strokes in May 1922. With Lenin out of action, Stalin formed a triumvirate (with Lev Kamenev and Grigory Zinoviev) to oppose Trotsky, whom they all feared as their main rival for the succession. Lenin became increasingly suspicious of Stalin. Between 23 December 1922 and 4 January 1923, he dictated a series of fragmentary notes for the forthcoming Twelfth Party Congress (later known as Lenin's Testament) in which he was highly critical of Stalin and recommended his removal from the post of general secretary.

Lenin had been shocked by his handling of the Georgian Bolsheviks, who had opposed Stalin's plan, as commissar of nationalities, to form a federation as the basis of the Soviet Union. In this plan the non-Russian nations would join Russia as 'autonomous' republics, denying them a formal right of secession from the union as Lenin had proposed in his own plans for a federation of equal Soviet republics before he was incapacitated by illness. Sergo Ordzhonikidze, the head of Moscow's Caucasian Bureau and Stalin's closest ally in the Caucasus, had been imposing his centralised control on the Georgian republic, purging 'nationalists' and 'deviationists' from the Party's membership. On one occasion in a private argument he had slapped the face of a Georgian Bolshevik opposed to Stalin's plan. Lenin was outraged when he found out. Stalin was a 'Great Russian chauvinist', he now realised, who could only bully and subjugate small nations, whereas what was needed was 'profound caution, sensitivity and a readiness to compromise'. His poor opinion of Stalin was confirmed in March when he learned of another ugly incident in which Stalin had subjected Krupskaya, Lenin's wife, 'to a storm of coarse abuse' and even threatened her.[4] Devastated by the incident, Lenin at once became ill. Three days later he had another stroke which robbed him of speech.

The Twelfth Party Congress finally convened in April 1923. The Testament was not read out to the delegates, as Lenin had intended, but was kept in store by Krupskaya, who hoped for his recovery. It was only after Lenin's death, in January 1924, that she presented his dictated notes to the Secretariat, asking for them to be published for the delegates of the Thirteenth Party Congress in May 1924. The Testament was not made known to the whole Congress, but was read out to the delegation heads in a small and orchestrated gathering where the triumvirate was able to persuade the delegates to accept Stalin's promises to mend his ways.

Trotsky was too weak to challenge this decision on the Testament (at the Thirteenth Congress he had come a lowly thirty-fifth in the voting for the Central Committee). Instead he vacillated between trying to conciliate his enemies in the name of Party unity and posing as the champion of the rank and file against the 'police regime' of the triumvirate. Support for Trotsky had come from a 'Group of Forty-Six', senior Bolsheviks who agreed with his pro-industrial stance on the NEP. But this merely exposed him to the charge of factionalism (a crime against the Party since Lenin's ban on factions). Branded as an oppositionist, and accused of 'Bonapartist' ambitions, Trotsky was condemned by a Party Plenum in October 1923. Kamenev and Zinoviev wanted him expelled from the Party, but Stalin, always eager to appear more moderate than he was, opposed this. Trotsky anyway was finished as a force. Removed from office in 1925, he was expelled from the Party two years later, exiled to Kazakhstan and finally deported from the Soviet Union in 1929.

Lenin had asked to be buried next to his mother's grave in Petrograd. But Stalin wanted to embalm the corpse and put it on display. In the Russian Orthodox tradition the uncorrupted body was a sign of holiness. Trotsky was horrified by the idea, which he compared to the religious cults of medieval Rus: 'Earlier there were the relics of Sergius of Radonezh and Serafim of Sarov: now they want to replace these with the relics of Vladimir Ilich.' Stalin forced the Politburo to accept his plan. Lenin's body was displayed in a temporary wooden mausoleum opened only one week after his death. On seeing it, many of the mourners bowed before it, fell to their knees, crossed themselves and said prayers to this new god.[5]

Stalin benefited from this cult more than any other Bolshevik leader. On 26 January 1924 he made a speech at the Soviet Congress of the Soviet Union in which, in the tone of an evangelist, he vowed repeatedly to continue Lenin's work, ending each successive incantation of the dead leader's principles and achievements with the same sacred oath: 'We vow to you, comrade Lenin, we shall fulfil your behest with honour!' The 'Great Oath' speech, as it became known, established Stalin as the leading apostle of the Leninist doctrine. His actions would be justified as a fulfilment of his oath. He used the defence of 'Leninism' to destroy his rivals, one by one.

With the defeat of Trotsky and his supporters (known as the Left Opposition), the pro-peasant approach to the NEP appeared set for many years. Although Zinoviev and Kamenev belatedly came round to Trotsky's side, their criticisms of the NEP (that it was strengthening the private sector at the expense of the state economy) carried little influence. Bukharin was supported by Stalin in his efforts to encourage peasant farms to sell more foodstuffs to the state. Some real progress was achieved. By 1926 agricultural production had regained the levels last attained in 1913, when Russia had been one of the biggest food exporters in the world. Through cooperatives, which offered better access to consumer goods, the peasant farms were marketing more grain in the socialised economy; they were improving their productivity, thanks to the agronomic aid they could receive from the cooperatives (land reorganisation, irrigation, better tools and fertilisers, and so on). Encouraged by the government's taxation policies, many villages were even forming simple collectives, known as TOZ, where the land was farmed in common but the livestock and the tools remained private household property. With more time, the TOZ might have formed a significant collective-farming sector within the market structures of the NEP.

But time for the NEP was running out. A poor harvest in 1927 led to a sharp fall in state grain procurements at a time when the Soviet press was filled with false reports (exploited if not engineered by Stalin) that the Polish nationalist government of Józef Piłsudski was planning an invasion of Soviet Ukraine and Belarus with the backing of the British government, whose relations with the Soviet Union had been tense for several years.* Stalin called for a return

---

* The British Conservative Party had won the 1924 election thanks in large part to the publication in the *Daily Mail* of the fake 'Zinoviev Letter' suggesting that the Comintern, which was headed by Zinoviev, had infiltrated the defeated Labour government and was using it to stir a Leninist revolution in Britain and its colonies.

to requisitioning. Only the methods of the Civil War could save the country from the capitalist powers and their allies, the kulaks, who were, he claimed, withholding grain to block the country's progress towards socialist industrialisation. Whereas the NEP was based on the idea that the 'kulak threat' was weakening, as all the 'anti-Soviet' forces were, in line with the country's socialist advance, Stalin introduced the novel theory, probably derived from his paranoid mentality and his calculation that he needed constant crisis to build his police state, that the struggle with the kulaks would intensify as the revolution neared its final victory. The idea was that, as they faced defeat, the 'counter-revolutionary' elements, like the kulaks, would fight with growing desperation through acts of terror and conspiracy. For the Party to disarm in its struggle with the kulaks, as Bukharin argued, was, Stalin warned in a clear threat to his erstwhile ally, to play into the hands of the revolution's 'enemies'. Against the protests of Bukharin, who tried to keep the market mechanisms of the NEP alive, requisitioning was brought back for the 1928 harvest. This time it was toughened by the application of Article 107 of the Criminal Code which allowed the food brigades to arrest peasants and confiscate their property if they failed to pay their grain quota. Known as the Urals–Siberian method, the relative success of this campaign persuaded Stalin to press ahead with more radical measures to break the 'kulak strike' by controlling food at the point of its production in collective farms.

Although small collectives, like the TOZ, had been steadily developing, Stalin now insisted that the peasants should be forced to join larger collective farms (*kolkhozes*) where not just the land but all the tools and livestock were collectivised. Beginning in the summer of 1929, armed brigades were sent into the countryside to set up the collective farms. Reinforced by army and police units, they went into the villages with strict instructions not to come back without organising a *kolkhoz*.

Most of the peasants were afraid of giving up a way of life their families had lived for centuries – a life based on the family farm, the peasant commune, the village and its church, all of which were to be swept away as legacies of 'backwardness'. In many villages there were demonstrations and riots, assaults on Communists, attacks on *kolkhoz* property and protests against church closures in which peasant women often took the lead. It was almost a return to the situation at the end of the Civil War, when peasant wars had forced the Bolsheviks to abandon requisitioning, only this time the regime was strong enough to crush the resistance. Realising their own weakness, the peasants ran away or slaughtered their livestock to prevent them being requisitioned for the collective farms. The number of cattle in the Soviet Union fell by 30 per cent in 1929–30, and by half from 1928 to 1933.

Any peasant who resisted was branded a kulak and sent to remote 'special settlements' controlled by OGPU where they were made to work in logging camps and mines. The Politburo set a target for OGPU to send a million kulak families to these penal settlements. OGPU in turn raised the figure to between 3 and 5 per cent of all peasant households and handed quotas down to provincial organisations, which frequently exceeded the target to demonstrate their vigilance.

The war against the kulaks was an economic disaster, on top of its immense human costs. It deprived the new collective farms of the best and hardest-working peasants (because these are what the kulaks in fact were) and ultimately led to the terminal decline of the Soviet economy. The *kolkhoz* system was a dismal failure. In the early years, few collective farms had tractors to replace the horses slaughtered by the peasantry. They were badly run by managers appointed for their loyalty. Under pressure to minimise their costs, they paid their workers a few roubles only once or twice a year, expecting them to live on a small food ration supplemented by their private garden plots, strictly limited in size, where they were allowed to keep a cow and a few chickens and to grow fruits and vegetables. Tied to the collective farm by an internal passport system, the peasants saw this enforced labour as the restoration of serfdom.

Roughly half the Soviet peasantry – around 60 million people in 100,000 villages – found themselves in the collective farms by the end of 1931. Almost everything the new farms produced was taken by the state, which now had no obstacle, like the peasant commune, to its rapacious requisitioning. The outcome was a widespread rural famine during 1932–3. The number of deaths is hard to calculate, but demographers suggest that up to 8.5 million people died of starvation or disease. The worst-affected areas were in Ukraine, where the levies on collective farms were particularly high. This has prompted some historians to argue that the 'terror-famine' was a calculated policy of genocide against Ukrainians, although that is hard to prove.[6] Certainly the famine, or *Holodomor* ('killing by starvation' in Ukrainian), has left a bitter legacy of hatred towards Russia among the descendants of Ukrainians who died from Soviet policies.

Although the gross harvest was dramatically reduced, the new collective farms delivered to the state a greater quantity of food compared to the peasant family farms which they replaced. On this basis collectivisation was hailed as a triumph by Stalin. Even if the *kolkhoz* peasants starved, the government would earn the capital it needed from its export sales of grain to import new machinery. This was why he had battled with Bukharin in 1928–9 – to end the state's dependence on the market mechanism with the peasantry so that it could maximise investment in the Five-Year Plan.

In its original version the Plan had envisaged optimistic but not completely unrealistic targets of industrial growth which could be met within the structures of the NEP. But Stalin pushed for higher rates. By the autumn of 1929, the Five-Year Plan was set to triple investment, double coal output and quadruple iron production. These were utopian rates of growth unattainable within the NEP.

The Plan created more chaos than organisation in the industrial sector. Statistics were falsified at every level of production, from the factory to the economic ministries, to cover up the failings of officials or secure more central investment. The official figures of the planned economy thus bore no relation to reality. Under intense pressure to meet their output targets, managers were forced to 'storm' production. This meant working round the clock in shifts, paying workers by results, and organising them in shock brigades. Factories competed with each other to fulfil their norms, which encouraged managers to hoard supplies, creating bottlenecks and dislocations in the planned economy. The shockwork system found its hero in the Donbass miner Alexei Stakhanov, who broke all records in 1935 by mining 102 metric tons of coal (fourteen times his quota) in six hours. He gave his name to a mass movement created by the state. The Stakhanovites were rewarded with consumer goods, better housing, higher rates of pay and often with promotion into management and the bureaucracy. They became loyal Stalinists. But the storming of production led to friction with the managers when shortages of fuel or raw materials slowed down the work rate of the shock brigades and reduced their pay. Workers accused their managers of 'sabotage' or 'wrecking'. They did not realise that the shortages were caused by the fantastic targets that had led to the hoarding of supplies and bottlenecks in the system. They were told that 'bourgeois wreckers and saboteurs' were the cause instead. It was the only way the regime could explain the chaos brought about by its planning.

The rates of growth that Stalin had demanded in the Five-Year Plan could not have been achieved without the use of forced labour, particularly in the cold and remote regions of the Far North and Siberia, where so many of the Soviet Union's precious economic resources (diamonds, gold, platinum and nickel, oil, coal and timber) were located but where nobody would freely go. The Gulag was the key to the colonisation of these areas. A vast slave economy organised by the police, the Gulag (an acronym for the Main Administration of Corrective Labour Camps and Colonies) oversaw the process of arresting 'enemies' and sending them to prison camps where they were worked to death on construction sites, building railways and canals, mining coal and gold by hand, and chopping down whole forests in the Arctic zone. Their labour made an incalculable contribution to the country's economic growth – far more valuable than any figures can communicate because of its added benefit of colonising these inhospitable regions with their precious resources.

The prototype of the Gulag system was the White Sea Canal (Belomorkanal), 227 kilometres of waterway between the Baltic and White seas, which employed 100,000 prisoners by 1932. It was a utopian project on a scale unseen since the building of St Petersburg. Prisoners were given primitive hand tools – crudely fashioned axes, saws and hammers – and were worked to exhaustion in the freezing cold. An estimated 25,000 prisoners died during the first winter. Their frozen corpses were thrown into the waterway's foundations where their bones remain today.

In August 1933, the canal was opened by Stalin. A few weeks later it was explored by a 'brigade' of leading Soviet writers, who sang its praises in a volume commissioned by OGPU to celebrate its completion. Edited by Gorky, who had recently returned from voluntary exile in the West to lend his support to Stalin's policies, the book's chief theme was how corrective labour could 'reforge' human beings, turning criminals into loyal Soviet citizens. It was a big lie – and a propaganda victory. The Belomorkanal was hailed as a symbol of the progress achieved by the Five-Year Plans. New factories, dams, canals, electric power stations, entire cities like Magnitogorsk, were being built at a fantastic rate. With the capitalist world in depression, these signs of progress led huge numbers of people to invest unbounded faith in the Soviet system. But would they have thought the same if they had known that the canal was built on bones?

The speed of change in the early 1930s was intoxicating. There were so many signs of the country's progress – or so it seemed from the Soviet press and other propaganda media – that people believed in the myth that a new world was being made.

Moscow was the symbol of this achievement. It was transformed in a few years from a rundown almost provincial city of churches into an imperial capital in the monumental architectural style with new apartment blocks, department stores, palaces of culture, parks and sporting arenas. Streets were cleared to build broad avenues for cars that rolled off the production lines. The Moscow metro was a marker of the better life to come. Its stations were like cathedrals, with spacious halls, marble floors and walls, lofty arches, chandeliers, mosaics and bas-reliefs depicting the achievements of the Five-Year Plans. The splendour of these public spaces – which stood in such stark contrast to the people's squalid 'living space' in communal apartments, where several families shared a few divided rooms and a kitchen – helped to foster popular belief in the public goals and values of the Soviet order. Millions of people were persuaded to believe – some with a religious fervour – that the hardships of their everyday existence were a sacrifice worth making for the building of a workers' paradise. Hard work today would be rewarded tomorrow.

The Five-Year Plans played a crucial role in this utopian projection. They aimed to accelerate the tempo of the whole economy. 'The Five-Year Plan in Four!' was their slogan. The Plans reconfigured time itself along a series of strategic targets on the path towards a Communist utopia. In this sense they built upon the age-old striving of the Russian people for a higher form of existence that lay at the heart of their religious consciousness, particularly their belief in the possibility of building a utopia on Russian soil. The creation of belief in the Soviet system required the replacement of religious ends with secular objectives tangible enough to motivate the people but meaningful in ways to satisfy the eschatological endeavour of the Russian collective psyche. By hailing the achievements of the Five-Year Plans, propaganda aimed to foster the belief that the utopia was imminent, that it could be reached by one last collective effort. The promise was renewed by every Five-Year Plan, of which there were twelve, but the utopia was never reached.

Belief was strongest in the young. For those indoctrinated in the Soviet school system, the Communist utopia was not a distant dream but a reality, which they would live to see. Nina Kaminskaya, a young law student in the 1930s, recalls a song which she and her friends would sing:

Believing in our country is so easy,
Breathing in our country is so free:
Our glorious, beloved Soviet land …
Our Soviet life is so good and bright
That children in ages to come

Will probably cry in their beds at night
Because they were not born in our lifetime.[7]

This sense of the approaching paradise was conveyed in the propaganda images of happy factory and *kolkhoz* workers that passed for Socialist Realist art. The paintings were not meant to represent some far-off future. They pictured present-day realities, recognisable to the masses, but in a mythical and ideal form to symbolise the signs of the coming Communist utopia. They were pictures of the present in the process of becoming the future. Like the icons of the Russian Church, which had let believers sense the sacred in the material world, they were meant to let their viewers sense the presence of the paradise towards which they were progressing under Stalin's leadership. The acceptance of this vision was the starting-point of Communist belief. But that belief had deep roots in the Orthodox religious consciousness, where the divine was not confined to the heavens but immanent in worldly existence.

The cult of Stalin was crucial to this belief in the Communist future. In the portraits of the 'Great Leader', the 'Teacher', 'Father' of the nation, which began to appear everywhere, Stalin's gaze is fixed ahead, beyond the frame, to a future only he can see. He looks calm and confident, certain of success in the heroic feats the Soviet people were accomplishing under his wise leadership. Whereas Lenin, in his cult, appeared as a human god or saint, a sacred guide for the Party orphaned by his death, the cult of Stalin portrayed him as a tsar, the 'little-father tsar' or *tsar-batiushka* of folklore, who would protect the people, like his children, and guide them to a better life. 'The Russians need a tsar', Stalin said on many occasions.[8]

In the 1930s, when the people suffered so much violence at the hands of the state, so much misery and uncertainty, they clung to their belief in Stalin. At no other time in the country's history has Cherniavsky's observation about Russian myths been so true or apposite: the harder life becomes, the more the Russians seek hope and salvation in myths transcending everyday realities. This explains why even Stalin's victims continued to believe in his goodness.

Born in 1917, Dmitry Streletsky was the oldest of four children in a peasant family in the Kurgan region of the Urals. In 1930 the family was stripped of all its meagre possessions and deported to a labour camp. The village Soviet, ordered by the district Party committee to find seventeen kulak families for deportation, had chosen his to make up the quota. For years they languished in terrible conditions in camps and penal settlements. Dmitry studied hard but could not go to university or hold down a proper job because of his kulak origins. Yet he never ceased believing in Stalin, and was himself, in his own words, an 'ardent Stalinist'. Looking back on his life decades later, he said in interviews: 'it was easier for us [the repressed] to survive our punishments if we continued to believe in Stalin, to think that Stalin was deceived by enemies of the people, rather than to give up hope in him ... Perhaps it was a form of self-deception, but psychologically it made life much easier to bear, believing in the justice of Stalin. It took away our fear.'[9]

Stalin faced a crisis in 1932. The year had begun with widespread strikes. The workers were protesting against cuts in their food rations, longer working hours and a fall in their real wages, which had been halved since 1928. Sacrifice today for a better life tomorrow – that had been the mantra of the Five-Year Plan. But the sacrifice was being made by them. 'There's no bread, no meat, no fats – nothing in the shops,' an OGPU official admitted to the British ambassador in an unguarded moment.[10]

There were rumblings of discontent in the Party. Anti-Stalin factions were forming. The most dangerous was organised by Martemyan Riutin, an Old Bolshevik, supporter of Bukharin, whose 200-page thesis 'Stalin and the Crisis of the Proletarian Dictatorship' circulated among the Party's rank and file. Better known as the Riutin Platform, the typescript was a blistering critique of Stalin's politics and personality, denouncing him as a mediocre thinker, 'unscrupulous intriguer' and 'gravedigger of the revolution' through his catastrophic policies, which, in forcing through collectivisation, had betrayed Lenin's voluntarist principles.[11] Riutin and his circle were arrested and exiled. Others were expelled from the Party for simply knowing of the group's existence and failing to report them to OGPU. The episode left Stalin with a paranoid belief that his 'enemies' were everywhere.

That conviction was intensified by the suicide of Stalin's wife, Nadezhda Allilueva, on 8 November. Stalin had been rude to her at a dinner in the Kremlin the previous evening to mark the fifteenth anniversary of the October Revolution. He knew that she sympathised with Bukharin (whose wife was her best friend) and that she was horrified by what she had learned about collectivisation from her fellow students at the Industrial Academy. Stalin had proposed a toast to the destruction of the 'enemies of the state'. Nadezhda did not raise her glass. Stalin goaded her, demanding to be told why she was not drinking. He threw orange peel and flicked cigarette butts at her across the table. Then she shouted at him to 'Shut up!' and stormed out. She went to her room and shot herself with a pistol. Among her things they found a note to Stalin in which she had written that she was opposed to everything he was doing. They also found a copy of the Riutin Platform.

Stalin was unhinged by his wife's suicide. It reinforced his fear of enemies. In April 1933 he announced a general Party purge. Almost one in five of the Party's 3.2 million members were expelled – not just 'socially alien elements', as in previous purges, but those considered 'unreliable'. It is striking that the leadership remained so insecure more than fifteen years after coming to power. Stalin could not trust the Party rank and file. Like Ivan the Terrible with his boyars, he needed constantly to test their loyalty. He wanted to create his own elite, workers promoted from the factory floor (*vydvizhentsy*) who would repay him in obedience. Trained as engineers and managers in evening colleges, the *vydvizhentsy* of the 1930s became the mainstay of the Stalinist regime. Their ascent was enabled by the purges of these years, when bosses were removed, allowing them to move into their jobs. In 1952, these *vydvizhentsy* made up half the Soviet leadership (57 of the top 115 ministers in the Soviet government), among them Khrushchev, Brezhnev, Gromyko and Kosygin.

By 1934, Stalin thought he had defeated his opponents. His personal dictatorship appeared secure. To his loyal supporters he was now known as the *khoziain*, 'the Master', a patrimonial term used for the tsars. On 26 January, Stalin told the opening session of the Seventeenth Party Congress that the 'anti-Leninist' opposition groups had been defeated. Bukharin and the others who had questioned Stalin's policies all recanted their 'errors'. *Pravda* dubbed it the 'Congress of Victors'.

In fact the Congress marked the last revolt against Stalin from within the Party's ranks. During the secret ballot to elect the Central Committee it was rumoured that Stalin had received at least 150 negative votes (the custom in Party elections was to vote for or against each candidate). The ballot papers were destroyed, and only three votes officially recorded against him. But opposition to his policies was obviously growing among the Party's regional secretaries, some of whom were looking to replace the general secretary with Sergei Kirov, the popular boss of Leningrad (as Petrograd had been renamed), who had polled better than Stalin. Whether Kirov knew of this alleged conspiracy is unclear. It is unlikely that he seriously considered joining it. Since the death of Stalin's wife, Kirov had become extremely close to the leader – practically a member of the family. But Stalin suspected treachery in everyone – a paranoia amplified by the anonymous ballot – and he was afraid of Kirov as a challenger.

On 1 December, Kirov was murdered in the Smolny Institute in Leningrad by a disgruntled Party member known to be a threat but allowed by the police to enter with a gun and find Kirov in his offices. Stalin's role in the assassination cannot be established. But there is no doubt that he used it to eliminate his political enemies.

Within hours of the murder, Stalin took control of the investigation and issued an emergency decree for summary trials and executions of suspected 'terrorists'. The city's 'former people' (as the elites of tsarist days were called) were rounded up in their thousands. None of them had been an actual threat, but they were convenient scapegoats. In the Party purge of 1935, a quarter of a million members were expelled, most of them investigated by the NKVD (as OGPU was renamed from 1934) and accused of being 'anti-Leninists'. The close involvement of the NKVD in a Party purge was something new. It set the pattern for the Great Terror.

Stalin was the driving force of this campaign. When Genrikh Yagoda, the NKVD chief, complained that his officials were uneasy about arresting so many Party comrades, Stalin told him to be more vigilant, or else 'we will slap you down'. In 1936 Yagoda was replaced by Nikolai Yezhov, an unscrupulous henchman, who fed Stalin's paranoid fears. He promoted the outlandish theory that, on Trotsky's orders from abroad, Zinoviev and Kamenev had organised a terrorist conspiracy to murder Stalin and other members of the Party leadership. The two Bolsheviks had already been tried in secret in 1935. But Stalin wanted a show trial to 'prove' the existence of this conspiracy. He charged Yezhov with 'building up the case'. Arrested suspects were tortured until they made the necessary confessions and agreed to speak the lines prepared for them in the courtroom. In August 1936, Zinoviev, Kamenev and fourteen other Party leaders were put on trial. All of them were shot.

A second show trial, in January 1937, witnessed the conviction of Piatakov, Radek and fifteen other former supporters of Trotsky. Then, in May, eight of the country's highest army leaders, including Marshal Tukhachevsky (deputy commissar of defence), General Uborevich (commander of the Belarusian Military District) and General Yakir (commander of the Kiev Military District), were arrested, tortured brutally and tried in secret in a military tribunal of the Soviet Supreme Court, where they were convicted of belonging to a 'Trotskyist-Rightist anti-Soviet conspiracy' as well as carrying out espionage on behalf of Nazi Germany. Within hours of their conviction all eight of them were shot. The army had been the one institution capable of standing up to Stalin in his quest for complete power (which is why the Trial of the Generals had been in secret). Now its leadership was virtually destroyed: of the 767 members of the high command, 512 were shot, 29 died in prison, 3 committed suicide and 59 were still in jail when the war with Germany began in 1941.

In the last and biggest of the show trials, in March 1938, Bukharin, Yagoda and Rykov, along with thirteen other Bolsheviks, were sentenced to be shot for conspiring with the 'Trotsky–Zinoviev terrorist organisation' to assassinate the Soviet leaders and spy at the behest of the Fascist states.

The show trials sent a signal through the Party ranks. It told them to report suspected oppositionists, anyone connected, however long ago or remotely, to 'enemies of the people'. When a leader was arrested, the NKVD investigated all his connections. The typical provincial town was ruled by a clique of senior officials – the district Party boss, the police chief, the heads of local factories, collective farms and prisons – who each had their own client networks in the institutions they controlled. These officials protected one another as long as their power-circle was maintained. But the arrest of one official would inevitably lead to the arrest of all the other members of the ruling clique, as well as their hangers-on, once the NKVD got to work revealing the connections between them.

The terror spread down through the Party ranks, Soviet institutions and society. Millions of people informed on their colleagues, neighbours, friends, sometimes even relatives. Some were motivated by malice, vendettas, jealousies, or by the prospect of material gain or promotion. Others acted from a sense of patriotic duty. They believed the propaganda about 'spies' and 'enemies'. But most informers were afraid of getting into trouble if someone they suspected was arrested and it was revealed that they had failed to report them. It was a crime to conceal one's contacts with 'enemies of the people'.

The duty to inform was a long-established principle in Russian governance, dating back to the sixteenth century, as we have seen. It was connected to the obligations of *krugovaya poruka*, the medieval principle of collective responsibility, which we have observed as a recurrent feature in the country's history. During the Great Terror, as the mass arrests of 1937–8 have become known, this tradition was reflected in the almost universal compliance of public institutions with the NKVD's instructions to rid themselves of 'enemies' within their midst. Whether they were factory collectives, research institutes or local Soviet committees, they eagerly displayed their vigilance in rooting out these suspect individuals to prevent the whole group being punished for their sins. Proof of guilt was not needed. Suspicion was enough. The concept of 'objective guilt' applied to crimes against the state – meaning that a person might act with sincere and innocent intentions and yet serve the counter-revolution through their behaviour. It was the objective consequence (the 'meaning') of a person's actions that determined guilt or innocence.

Most of the arrests were carried out, not as a result of individual denunciations, but with lists prepared by the police for the mass repression of entire social groups. The 'kulak operation' (Order 00447) accounts for almost half of the arrests (670,000) and more than half the executions (376,000) in 1937–8. Most of the victims were former kulaks and their families who had returned from three- or five-year sentences in the special settlements and Gulag labour camps.

If there was a rationale for this Great Purge it was Stalin's fear of a fifth column in the coming war, which he thought was unavoidable. He was acutely conscious of the dangers faced by wartime governments (the Bolsheviks themselves had come to power by exploiting Russia's war campaign). Stalin was particularly afraid that 'malicious kulaks' who had returned embittered from the labour camps might pose a threat in time of war. He also deemed certain ethnic groups 'unreliable' in the event of war – and the 'national operations' or wholesale deportations he instituted account for another 350,000 arrests and 200,000 deaths.[12]

'To win a battle,' Stalin warned in 1937, 'several corps of soldiers are needed. But to subvert this victory on the front, all that is needed are a few spies somewhere in army headquarters.' On this reasoning, if only 5 per cent of those arrested turned out to be truly enemies, 'that', Stalin said, 'would be a good result'.[13]

What did people make of this madness? How did they reconcile their belief in the Soviet system with the arrest of relatives and friends whose guilt had seemed impossible to them? People dared not question the arrests. They suppressed their doubts, or found ways of rationalising them to preserve the basic structures of their Soviet identity. They told themselves that their own relatives had been arrested 'by mistake'. The police, they reasoned, were bound to make some errors because there were so many hidden enemies. It was not Stalin's fault. He would surely put things right if they wrote to him, as many people did, continuing the old tradition of petitioning the tsar to correct the abuses of his officials. How far people were prepared to extend this logic to other families is hard to tell. Maybe they believed in the innocence of their closest friends, the people they knew well. But did they think the same of casual acquaintances? Perhaps they were guilty of some crime they could not know of? There was no smoke without fire. In this way society was atomised. People were afraid of making contact with the families of 'enemies of the people'. They crossed the street to avoid them. The solidarities of the workplace and the neighbourhood – which might have served to slow down the arrests or mitigate their damage – dissolved in this toxic atmosphere of universal mistrust, anxiety and fear.

But how long could the arrests go on for without undermining people's trust in Soviet justice? At the rate set in 1937, when 1,500 Soviet citizens were shot on average each day, it would not be long before doubts began to spread. In January 1938, Stalin warned the NKVD not to carry on arresting people solely on the basis of denunciations without checking their veracity. Yezhov's power was gradually reduced. In November he was replaced by his deputy, Lavrenty Beria, who announced a full review of the arrests in Yezhov's reign. Over the next year, 327,000 prisoners were let out of the Gulag's labour camps and colonies. Yezhov himself was exposed as an 'enemy of the people'. It was said that he had tried to undermine the government by spreading discontent through false arrests. He was later shot in a basement near the Lubianka, the NKVD headquarters. The effect of Beria's review was to stabilise belief in the justice of the purge. People reasoned that the mass arrests had all been Yezhov's fault, that Stalin had corrected his mistakes, and so those left in the camps, as well as those arrested from this point, must be guilty of some crime against the state.

10

MOTHERLAND

Alexander Nevsky had its premiere on 1 December 1938. Eight hundred copies of the film were made. On the first day, in Moscow alone it was shown in seven cinemas to 45,000 people.[1] Its release was accompanied by a massive state publicity campaign explaining how the obscure prince of Novgorod had saved Russia from the Teutonic Knights in the thirteenth century. Stalin was delighted with the film. Its patriotic message of national unity against foreign invasion was carried with tremendous emotional power by the cinematic arts of Eisenstein and the programmatic music of Prokofiev. At a time when the Soviet Union was readying for war with Nazi Germany, the contemporary parallel was obvious. 'We want our film to mobilise the people in the struggle against Fascism,' declared Eisenstein.[2] He had planned to begin the film with a quotation from *Mein Kampf* in which Hitler had invoked the memory of the Teutonic Knights to call for Germany's expansion (*Drang nach Osten*) into Slavic lands. That idea was dropped. But the film retained some visual reminders of the German threat. The Teutonic infantry are seen in helmets like the *Stahlhelm* worn by German soldiers in the First World War. The mitres of their bishops are marked with swastikas.

Nevsky was not the only ruler from the tsarist past to be celebrated on the Soviet screen. A two-part biopic of *Peter the Great* was released in 1937, and Eisenstein would follow up his Nevsky triumph with *Ivan the Terrible*. Stalin led this rehabilitation of the tsars. They had done 'much that was bad', he said in a speech to mark the twentieth anniversary of the October Revolution. 'But they did do one good thing – they put together an enormous state.'[3] He saw himself as a national leader in the combined mould of Nevsky, Peter and Ivan – a view of him reflected in these films.

On Stalin's orders, history was restored to a prominent position in the school curriculum from 1934. The new textbooks gave more attention to the positive achievements of the tsars, above all in 'uniting all the *Russian* [sic] lands' of the Soviet Union, as Stalin instructed. This was a far cry from the way the subject had been taught in the 1920s when the main book used in schools, Mikhail Pokrovsky's *Russian History*, had given primacy to the international class struggle. Pokrovsky had pioneered the Marxist school of history. But following his death in 1932, he was attacked for over-emphasising social forces at the expense of patriotic heroes like Nevsky. History was to teach devotion to the motherland.

Stalin realised that patriotic pride was a more solid base of popular belief than Marxist ideology. After the mass upheavals of the Five-Year Plan, he recognised the need to reunite the country around familiar national symbols and ideas. This was connected to a general retreat from the utopian policies of the 1920s, when the Bolsheviks had launched a cultural revolution to break free from the tsarist past and foster a more international proletarian culture. They had attacked the Russian Church, along with the 'bourgeois–patriarchal family', the most familiar institution of them all, whose oppressive influence they had sought to undermine by opening kindergartens, laundries and canteens to free women from domestic slavery and help them enter the workplace. Under Stalin's leadership the Bolsheviks continued with their atheist campaigns against the Church, but they adopted new 'pro-family policies' (for example, the outlawing of abortion, more state child support, the prosecution of homosexuals) to boost the birth rate, which had fallen sharply since the launching of the Five-Year Plan. Like Fascist Italy and Nazi Germany, Stalin's Russia needed more young people for its military.

The new nationalist emphasis also meant a turnaround in Moscow's policies towards the non-Russian nationalities. During the 1920s the Party had encouraged the development of national cultures in the Soviet republics ('national in form, socialist in content' was the slogan). The aim was to liberate the non-Russians from the 'Great Russian chauvinism' of the Tsarist Empire (the 'prison of peoples', as Pokrovsky had called it). Under the policy of *korenizatsiia* (indigenisation), essentially a form of affirmative action for the non-Russians, every nationality was to have its own territorial autonomy with rights to use its native language in books, newspapers, schools, universities and public offices. The result was the growing domination of the state administration in these territories by the indigenous elites.[4]

Stalin had reversed these policies. As he tightened his control of the Party structures, he grew more suspicious of the non-Russian territorial leaders, purging them as 'bourgeois nationalists' if they deviated from the Moscow line and appointing Russians in their place. In the Soviet 'family of peoples' the Russians were now firmly at the head. 'The Great Russian people lead the struggle of the Soviet people for the happiness of mankind. They are the first among equals,' proclaimed the journal *Bolshevik* in 1938.[5] From that year, learning Russian was made compulsory in Soviet schools. It became the only language of command in the Red Army, where ethnic units were abolished at this time. Stalin was afraid of the non-Russian borderlands in the event of war. The 'national operations' of the Great Terror wiped out whole communities of Soviet Poles, Latvians, Estonians, Finns, Chinese and Koreans (all redefined as 'nationalities of foreign governments') whom he feared could become spies.

By 1939 Stalin knew that war was imminent. He doubted that the Western powers were prepared to fight against the Axis powers (Germany, Japan and Italy). They had failed to act against the German occupation of the Rhineland, Austria and Czechoslovakia. They appeared set on a policy of appeasement, hoping that the Nazis' military aggression would be directed east, against the Soviet Union. Such considerations were invoked to justify the Soviet

Non-Aggression Pact with Nazi Germany, signed in Moscow on 23 August by Molotov and Ribbentrop, the two foreign ministers. The country needed more time to build up its armed forces. Soviet troops were involved already in a border conflict with the Japanese in Mongolia and Manchuria. They were unable to fight on two distant fronts.

These same reasons have been given by successive Russian governments to justify the shocking pact – an obvious betrayal of Soviet principles. The 'leading role' of the USSR in 'the struggle against Fascism' – the basis on which socialists around the world aligned themselves with Moscow – had turned out after all to be a lie. The Soviet entry in the war, from 1941, revived this myth, justifying the pact as a necessary measure for the country's survival in the minds of most Russians. But there was more to Stalin's thinking than national defence. He also had a hidden long-term plan. On 7 September, he told his inner circle that they would wait for the Western powers and Nazi Germany to exhaust themselves in a long war before they joined the fighting to 'tip the scales' and emerge as the victors. The capitalist system (in which he included the Fascist states) would be weakened, enabling the Red Army to export the Soviet revolution as it marched into Europe.

The Nazi–Soviet Pact contained a secret protocol, revealed only after 1945, which partitioned Poland between the two states and gave the Soviet Union control of the Baltic states, Finland and parts of Romania – territories the Russian Empire lost in 1917. None of them was needed for the Soviet Union's survival – the reason given for the pact. They were territorial gains, the price Stalin demanded for his collaboration with Hitler, and he hoped to add to them control of the Turkish Straits through the conquest of Bulgaria.

Once the Germans began their invasion of Poland from the west, on 1 September, the Red Army entered Poland from the east. Over the next eighteen months the Soviet invaders arrested and deported around 400,000 Poles deemed hostile to the Soviet regime. They executed 15,000 Polish prisoners of war and 7,000 other 'bourgeois' prisoners in the Katyn Forest near Smolensk. The Soviet invasion of the Baltic states was accompanied by similar repressions – a 'cleansing operation' of 'anti-Soviet elements' in which 140,000 Latvians, Estonians and Lithuanians were killed or deported by the Red Army. But in Finland the Russians were resisted by the Finns in a three-month Winter War for which the Red Army had not been prepared. A quarter of a million Soviet troops were killed or wounded before the Finns were overwhelmed.

After the signing of the pact with Germany, *Alexander Nevsky* was withdrawn from Soviet cinemas. It had been seen by 50 million people in the Soviet Union, and by many more abroad. But its anti-German message was now out of line with Stalin's policy of keeping in with Germany. Under the pact, the USSR agreed to send to Germany millions of tons of war materiel – foodstuffs, fuel, cotton, minerals – more than half of all its exports between the signing of the pact and the German invasion of the Soviet Union in June 1941.

Stalin had been fooled. Convinced that Hitler would not attack the Soviet Union until he had beaten the British, he ignored intelligence reports of German preparations in the east, discounting them as a British ploy to lure the Soviet Union into war. 'You can send your "source" from German aviation headquarters back to his fucking mother. This is disinformation, not a "source",' he wrote to his state security commissar, who on 17 June had warned of an imminent attack.[6] When, four days later, the Germans launched their invasion, known as Operation Barbarossa, the Soviet defences were completely unprepared. They fell back in disarray. By 28 June, six days after the invasion had begun, German forces had advanced in a huge pincer movement to capture Minsk, 300 kilometres into Soviet territory, and were on the road to Moscow, while further north they cut through the Baltic states to threaten Leningrad.

Hitler had three basic aims in this 'race war': to destroy the 'Jewish Bolshevik regime'; to turn the Soviet Union into a free supplier of raw materials for the Third Reich; and, once all the Jews and 30 million other Soviet people had been killed or starved to death, to turn the surviving population into slaves. Hitler wanted the destruction of Russia. He viewed the Russians, like the Slavs, as 'sub-humans', incapable of building their own civilisation. He once said, in terms reminding us of the early German historians of Russia we met in the first chapter, that 'unless other peoples, beginning with the Vikings, had imported some rudiments of organisation into Russian humanity, the Russians would still be living like rabbits'.[7]

Stalin was shaken by the collapse of the Soviet front. It was not until 3 July that he made his first war speech to the country on the radio. Pausing frequently, he addressed the people, not as 'comrades', but as 'brothers, sisters, friends', and called on them to unite in this 'war of the entire Soviet nation'.[8] It was an entirely different tone from the divisive, class-embattled language of the pre-war years, a tone suggesting that he shared the people's suffering. A million people from Leningrad and Moscow – many of them no more than students – volunteered at once to go off to the front. They had little training, no medical support, and only half of them were armed. People's Militias were quickly formed to defend towns and factories. It was thanks to the patriotic spirit of the Soviet people, not to the Party, that the country managed to escape defeat in 1941.

By the beginning of September, the German forces had surrounded Leningrad. Wanting to preserve his northern troops for the crucial battle of Moscow, Hitler ordered them to starve the city rather than to conquer it. In military terms the fate of Leningrad was not decisive for the outcome of the war. But as the birthplace of the revolution it had a symbolic importance, making it impossible to abandon. Stalin sent his top commander, General Zhukov, to defend it. The evacuation of the city's population was badly organised. A mere 400,000 left before the Germans closed the exit routes. But many people chose to stay and fight. A million Leningraders – one-third of the city's population – died from cold, starvation and disease before the siege was lifted in January 1944.

Meanwhile, the Germans moved into Ukraine, whose agriculture, coal and industry were essential for their war machine, while their main force advanced on Moscow. By 10 October, when Zhukov arrived from Leningrad to take control of the capital's defence, they had reached the outskirts of Moscow. Stalin ordered the evacuation of the government to Kuibyshev. Panic spread as the bombing of the city became more intense. At railway stations there were ugly scenes as crowds struggled to board trains heading east. Stalin made a radio broadcast pledging to defend the city to the end – and its people responded. A quarter of a million Muscovites dug defences on the city's edge, carted supplies to the front and cared for injured soldiers in their homes. Many fought alongside army units, scratched together from the shattered forces of the Western Front and reinforcements from Siberia.

This new spirit of determination was symbolised by Stalin's bold decision to go ahead as usual with the military parade for Revolution Day (7 November) on Red Square. He went against the advice of his air force commanders, who feared that the Germans would try to bomb the parade from the air (a few days earlier German planes had scored a direct hit on the Kremlin, killing 41 and injuring 146 people).[9] In his speech from the Lenin Mausoleum, Stalin called upon the soldiers to take inspiration from the military heroes of 'our great ancestors' – naming Alexander Nevsky, Dmitry Donskoi, Minin and Pozharsky, Suvorov and Kutuzov, the generals who had fought against Napoleon – in the defence of 'our glorious motherland'.[10] From Red Square the soldiers marched directly to the front.

The speech had a critical effect. Emboldened by its patriotic spirit, the Russians fought with grim determination for their capital. Gradually they overcame the German troops, who were unprepared for the Russian winter and exhausted after fighting for five months without a break. The defence of Moscow was vitally important. Hitler's capture of the capital would not have meant the end of the fighting (the Red Army could retreat to the Urals and beyond) but it could have toppled the Soviet regime, and would have led to millions of extra deaths in a more protracted war for the defence of Russia.

No one can deny the extraordinary courage of the Soviet people in the war. But who can explain it? Why did so many Soviet soldiers fight with such determination and self-sacrifice? Foreigners were astounded. 'The front abounded in examples of the personal heroism and unyielding tenacity and initiative of the common soldiers,' noted Milovan Djilas, the Yugoslavian Communist, on a visit to the Ukrainian Front in 1943. 'Russia was all last-ditch resistance and deprivation and will for ultimate victory.'[11] Was there something in the Russian character that explains this sacrifice, as some naive commentators have maintained? Or was it the result of a discipline imposed by the totalitarian state?

Terror and coercion provide only part of the answer. At the height of the Soviet collapse, on 28 July 1942, as the Germans threatened Stalingrad, Stalin issued Order 227 ('Not One Step Backwards!') calling on the troops to fight to the death without retreat. To enforce the command special units swept behind the front lines and shot any troops who lagged behind. The impact of this terror system was limited, however. Order 227 was used at desperate moments, like the battle for Stalingrad, but otherwise it was ignored by commanders, who learned from experience that military effectiveness was not best served by drastic punishments.

The cult of sacrifice was a more important factor than terror. It was the Soviet system's main advantage over Western liberal societies where the loss of human life was given greater weight in the reckonings of the command. Since the launching of the Five-Year Plan, the Soviet people had been told that sacrifice today was needed for the building of the Communist utopia. By 1941, they were more prepared than other peoples for the hardships of the war – the sharp decline in living standards, the breaking-up of families, the death and disappearance of their relatives – because they had been through these during the 1930s. The most selfless sacrifice was made by teenagers. Brought up on tales of Soviet heroes (record-breaking pilots and Stakhanovites, courageous soldiers of the Civil War, Communists who went to fight in Spain), they volunteered in huge numbers. Among them was Rita Kogan, one of a million Soviet women who fought in the Red Army and its partisan units. Born into a Jewish family in Belarus, she was in her final year at school when the war broke out:

> I was just 18 in 1941 … I saw the world in terms of the ideals
> of my Soviet heroes, the selfless pioneers who did great things
> for the motherland … I had no idea what war was really like,
> but I wanted to take part in it, because that was what a hero
> did … I did not think of it as 'patriotism' – I saw it as my duty
> … I could have simply worked in the munitions factory and
> sat out the war there, but I was an activist … I did not think of
> death and was not afraid of it, because, like my Soviet heroes,
> I was fighting for my motherland.[12]

Her generation fought with reckless bravery. Only 3 per cent of the eighteen-year-olds mobilised in 1941 would still be alive in 1945.

The Soviet command economy was made for war. Its ability to organise production for the military campaign – to move and build new factories overnight, to subject workers to martial law and to work to death a million Gulag slaves mining fuel and minerals – gave it an advantage over the Nazis, who were unable to demand so much from the Germans. There was almost no limit to the number of lives that the Stalinist regime was willing to expend to achieve its military goals. It went far beyond the traditional reliance of the Russian army on large quantities of troops to defeat the enemy. Only by considering this ruthless disregard for human life can we explain the shocking losses of the Red Army – around 12 million soldiers killed between 1941 and 1945 – three times the number of German military losses between 1939 and 1945.[13]

The defeat of Nazism was a victory of the Soviet people, above all. They were fighting not for Communism – 'for us', as Stalin put it to the US envoy Averell Harriman – but 'for their motherland'.[14] Stalin and the Party were conspicuously absent from Soviet wartime propaganda. Revolutionary symbols were replaced by older images of Mother Russia (*Rodina-Mat*, literally 'Homeland Mother') that carried greater weight among the troops. The Communist 'Internationale' was replaced by a new Soviet national anthem, whose lyrics hailed the union of the peoples bound together by Great Rus. New Soviet medals were embossed with the names of military heroes of the tsarist past: Nevsky, Suvorov, Kutuzov, Nakhimov, the martyr–hero of Sevastopol during the Crimean War. *Alexander Nevsky*, the film by Eisenstein, was brought back to cinemas and shown endlessly throughout the war. Perhaps most importantly, the persecution of the Russian Orthodox Church was brought to a temporary halt and an agreement reached with its new patriarch, elected after eighteen years of prohibition by the Bolsheviks in September 1943. In exchange for the patriarch's support and loyalty, Stalin ordered the release of thousands of imprisoned priests, allowed churches to reopen and restored church property, including the Trinity Lavra of St Sergius, the centre of the Russian Church, closed by the Bolsheviks in 1920, since when its buildings had been used for a wide variety of purposes, among them the training of radio engineers.

What did the soldiers understand by 'motherland'? The word *rodina*, usually translated as the 'motherland', can be used in Russian for a family household, kinship group, a village, town or city, or more generally for the nation. The Red Army soldiers were mostly peasant sons. When they wrote home from the front they made no distinction between fighting for Russia, as their *rodina*, and fighting for their homes and families. Wartime propaganda played to these emotions. The best-known poster of the war – 'Mother Russia Calls' – shows a middle-aged woman holding out a draft form, calling on her sons to defend her from the enemy. She symbolised the mother every soldier believed he was fighting for.

Many soldiers found an expression of their patriotic feelings in *Vasily Terkin*, Alexander Tvardovsky's narrative poem, printed in the front-line newspapers throughout the war. Terkin is a peasant lad. He never mentions the Party or Stalin. His attachment to the motherland is focused on his village in Smolensk. But he also has a sense of fighting both for Russia and for the liberation of the world:

> Today we answer for Russia,
> For the people,
> For everything in the world.
> From Ivan to Foma,

Dead and alive,
We together are we,
The people, Russia.[15]

Hatred of the enemy was equally a part of these patriotic emotions. The Germans had committed so many atrocities on Soviet soil that it was not difficult to fan the popular desire for revenge. According to a study of the Red Army's rank and file, it was hatred of the Germans, more than anything, that made the soldiers want to fight. The poem 'Kill Him!' by Konstantin Simonov was read to soldiers by their officers before they went into battle:

If you cherish your mother,
Who fed you at her breast
From which the milk has long since gone,
And on which your cheek may only rest;
If you cannot bear the thought,
That the Fascist standing near her,
May beat her wrinkled cheeks,
Winding her braids in his hand;
…
Then kill a German – make sure to kill one!
Kill him as soon as you can!
Every time you see him,
Make sure that you kill him every time![16]

Stalingrad became the symbol of this patriotic spirit. Even as the city was reduced to ruins under the bombardment of the German tanks, artillery and planes, the Soviet soldiers fought for every street, as if defending their own homes. They went on fighting for three months, from August to November 1942, when the Red Army under Zhukov launched its counter-offensive and forced the Germans to retreat towards the Don. These weeks of fighting were the turning-point of the whole war. From the Don, the Soviet army pushed on towards Kursk, where it concentrated 40 per cent of its infantry and three-quarters of its armoured forces to defeat the bulk of the German army in July 1943. Kursk definitively ended German hopes of a victory on Soviet soil.

As the Red Army drove the Germans back towards the western borderlands, it carried out a second war against Ukrainian nationalists, many of them followers of Stepan Bandera, whose guerrilla bands had been employed by the Nazis to fight behind the Soviet lines. NKVD units rounded up civilians in areas where Bandera's partisans had been active, and in a policy of ethnic cleansing sent them east to Gulag camps. Similar campaigns were carried out in Poland and the Baltic states. There were also wholesale deportations of Soviet ethnic groups (Kalmyks, Chechens, Ingush and Crimean Tatars) deemed collectively responsible for those few among them who had worked for the Germans.

The Red Army moved into the western borderlands as imperial conquerors. It was guided from the top by a strong sense of Russia's rightful domination of the non-Russian population in these territories. Once it entered German soil, the Soviet troops were driven forward by hatred of the Germans and by their desire for revenge – an impulse culminating in the rapes of German women on their final march towards Berlin. Around 2 million German women are believed to have been raped by Soviet soldiers, whose actions went unpunished by their commanders. When Djilas, at a dinner, expressed his concerns about hundreds of reported rapes by Red Army soldiers in Yugoslavia, Stalin interrupted him:

> 'Yes, you have, of course, read Dostoevsky? Do you see what a complicated thing is man's soul, man's psyche? Well then, imagine a man who has fought from Stalingrad to Belgrade – over thousands of kilometres of his own devastated land, across the dead bodies of his comrades and dearest ones! How can such a man react normally? And what is so awful in his having fun with a woman, after such horrors?'[17]

On 24 May 1945, at a reception for the Red Army's commanders in the Kremlin, Stalin proposed a toast 'to the health of our Soviet people, and in the first place, the Great Russians. (*Loud and*

prolonged applause and shouts of "Hurrah.") ... I propose a toast
to the health of the Russian people because it has won in this war
universal recognition as the leading force of the Soviet Union
among all the peoples of our country.'[18]

The victory of 1945 gave rise to a new brand of Russian
nationalism – more imperial than before. Russia emerged from the
war in Stalin's view as the undisputed leader of the Soviet peoples.
Djilas noticed that he spoke of Russia (Rossiia) instead of the Soviet
Union.[19] The primacy he gave to the 'Great Russians' (a term Stalin
favoured) justified his post-war policies of Russification in the
non-Russian republics and the newly annexed territories of west
Ukraine, Moldova and the Baltic, as it would in the east European
Soviet satellites. In all these lands the Russian language became
compulsory in schools and universities, fluency in it a requirement
for almost any job where higher education was called for. Russian
books and films, music, street names, history – they were imposed
everywhere.

This triumphalism was expressed in the architectural forms
which dominated plans for the reconstruction of Soviet cities after
1945. The 'Soviet Empire' style copied the neo-classical and Gothic
motifs of its Russian Empire model, which had flourished in the
wake of 1812. It can be seen most clearly in the 'Stalin Cathedrals',
the seven monumental wedding-cake-like structures (such as
the Foreign Ministry and the Moscow University ensemble)
which shot up around Moscow after 1945. But it was also visible
in palaces of culture, cinemas and circuses, even metro stations,
such as Komsomolskaya on the circle line. Komsomolskaya's huge
subterranean Hall of Victory, conceived as a monument to Russia's
military heroes of the past, is a curious mixture of the baroque and
the Byzantine.

Although the Comintern had been disbanded in the war, a new
messianic role for Russia had emerged. As the first and only socialist
society, its survival had been seen by Communists around the world
as the main objective of the war. With the defeat of Nazi Germany
its prestige was at its height, strengthening the case for exporting
revolution to those countries occupied by the Red Army, as Stalin

had envisaged when he made the pact with Hitler in 1939. No one better understood the dynamic between war and revolution than the Bolsheviks. They had used the revolutionary forces unleashed by the last war to seize power in 1917. Now they saw a chance to do the same in the war-torn territories they had liberated from Hitler.

Stalin saw the victory over Hitler as a prelude to Russian foreign expansion. 'This war is not as in the past,' he explained at dinner with Djilas in early 1945. 'Everyone imposes his own system as far as his army can reach.' Stalin believed that the Soviet Union had proved its invincibility, and that under Russian leadership it was strong enough to liberate the capitalist world. Until his break with Tito and the Yugoslavs in 1948, he embraced a Pan-Slav policy, as Russia's later nineteenth-century tsars had done, convinced as he was that Slavic unity would keep the Germans down and extend Russian power to the centre of Europe. 'If the Slavs keep united and maintain solidarity,' he explained to Djilas, 'no one in the future will be able to move a finger. Not even a finger!' He emphasised the last point, recalled Djilas, by 'cleaving the air with his forefinger'.[20]

Hubris yielded to a new imperial myth of Russia as the liberator of mankind. Born in the victory of 1945, the myth was linked by its propagandists to earlier historical episodes when Europe had been 'saved' by Russia's selfless sacrifice – at Kulikovo, when the Muscovites had beaten the Mongols, or in the war against Napoleon. The war dead were mobilised for the construction of this messianic myth – their deaths invoked as proof, not of Soviet inefficiency and callous disregard for human life, but of Russia's sacrifice, the price it paid to save humanity. At first Stalin allowed a published figure of only 7 million dead, around one-quarter of the estimated deaths accepted by historians today.[21] It was only in the 1960s, when a fuller picture of the losses could be given, that the endlessly repeated statistic of '20 million dead' entered Soviet propaganda as a symbol of the country's unique sacrifice for the liberation of the world.[22]

Indeed, no other country had sacrificed so much for the defeat of Nazism. Apart from the millions of its war dead, Russia's towns and cities were destroyed. The economy was in a mess. The collective farms had lost almost half their pre-war livestock and 38 per cent of their male workers.[23] In the central agricultural zone there was widespread famine in 1946. To get the country on its feet again a new Five-Year Plan was soon imposed.

In February 1946, in a speech that marked this return to the planned economy, Stalin argued that the war had put the Soviet system to the test. Its victory had proved the superiority of the Soviet multinational state, the Red Army and the planned economy, without which the 'bravery of our troops' would not have been enough to defeat the enemy.[24] The victory was, in other words, the Party's achievement, and without the Party's leadership the people would be defenceless. Over the next forty years, this myth would be used to legitimise the Soviet system, justifying everything it had accomplished after 1917.

Stalin still had doubts that the Soviet people would fight for the system if there was a new war with the West. He retained the view that they would first be fighting for the motherland. Russian nationalism, for this reason, was heavily promoted by the post-war Soviet regime. Its main aim was to seal the country off from Western influence during the Cold War. Absurd claims for Russia's greatness began to appear in the Soviet press. 'Throughout its history,' declared *Pravda*, 'the Great Russian people have enriched world technology with outstanding discoveries and inventions.'[25] The aeroplane, the steam engine, the radio, the incandescent bulb – there was scarcely an invention for which the Russians were not responsible. Timofei Lysenko, the director of the Soviet Institute of Genetics, even claimed to have developed a new strain of wheat that would grow in the Arctic – a bogus claim that was responsible for millions of deaths in Maoist China where the pseudoscience was adopted during the 1950s. Pride in Russian culture knew no bounds. Its literature and music were 'far superior' to their Western counterparts, Stalin's chief of culture Andrei Zhdanov argued, 'because they reflect a culture many times higher.'[26]

Stalin used this nationalist programme to tighten the regime's ideological grip on the intelligentsia, whose reverence for the West he mistrusted. He soon clamped down on the ideas of reform that had surfaced in the war, when the country was exposed to foreign books and films imported by the Lend-Lease agreement with America. Zhdanov oversaw the purge of Western ('anti-Soviet') tendencies in all the arts and sciences (hence the clampdown became known as the Zhdanovshchina). It began in August 1946, when the Central Committee published a decree censoring the journals *Zvezda* and *Leningrad* for publishing the work of two great Leningrad writers, Mikhail Zoshchenko and Anna Akhmatova. Zoshchenko was the last of the Soviet satirists, a literary tradition dictators cannot tolerate. As for Akhmatova, she had acquired an immense moral stature in the war, when her poetry, rarely published in the Soviet Union, was widely circulated in handwritten copies, even by the troops. Stalin envied her authority.

These attacks were followed by a series of repressive measures against 'anti-Soviet elements' in all the arts and sciences. The State Museum of Modern Western Art was closed down. A campaign against 'formalism' and other 'decadent Western influences' in Soviet music led to the blacklisting of Shostakovich, Khachaturian and Prokofiev, among other composers. In July 1947, the Central Committee published an attack on two Soviet scientists, Nina Kliueva and her husband, Grigory Roskin, for sharing information about their cancer research on a US tour. Accused of 'servility' towards the West, they were dragged before an 'honour court', a new institution to examine 'anti-patriotic' acts, where they were made to answer hostile questions before 800 spectators.

There were also attacks on the Soviet Jews, whose fortunes were connected to the Cold War alignment of Israel. Stalin had supported the idea of a Jewish state in Palestine. He hoped it might become a Soviet satellite. When Israel sided with America, he grew fearful of pro-Israeli feeling among the 2 million Soviet Jews. In 1948, Solomon Mikhoels, the popular director of the Jewish Theatre in Moscow, was killed by the MVD (as the NKVD had been renamed), his body later dumped on a roadside and run over by truck to disguise the killing as an accident. The next year saw the start of a campaign against 'cosmopolitans' (that is, Jews) in the other cultural spheres, with expulsions from the Party, the Writers'

Union, universities and research institutes. The anti-Semitic campaign climaxed with the Doctors' Plot in 1952.

The idea of a plot had its origins in 1948, when Lidiia Timashuk, a doctor in the Kremlin Hospital, wrote to Stalin two days before Zhdanov's death, claiming that his medical staff had failed to recognise the gravity of his condition. The letter was ignored and filed away, but four years later it was used by Stalin, by now completely paranoid, to accuse the Kremlin doctors of belonging to a 'Zionist conspiracy' to murder Zhdanov and the rest of the leadership. Hundreds of doctors and officials were arrested and tortured into making false confessions of belonging to a huge international conspiracy linking Soviet Jews to Israel and the USA. The country was returning to the atmosphere of 1937 with the Jews in the role of 'enemies of the people'.

In December 1952, Stalin told a meeting of the Central Committee that 'every Jew is a potential spy for the United States'. Thousands were arrested, expelled from jobs and homes and deported as 'rootless parasites' from the major cities to remote regions of the Soviet Union. Stalin ordered the construction of a vast network of labour camps in the Far East where the Jews would be sent. Had it not been for his death, at the height of this hysteria, there might well have been a holocaust on Soviet soil.

Stalin had suffered a stroke and lay unconscious for five days before he died on 5 March 1953. He might have been saved if medical assistance had been called in time. But in the panic of the Doctors' Plot none of Stalin's inner circle dared take the initiative. He became the final victim of his system of terror.

Huge crowds came to the Hall of Columns near Red Square where his body lay in state. Hundreds were killed in the crush. There were scenes of mass grief and hysteria. For thirty years the people had regarded Stalin as their moral reference point, their teacher, national leader, guarantor of justice and order. He had been their tsar, a god on earth, the embodiment of their hopes and ideals, and they had needed to believe in him during the hard times they had lived through. The grief they showed was a natural response to the fear and confusion they were bound to feel on his passing.

A collective leadership assumed control. Beria was the dominant figure. But senior Party and military leaders were opposed to his programme, which involved the dismantling of the Gulag and a relaxation of Soviet policies in western Ukraine, the Baltic region and East Germany. On 26 June, Beria was arrested in a Kremlin coup organised by Khrushchev with senior army personnel. Tried in secret, he was later shot.

Nikita Khrushchev emerged from the coup at the head of the collective leadership. A flamboyant and tempestuous character of humble peasant origins, he had risen through the ranks as a loyal executioner of Stalin's policies. He was deeply implicated in the repressions of the 1930s, first as the Moscow Party boss and then in Ukraine, where he had been responsible for the arrest of a quarter of a million citizens. Perhaps it was guilt that would lead him to expose the crimes of Stalin's reign in his 'Secret Speech' of 1956.

The Gulag population reached its peak in 1952, when there were around 2 million prisoners in its labour camps and colonies. After Stalin's death, prisoners began to be released – first those, mainly criminals, on shorter sentences, and then the 'politicals', whose cases were reviewed by the Soviet Procuracy, a long and complex process obstructed by authorities reluctant to acknowledge their mistakes. With so many prisoners returning, the regime needed to explain what had gone on. But how much of the truth could be revealed? All the leaders were afraid of what might happen if the full extent of the terror was exposed. Would they be held accountable? Wouldn't people ask why they had failed to stop the mass arrests?

A commission was appointed to report on the repression of Party members between 1935 and 1940. The Politburo was so shocked by its findings that it decided to report them (though not the full extent of the terror in the country as a whole) to the Twentieth Party Congress, the first since Stalin's death, in February 1956. The text was prepared collectively and delivered by Khrushchev. The speech gave details of the Party purges and of Stalin's blunders in the war, attributing them both to the dictator's deviation from

Leninist principles and to the 'cult of the personality', which had made resistance to his policies impossible. By emphasising that the current leadership had only just found out these details from the commission, Khrushchev tried to absolve it and shift the guilt on to Stalin. There was no question of blaming the Party leadership. The whole purpose of the speech was to restore belief in the Party by presenting Stalinism as an aberration from the October Revolution's socialist ideals.

Khrushchev ended with a plea for his revelations not to be communicated outside the Party. But the text of his speech was read to millions of Party members in meetings right across the Soviet Union and was sent to the Communist governments of eastern Europe. Published by the Poles, it was printed in the *New York Times*. And from the West, it filtered back to the Soviet Union. In the climate of the Khrushchev 'Thaw', when censorship was gradually relaxed, it encouraged a more general evaluation of the Party's record by the Soviet intelligentsia. 'The congress put an end to our lonely questioning of the Soviet system,' recalled Liudmilla Alexeeva, later to become a well-known dissident but at that time a Moscow University student. 'Young men and women began to lose their fear of sharing views, information, beliefs, questions. Every night we gathered in cramped apartments to recite poetry, read "unofficial" prose and swap stories that, taken together, yielded a realistic picture of what was going on in our country.'[27] The Party faced a moral crisis of authority. For the first time in its history it was admitting that it had been wrong – not wrong in a minor way but catastrophically wrong – and had lied about it all along. How could it rebuild its credibility?

The Thaw had begun in literature, a surrogate of politics throughout modern Russian history. Once the hand of Stalinist conformity had been removed, writers strived to portray Soviet life with more sincerity. Ilya Ehrenburg's novel *The Thaw* (1954) – which gave its name to this period – tells the story of a woman oppressed by her husband, a despotic factory boss, who at last finds the courage to leave him during the spring thaw. The high point of this literary renaissance came in 1962 with the publication of

Alexander Solzhenitsyn's *One Day in the Life of Ivan Denisovich*, the first novel on the subject of Stalin's labour camps, in the journal *Novy Mir* (New World). It was read by millions. But if condemnation of the Gulag was allowed, the October Revolution remained beyond questioning. *Doctor Zhivago*, Boris Pasternak's epic novel set against the backdrop of the revolution and the Civil War, was rejected in 1956 by several journals, including the progressive *Novy Mir*, on the grounds that it was 'anti-Soviet'. Smuggled to Milan, where it was published in Italian, the novel soon became an international bestseller. Pasternak was nominated for the Nobel Prize in 1958. But under pressure from the Soviet government he was forced to turn it down.

The Thaw entailed the partial opening of Soviet society to the West. For the first time, foreign tourist groups arrived. The Khrushchev government saw tourism as a way of earning dollars while demonstrating Soviet achievements to the world (the Sputnik programme of space exploration had just been launched). In 1957, Moscow hosted the World Festival of Youth. The Kremlin's aim was to win over the young people of the capitalist countries to the Soviet way of life. But the outcome was the opposite. With their jeans and easy-going manner the visitors converted Soviet youth to the Western way of life. Rock and roll and its attendant fashions captured the imagination of a generation of Soviet students too sophisticated for the dull, conformist culture of the Komsomol, the Communist Youth League. On their short-wave radios, they listened to the Voice of America and Radio Free Europe, where rock and jazz were the draw for news and information about the freedoms of the West. This generation formed its picture of the West through Hollywood, whose films, shown in Soviet cinemas as part of the thaw, had a massive influence. According to the poet Joseph Brodsky, the *Tarzan* films 'did more for de-Stalinization than all of Khrushchev's speeches at the Twentieth Party Congress and after'.[28]

By 1960, more than half the population was under thirty years of age. The October Revolution was not something they could relate to – for them it was ancient history – while the Great Patriotic

War was something that their parents had lived through. It was a challenge to engage this generation in the system's values and beliefs.

Khrushchev tried to do so through the Komsomol. He attached importance to mass participation in policy campaigns designed to reawaken the enthusiasm of the Revolution's early years. In the Virgin Lands campaign of 1954–63, young men and women from the Komsomol volunteered in their tens of thousands to work in new collective farms on the unfarmed steppelands of Kazakhstan. Forty million hectares of arid land were brought into production by 1963. Grain output rose. But harvest yields were variable and steadily declined after 1958, because the soil was too poor to grow wheat.

Khrushchev was removed in 1964. Apart from the failure of his Virgin Lands campaign, he was blamed for the food shortages that had resulted, in 1962, in a workers' uprising in Novocherkassk in southern Russia, which had been suppressed by the army with dozens of protesters killed. Khrushchev's political reforms had alienated the regional Party bosses by weakening their economic powers and subjecting them to regular elections to the Central Committee, a body under Stalin they had occupied as a sort of natural right, enabling them to build up their own patron–client networks in the provinces. Khrushchev's erratic leadership, his tendency to act on intuition and then attack his critics, his meddling in affairs where he lacked expertise, and his dangerous confrontation with the USA in the Cuban Missile Crisis – all this lost him the support of Party colleagues who wanted a more stable and collective style of government.

Leonid Brezhnev emerged as *primer inter pares* of the colourless regime that replaced him. It gave the appearance of 'collective leadership' – a myth used by all the Soviet leaders to symbolise their accountability, to enforce Party discipline and, in Brezhnev's case, to regain the cadres' trust by promising stability. The Politburo's decisions were henceforth reached collectively, and their names listed alphabetically. Slowly Brezhnev became dominant. He was a creature of the system, a grey and mediocre functionary. Even his passions were conventional (fast cars, hunting, women and football). Like so many Party apparatchiks promoted during Stalin's purges and the war, he had more practical than intellectual capacities (according to his brightest minister, Alexander Yakovlev, his main talent was an uncanny ability to 'recognise precisely who was his friend and who was his enemy').[29] He was good at building political alliances and networks of support among the regional Party leaders, many of them comrades from the 1930s, when he had risen from the factory floor to become the propaganda chief of the Dnepropetrovsk Party organisation in Ukraine. What united them was the preservation of the status quo. They wanted to prevent the shake-up of the Party that Khrushchev had begun, to restore a stable system that would keep them at the top. As long as Brezhnev was in power, the leaders were allowed to grow old in their posts. The average age of the Politburo rose from sixty in 1964 to over seventy in 1982.

In contrast to the Khrushchev government, which had appealed to Leninist ideas in its efforts to restore authority, the Brezhnev government turned to Russian nationalism to shore up its base of political support. This was the moment when the regime built up the official cult of the Great Patriotic War, whose memory previously had been downplayed. Until 1965, Victory Day had not even been a Soviet holiday. It had been left to veterans' groups to organise their celebrations and parades. But from the victory's twentieth anniversary, 9 May was commemorated with a huge display of military might and with all the Party leaders, lined up on the top of the Lenin Mausoleum, saluting as the massed ranks of the Red Army marched past on Red Square. Two years later, the Tomb of the Unknown Soldier was erected near the Kremlin Wall – a sacred site for foreign dignitaries (and Soviet bridal couples) to pay homage to the '20 million dead'. In Volgograd (previously Stalingrad) a monumental complex of mourning was completed the same year. At its centre was a colossal statue, *Mother Russia Calls*, her sword held aloft summoning the people to action.

The Brezhnev government encouraged two main strands of Russian nationalism, both reflected in the literary sphere. One was represented by a group of 'village prose writers', among them Fedor Abramov, Valentin Rasputin and Solzhenitsyn (until his falling out with the regime and exile to the West after the foreign publication of his *Gulag Archipelago* in 1973). The group had first emerged in the Khrushchev era, mainly at the journal *Novy Mir*. Their stories served as a condemnation of the legacies of collectivisation – the destruction of the village and its church, the depopulation of the countryside, deforestation, pollution, the decline of rural living standards – and as a lament for the old Russian values and traditions of the peasantry. A second more assertive strand of nationalism was found at the journal *Molodaya Gvardiia* (Young Guard), the official organ of the Komsomol, which enjoyed the support of the neo-Stalinist wing of the Party leadership, including Mikhail Suslov, Brezhnev's chief of ideology. The journal shared the same concerns as the village prose writers, but it also used its Politburo protection to push for more aggressive policies. Its writers were united by their nationalist view of history, in which Russia was defined by its strong authoritarian state and anti-Western traditions. Encouraged by Suslov, they argued that the Party should adopt Russian nationalism as its basic ideology alongside Marxism-Leninism. When Alexander Yakovlev, the head of the Party's Propaganda Department, criticised the journal's nationalist views as anti-Leninist, he was sacked from his position and sent in punishment to Canada as the Soviet ambassador (he returned ten years later, after Suslov's death in 1982, and went on to become the main ideologist of Gorbachev's reforms).

These and other nationalist groups received protection from the Party leadership. Nationalism was regarded as an antidote to the growing influence of Western ideas and culture. It lent support to military spending, which by 1982 accounted for around one-sixth of the country's GNP, largely due to the 1979 invasion of Afghanistan, intended to prop up its unstable Communist regime, and the nuclear arms race with America. Nationalist support was important too for Brezhnev's policies, which he made his top priority, to reverse the decline of living standards in the countryside. Between

1965 and 1970 there was a four-fold increase in state subsidies to the collective farms.

No amount of investment could turn around the fortunes of collectivised farming, however. Machines were badly made and always breaking down, sometimes going years without repair (concerned to find out what was going on, in 1980 Brezhnev at last ordered an investigation, which found that less than 1 per cent of new agricultural machines had been made according to the technical requirements).[30] The *kolkhoz* workers were given no incentives in those sectors where the state took all the crops (cereals, sugar beet, cotton, flax and cattle production). Despite the rise in state procurement prices, they remained very poorly paid. Many lived in squalid poverty, without running water or electricity, in settlements neglected by the *kolkhoz* management. They focused all their energies on their tiny garden plots – the last refuge of the peasant economy – where they grew fruits and vegetables, or kept pigs and poultry, which they sold on roadsides or in peasant markets in the towns. The Brezhnev government lifted the restrictions on the size of these private allotments to get more food to consumers. By the end of the 1970s, they took up 4 per cent of the country's agricultural land, but produced 40 per cent of its pork and poultry, 42 per cent of its fruit and over half its potatoes.[31] The prices in the peasant markets were too high for most people to afford, except on special occasions.

There were shortages of everything in the state shops. Long queues formed if some hard-to-come-by product (and it could be anything) by chance appeared. People became disenchanted, cynical about the propaganda claims of the regime. No longer fearful of repression, they let off steam by telling jokes:

A man goes into a shop and asks: 'You don't have any meat?'
'No,' replies the sales assistant, 'we don't have any fish. It's the shop across the street that has no meat.'

The one product not in short supply was alcohol. Consumption more than doubled in the Brezhnev years. By the early 1980s, the average *kolkhoz* family was spending one-third of its household income on vodka. Alcoholism was the national disease. It had a major impact on crime rates (10 million people every year were detained by the police for drunkenness) and male life expectancy, which declined from sixty-six in 1964 to just sixty-two in 1980. Brezhnev's children were both alcoholics. But his government was unconcerned by the problem. It increased vodka sales to extract money from the population, which had little else to buy. Better to have people drunk than demonstrating against shortages.

Oil revenues rescued the regime from probable food riots and possible collapse in the 1970s. They gave a lease on life to the Soviet economy, which would have been in serious trouble without a five-fold increase in crude oil prices as a result of the crisis caused by the Arab producers' embargo on oil sales to pro-Israeli states during the Yom Kippur (Arab–Israeli) War of October 1973. The Soviet Union doubled oil production in the 1970s, mainly by developing new fields in Siberia. With its dollar earnings from the sale of oil and gas, the government was able to buy consumer goods and foodstuffs from the West. Before the revolution, Russia had been a major agricultural exporter. But within sixty years of 1917 it had become the biggest food importer in the world. One-third of all baked goods were made from foreign cereals. Cattle farming was entirely dependent on imported grain.

There comes a moment in every old regime when people start to say, 'We cannot go on living like this any more.' That feeling started in the 1970s. But there was no social force to bring about a change. The people were too cowed, too passive and too conformist, to do anything about their woes. Very few were involved with the dissidents – human rights campaigners, Jewish *refuseniks* (denied permission to emigrate abroad), dissenting priests and liberal intellectuals like Andrei Sakharov, the Nobel physicist, who formed an active underground through *samizdat* (self-publishing) and *tamizdat* (publishing abroad). Harassment and surveillance by the KGB (as the MVD had been renamed) deterred those who sympathised with them – perhaps a majority of the intelligentsia – from having any contact with the dissidents.

*

The push for change came from the only place where it was possible: the Party leadership. Mikhail Gorbachev was one of many Bolsheviks – all of them the children of the Twentieth Party Congress – who believed in Khrushchev's vision of a Leninist renewal to revitalise the Soviet project. They had spent the Brezhnev years working in the research institutes connected to the Central Committee, and had been talking about *perestroika* (structural reform), the catchword of the Gorbachev era, since the Khrushchev period. *Glasnost* (openness) too was a concept that went back in Party circles to the 1960s, when it had been used to argue that the work of government should be open to the media.

Gorbachev was born in 1931 to a peasant family in Stavropol in south Russia. His paternal grandfather was sent into exile in Siberia for failing to fulfil the sowing plan for 1933 – a year of famine when three of his six sons and half the population of his village died of starvation. His other grandfather, a *kolkhoz* chairman, was arrested as a 'Trotskyist' in 1937. Gorbachev concealed this 'spoilt biography' until 1990. But the stigma of repression was no doubt at the root of his commitment to overcome the legacies of Stalinism.

With a good school record and Komsomol report, Gorbachev was awarded a place to study law at Moscow University. He was the first Soviet leader with a university degree. Joining the Party in 1952, he was fairly orthodox in his Stalinist opinions at this time. He did not yet connect his family's suffering to Stalin's policies. But his worldview was transformed by Khrushchev's Secret Speech. One of his closest friends at university, Zdeněk Mlynář, another major influence on Gorbachev, would go on to become a central figure in the socialist reformist government of Alexander Dubček suppressed by the Soviet invasion of Czechoslovakia in August 1968.

In 1970, at the age of thirty-nine, Gorbachev became the Party secretary of the Stavropol region, the youngest regional Party leader in the Soviet Union. It was a useful position on the ladder to the top. Known for its spas, Stavropol was a place where Kremlin bosses came for holidays. Gorbachev took full advantage of the opportunity to impress them with his efficiency, intelligence and charm. Yuri

Andropov, the chief of the KGB, was a frequent visitor. He brought Gorbachev to the attention of Brezhnev, who called him to Moscow, putting him in charge of coordinating agricultural policies.

On Brezhnev's death, in 1982, Andropov became the Party's new leader. He signalled his intention to tighten discipline in the workplace, to fight corruption in the administration and to decentralise the Soviet economy in order to increase productivity. Andropov was a moderniser who believed the system could be made to work if only it was run more rationally, like a police state. He rewarded young reformers, promoting Gorbachev and Nikolai Ryzhkov to counteract the influence of Konstantin Chernenko, leader of the Brezhnevite old guard. After only fifteen months in office, Andropov died from a long illness. He had nominated Gorbachev to succeed him, but Chernenko took his place. Within weeks he too became terminally ill. The Bolsheviks were dying of old age.

The selection of Gorbachev as Chernenko's successor, in March 1985, did not at first appear so radical. Without a pro-reform majority, Gorbachev was conscious of the need to proceed carefully if he was to avoid Khrushchev's fate. In his first year in power he talked only of a 'quickening' of the economy (*uskorenie*), an echo of the Andropov approach. It was not until the January 1987 Plenum of the Central Committee that Gorbachev announced the launching of his *perestroika* programme, describing it as a 'revolution' in its radical restructuring of the command economy and political system, but invoking Lenin to legitimise his bold initiative. He was a sincere Leninist. Where other Party leaders paid lip-service to Lenin, Gorbachev believed that his ideas, particularly those he had developed in the NEP, were still helpful for the challenges the country faced.

Economically, *perestroika* had a lot in common with the NEP. It rested on the assumption that market mechanisms could be added to the structures of the socialist economy to stimulate production and satisfy consumer needs. State controls on wages and prices were loosened in 1987. Cooperatives were legalised the following year, resulting in an NEP-like sprouting up of cafés, restaurants and small shops or kiosks, selling mostly vodka, cigarettes and pornographic videos imported from abroad. But these measures failed to ease the shortages of food and household goods. Only the dismantling of the planned economy could have solved the crisis – a reform too far in 1987 and yet too late in August 1990 when a 500-Day transition to a market-based economy was introduced.

Glasnost was the really revolutionary element of the Gorbachev reforms, the means by which the system unravelled ideologically. The Soviet leader intended it to bring transparency to government and break the power-hold of the Brezhnevite conservatives opposed to his reforms. The need for *glasnost* had been reinforced by the shameful cover-up of the Chernobyl nuclear disaster in April 1986. But its consequences quickly spiralled beyond Gorbachev's control. By relaxing censorship, *glasnost* meant that the Party lost its grip on the mass media, which exposed social problems previously concealed by the government – poor housing, criminality, ecological catastrophes – undermining public confidence in the system. Revelations about Soviet history had a similar effect. One by one the legitimising myths of the regime – the achievements of Soviet industrialisation, the creation of a socialist society, the Party's leading role in the defeat of Nazism, even the idea of mass support for the October Revolution – were questioned as the facts emerged from the newly opened archives and books published in translation from abroad.

Glasnost politicised society. Public bodies formed. By March 1989, there were 60,000 'informal' groups and clubs in the Soviet Union. Here were the stirrings of a civil society, something that the country had previously lacked to sustain democracy. Groups held demonstrations in the streets, many of them calling for political reforms, independence for Soviet republics and an end to the Communist monopoly of power (enshrined in Article 6 of the Soviet constitution). The cities were returning to the revolutionary atmosphere of 1917.

The one-party state began to crumble as reformers in the system lost the will to defend it or made their support for the opposition known. Yakovlev, the intellectual architect of Gorbachev's reforms, began to talk like a European social democrat. Boris Yeltsin, the Moscow Party boss, called on the Party to renounce its Leninist inheritance. Gorbachev was moving in the same direction too. His views developed as he came to understand the unreformability of the system. He was beginning to talk about the need for checks and balances within the state, supporting contested Soviet elections and slowly coming round to the demands of the radicals to abolish Article 6.

Communist hardliners were alarmed by the speed with which the system seemed to be unravelling. Political reform was threatening to become a revolution undermining everything the Party had achieved since 1917. Their opposition to Gorbachev's reforms was articulated by Nina Andreeva, a chemistry lecturer in Leningrad, in an article entitled 'I Cannot Give up Principles'. Approved by several Politburo members, the article was published in the newspaper *Sovetskaya Rossiia* in March 1988. It attacked the 'blackening' of Soviet history, defended Stalin's achievements 'in building and defending socialism' and called on the country's Communists to defend their Leninist principles, 'as we have fought for them at crucial turning points in the history of our motherland'.[32]

Gorbachev decided to fight back, pushing ahead with a series of more radical reforms. At an All-Union Party Conference, in June 1988, he forced the introduction of contested elections for two-thirds of the seats in a new legislative body, the Congress of People's Deputies, which would meet twice a year and elect a reformed Supreme Soviet of the Soviet Union, the country's highest parliament. This was not yet a multi-party democracy (87 per cent of the elected deputies were Communists), but voters could remove incumbent leaders if they were united against them (the entire Party leadership of Latvia and Lithuania suffered a humiliating defeat in the Congress elections in early 1989).

The Congress of People's Deputies became a democratic platform against the one-Party state. The opening sessions at the end of May were watched by 100 million people on TV. An Inter-Regional Group was formed within the Congress by reformists in the Party and non-Party democrats whose main demand was the scrapping of Article 6. Gorbachev agreed with the proposal and steered it through the Politburo in February 1990. He had started his reforms to save the one-party state, but was now dismantling it.

Nationalist movements were unleashed. The Baltic nations were the first to call for independence, followed by the Georgians and Armenians and substantial segments of the population in western Ukraine and Moldova (regions which like the Baltic states had been annexed in the war). Slower to react were the Central Asian republics where the elites depended on the Soviet system and the popular alternative was likely to be Islamic.

Gorbachev's reforms helped the nationalist leaders in two ways. First his creation of the post of Soviet president, which he occupied from 1990, encouraged them to form a presidential office of their own in the republics. Yeltsin was the major beneficiary. His election as Russia's president, in June 1991, gave him more authority in Russia than the unelected Soviet president. He became a symbol of Russian independence from the Soviet Union. Secondly, the introduction of contested elections for the Supreme Soviet of each republic allowed nationalists to win control of these new parliaments and use them to declare their independence from Moscow. In the Baltic states nationalists swept to victory in the 1990 Supreme Soviet elections.

Police repressions also fuelled the independence movements in Georgia and the Baltic states. In Tbilisi nineteen demonstrators were killed and hundreds wounded by the Soviet police in April 1989. In Lithuania and Latvia seventeen were killed in the crackdown of January 1991. These last repressions had been instigated by Communist hardliners in the KGB and military. They were trying to provoke a violent response by the nationalists which they could use to impose a state of emergency and prevent the break-up of the Soviet Union. Rather than resist the hardliners and run the risk of splitting the Party, Gorbachev made concessions, promoting two of them, Boris Pugo as minister of the interior and Gennady Yanaev as his Soviet vice-president.

Gorbachev needed the support of the hardliners for his plans to reconstitute the Soviet Union. The Soviet president proposed to negotiate a new union treaty with the republics, whose participation was dependent on a plebiscite. He wanted to agree a federal structure that would keep the Soviet Union together as a voluntary union, as Lenin had originally planned. Six republics were determined to break free and refused to vote on the matter (Georgia, Armenia, Moldavia and the three Baltic states). In the nine other republics, where a plebiscite was held, three-quarters of the people voted for maintaining the federal system of the Soviet Union. A draft treaty was negotiated between the Soviet government and the nine republican leaders (the '9+1' agreement). It was signed on 23 April 1991 at Novo-Ogarevo near Moscow. In these negotiations Yeltsin (in a strong position after his election as the Russian president) and Leonid Kravchuk (angling to become the Ukrainian president by reinventing himself as a nationalist) extracted many powers for the republics from the Soviet president.

By August, eight of the nine republics had approved the draft treaty (the one exception was Ukraine, which had voted for the union but was holding out for guarantees of Ukrainian sovereignty). The draft treaty promised to convert the USSR into a federation of independent states, not unlike the European Union, with a single president, foreign policy and military force. It would be called the Union of Soviet Sovereign Republics (with 'Sovereign' replacing the original USSR's 'Socialist'). On 4 August, Gorbachev left Moscow for a holiday in Foros in the Crimea, intending to return to the capital to sign the new union treaty on the 20th.

Although the treaty was meant to save the union, the hardliners feared it would encourage its break-up. They decided it was time to act. On 18 August, a delegation of conspirators flew to Foros to demand the declaration of a state of emergency, and when Gorbachev refused their ultimatum, placed him under house arrest. In Moscow a self-appointed State Committee of the State of Emergency (including Yanaev and Pugo) declared itself in power. A tired-looking Yanaev, his hands seized by alcoholic tremors, announced uncertainly to the world's press that he was taking over as the Soviet president.

The putschists were too hesitant to have any real chance of success. Perhaps even they had lost the will to take the necessary measures to defend the system at its very end. They failed to arrest Yeltsin, who made his way to the White House, the seat of the Russian Supreme Soviet, where he organised the parliament's defence. They failed to give decisive orders to the tank divisions they had brought in to Moscow to put down resistance to the coup. The senior army commanders were in any case divided in their loyalties. The Tamanskaya Division, stationed outside the White House, declared its allegiance to Yeltsin, who climbed on top of one of the tanks to address the crowd. Without a bloody struggle there was no way from this point that the putschists could succeed in an attack on the White House. They did not have the stomach for a fight.

The coup soon collapsed. Its leaders were arrested on 22 August (Pugo shot his wife and then himself just before they came for him). Gorbachev returned to the capital. But his position had been undermined. Many thought he had been on the putschists' side or had been complicit in some way (he fell victim in this way to the same fate as Kerensky after the Kornilov coup attempt in August 1917). The putsch had discredited the Communist Party and handed the initiative to Yeltsin as the president of Russia and 'defender of democracy'. On 23 August, he issued a decree suspending the Party in Russia pending an investigation into its role in the putsch (it was banned by him in November). Late that night, crowds in Moscow toppled the statue of Dzerzhinsky outside the KGB headquarters at the Lubianka. The next day, Gorbachev resigned as the Party's general secretary.

He still wanted to revive the union treaty talks. But Yeltsin turned against them, seeing the disbanding of the Soviet Union as a victory for his Russian government. The other republics, especially Ukraine, were now wary of any sort of union with Moscow, the power-centre of the KGB and the armed forces. When the Novo-Ogarevo talks resumed in mid-November, Yeltsin and Kravchuk demanded more concessions from the Soviet president. It looked as if the USSR would be converted into a Union of Sovereign States. But in a referendum on 1 December the Ukrainians voted by a huge majority for independence. Their departure blew a massive hole in the Soviet ship of state, an act that would not be forgotten by those who saw its sinking as a tragedy. A week later, Yeltsin, Kravchuk and the Belarusian leader Stanislav Shushkevich met in Belarus to announce the dissolution of the Soviet Union. Effectively, it was a coup by the leaders of the three republics.

In a farewell address broadcast from the Kremlin on Christmas Day, Gorbachev declared that he could not support the abolition of the Soviet Union. It had not been ratified by constitutional procedures or even by a democratic vote. Popular opinion had been in favour of a union, but the nationalist leaders had gone against the people's will.

II

ENDS

How does the story of Russia end? How far will the country's future be shaped by its past? In many ways the country appears to be trapped in a repeating cycle of its history. Twice in the twentieth century, in 1917 and 1991, the autocratic state has broken down, only to be reborn in a different form. The public forces unleashed in the state's collapse have turned out to be too weak and divided to sustain a democratic government. This has been a recurring pattern throughout Russian history. The autocratic state has been challenged many times by popular revolts but has always re-established its power.

Why did this occur again in 1991? How can we explain the failure of democracy in Russia under Yeltsin, and the re-emergence of dictatorship under Putin's leadership? Many views have been expressed by pundits of all sorts. The literature is large and grows by many volumes every year. But its perspective is narrow. Most of it reflects the viewpoint of the liberal intelligentsia in Moscow and the other big cities, a small and isolated caste whose influence was never as significant as it and its allies in the West believed. Western analysts have also focused too much on Putin as the embodiment of the 'kleptocracy' or 'mafia state' – descriptions of a system that is too complex to be explained by the corrupt pursuit of personal wealth or the machinations of one man and his oligarchic entourage. Much of what is called the 'Putin system' was already in existence in the Yeltsin years in any case. A deeper problem of this literature is its ahistoricism. Contemporary Russian politics are too often analysed without sufficient knowledge of Russian history. Yet an understanding of the country's past is essential to make sense of the developments in Russia during the last thirty years. History and myth – and the Putin regime's use of both – should be reconsidered if we want to understand where Russia's story is heading.

The events of 1991 were not a revolution but an abdication of power by the Communist Party. There was no mass uprising or opposition movement to bring down the Soviet regime in Russia. There were no parties, no trade unions or civic forum groups ready to take power, as they did in the east European revolutions of 1989. The crowds defending the White House against the putsch were not as large as later claimed, when there were accounts of 40,000 people standing in the rain on the night of 20–21 August to defend the Yeltsin government against the tanks.[1] In fact on that night there was just a 'tiny rag-tag army' on the barricades and only 'several thousand' in the general vicinity of the White House, according to the most reliable accounts by foreign TV journalists. Meanwhile life went on as normal in the rest of the city (one reporter thought there were more people in the queue at Moscow's new McDonald's than at the White House).[2] Three young men were killed by tanks, which, ironically, were on their way out of the capital, having received orders to withdraw. These needless deaths were enough to break the resolve of the putschists, even in the KGB.[3] Larger crowds turned out the next day, 21 August, *after* all the tanks had been withdrawn; and many tens of thousands appeared at the victory rallies held in Moscow, Leningrad and other cities later on.

If this was a victory for democracy, it was not perceived as such for long. By 1994, only 7 per cent of the Russian people thought that the downfall of the Soviet regime was a democratic victory, according to the trusted polling group of Yuri Levada. The rest saw it as a 'power struggle' between leaders, or a 'tragedy with terrible effects' for the country.[4]

Without a democratic revolution, the old elites soon re-emerged at the top of the post-Soviet system. The KGB renamed itself the

Federal Counter-Intelligence Service (later changed to the Federal Security Service, or FSB) without changes in its personnel. Yeltsin filled his government with former Communists and set about reclaiming the old Soviet bodies (the army, the state bank, the Soviet seat in the United Nations) for Russia. There were none of the lustration laws like those in eastern Europe and the Baltic states to bar from public office those involved in the old repressive organs of the Soviet regime. Even the leaders of the August putsch were amnestied in February 1994. Some went straight from jail to leading positions in Russia's largest banks and companies.

In business, too, the Communist elites were quick to take advantage of the legal loopholes created by the Gorbachev reforms to emerge as millionaires from the wreckage of the Soviet economy. The mass privatisation programme was a social disaster. Hurried through in 1992 by Yeltsin's wide-eyed young free marketeers, Yegor Gaidar, the prime minister, and Anatoly Chubais, his deputy, the programme involved giving vouchers to the population which could be used to buy shares in the privatised state companies. Most people had no clue what they should do with these vouchers. They had never heard of shares before. They were struggling to make ends meet as a result of the government's decision, in January 1992, to lift price controls on basic goods ('shock therapy') which had sent prices rocketing. Many people sold their vouchers straightaway, often for no more than the price of a few tins of food or a bottle of vodka. Because the voucher value was not linked to inflation, enterprises could be picked up for a song by businessmen with access to loans from the state bank, which was happy to lend large sums to its friends in business. Gazprom, Russia's gas monopoly, had a voucher value of $228 million – just 0.1 per cent of the valuation made by Western banks.[5]

The worst scandal was the scheme of 'loans for shares' introduced in 1995. Yeltsin's government was strapped for cash to pay its public workers, many of whom had not received their salaries for months. Facing re-election in 1996, it was in danger of losing power to a resurgent Communist Party, which had emerged as the largest party in the Duma elections of December 1995. Yeltsin's ratings were at an all-time low, a long way behind Gennady Zyuganov, the Communist leader. People were fed up with the collapse of the economy, the loss of basic services, rising criminality and corruption. They called democracy (*demokratiia*) 'shitocracy' (*dermokratiia*). Chubais brought together the leading oligarchs and offered them a deal allowing them to pay – in the form of 'loans' to Yeltsin's government – for 'temporary ownership' of the controlling shares in state oil and mining companies. The shares were sold through rigged auctions to ensure that these national assets ended up in the hands of tycoons – a new boyar class of oligarchs – handpicked by the Yeltsin government. Mikhail Khodorkovsky, who had made his fortune as a Komsomol official, acquired 45 per cent of the shares in Yukos, one of Russia's biggest oil giants, at the bargain price of $159 million. Vladimir Potanin, a former Communist official at the Ministry of Foreign Trade, purchased 38 per cent of Norilsk Nickel, the world's second largest nickel producer, for $100,000 more than the auction's opening price of $170 million. These acquisitions became permanent when, as everyone had expected, the government defaulted on the loans.[6]

Through this scheme Yeltsin raised $500 million for his campaign. With the help of US advisers and Yeltsin's favourite media moguls Vladimir Gusinsky and Boris Berezovsky, owners of the country's two main TV stations, his team overwhelmed the media with scare stories about the Communists. It brought a sweeping victory. But real power now lay with the oligarchs. They started to behave as if they were the government, demanding posts from Yeltsin, who had suffered several heart attacks during the campaign and was barely able to carry out the functions of a president (heavy drinking did not help). The state was in danger of breaking into fiefdoms controlled by the oligarchs.

This was the context in which Putin was manoeuvred into power by the FSB, whose mission, as it saw it, was to 'save the state' by replacing Yeltsin with a stronger leader, more in line with its own statist principles. Putin was not its first choice. The FSB had pinned its hopes on the prime minister, Yevgeny Primakov, who had been the KGB's director of foreign intelligence before 1991. But Yeltsin fired

Primakov in May 1999, after it had become evident that Primakov would not grant immunity to Yeltsin or his family, should he be elected president in the 2000 elections. There had been mounting allegations of corruption against Yeltsin and his daughter involving money-laundering through a Swiss-based company called Mabetex. Yeltsin wanted a successor who would protect him. His choice fell on Putin, Berezovsky's favoured candidate, whom he made prime minister in August 1999, announcing at the same time that he wanted Putin to succeed him as the president. One of Putin's first acts in that office was to grant immunity to Yeltsin and his family.

Putin was born in Leningrad in 1952. His family had suffered, like so many from that city, in the war. His father had been badly wounded at the front, while his elder brother had died in childhood during the siege. Putin joined the KGB at the age of twenty-three and ended up in Dresden as a spy. When the Berlin Wall came down, he was in the basement of the Soviet compound burning secret documents. None of the democratic spirit of these years affected him. He experienced the collapse of the Soviet system as a humiliation for his motherland, and took from it the lesson that uncontrolled democracy could only end in chaos and the weakening of the state. It was a lesson that would guide him as the Russian president.

Putin returned to Leningrad in 1990, and began to work for his former law professor, Anatoly Sobchak, the mayor of St Petersburg, as the city was renamed in 1991. Putin was in charge of granting licences to businesses and headed up a programme to export Russian goods in exchange for foodstuffs imported from abroad. The food never came, and he was accused of taking bribes worth millions of dollars from the racketeers.[7] Thanks to Sobchak's protection the charges against him were dropped. Many of the people who defended him went on to perform important roles in his regime, including Dmitry Medvedev, the prime minister and president, Sergei Stepashin, the justice minister, and Nikolai Patrushev, the head of the FSB during Putin's first two presidential terms.

It was Putin's loyalty that recommended him to Yeltsin and his bosses in the FSB. Appointed to his first job in the Kremlin in 1996, within two years he had risen to become director of the FSB. The grey official was unknown by the public that elected him as president. But that was the key to his success. His victory depended, not on an assessment of his policies (no one knew what he stood for) but on how he came across on television screens: sober, clean-cut, competent, someone who would not bring shame to Russia on the international stage – in sum, Yeltsin's opposite.

People were confused by the loss of Communism as a system of beliefs and practices. They fell into a moral vacuum. For some, religion filled the gap. For others monarchism was a substitute. There was even talk of the Romanovs returning to the throne. Cults of every kind, hypnotists with magic healing powers, found a ready following. The need to believe in something, anything, that offers hope, is a constant thread of Russian social history, as we have seen. The harder life in Russia is, the more its people hold on to beliefs that give them faith in salvation.

The Russians were affected more than other nationalities by the ideological collapse. The Ukrainians, the Baltic nations, Georgia, Armenia and even Kazakhstan were able to rebuild themselves as nation states by imagining the Soviet collapse as a national liberation from foreign ('Russian') rule. But the Russians did not have this possibility. They had never been a nation state. Their identity had been subsumed in the Russian Empire, and then in the Soviet Union, where they were regarded as the leading nationality. Russia had existed as an empire for so long that it could not simply reinvent itself as a nation after 1991.

There were no symbols or ideas around which the Russians could unite. They were too divided by their history. The imperial tricolour (white–blue–red) introduced by Peter the Great was readopted as the national flag in 1993, but nationalists preferred the black–yellow–white flag of Alexander II, said to be the colours of Byzantium, while Communists adhered to the Red Flag. The Soviet national anthem was replaced by Glinka's 'Patriotic Song'. But it proved unpopular. It failed to inspire Russian athletes or footballers, whose lacklustre performances on the international stage became a source of national shame. So the Soviet anthem was brought back with newly written words ('Russia – our sacred state'). New national holidays were established. Those of the Russian Church were all restored. But the Soviet holidays were still observed. Ideologically it was a mess. The vacuum created by the Soviet collapse was being filled with debris from every period of Russian history.

A good illustration of this eclectic attitude to Russia's past was one of Putin's first political billboards. It was posted throughout Moscow by his United Russia Party in the wake of the December 2003 parliamentary elections. Against the national tricolour and the slogan 'A Strong Russia Is a United Russia', it showed the map of Russia filled with portraits of 145 national figures (one for each million of the population) from the country's history: Alexander Nevsky, Peter the Great, Nicholas II, Stolypin, Tolstoy, Tchaikovsky, Lenin, even Stalin, all of them were there. This was more than an all-inclusive mix designed to appeal to everyone.[8] It was a statement of Putin's ideology, based on his reading of Russian history, a subject in which he considers himself to be an authority.

Putin's view of the country's history is statist and conservative. His reading of it tells him that Russia has been strong when its people were united behind a strong state; weak when the people were divided and lost sight of the 'Russian principles' that united and distinguished them. This was the view he first mapped out in his 'Millennium manifesto', published in December 1999. The liberal freedoms the Russians had obtained since 1991 were universal values, he declared, but Russia's strength lay in its 'traditional values' – patriotism, collectivism and submission to the state. 'For Russians,' he explained, 'a strong state is not an anomaly to fight against. On the contrary, it is the source and guarantor of order, the initiator and main driving force of any change.'[9] While this concept of the state was obviously nationalist (his stated aim was to restore Russia as a major power in the world), it was not aligned to any ideology or period of Russian history. At times he invoked the evolutionary principles of Stolypin, at other times he borrowed from the tsars, the Slavophiles, White emigré and Eurasianist philosophers, the Russian Church or the KGB handbook.

Putin's reassertion of the state began by taking back control of the television stations owned by Gusinsky and Berezovsky, who were forced to sell their interests and flee abroad. Both stations had been critical of Putin's war in Chechnya and his manipulation of the Chechen terror threat to boost his polling for the 2000 presidential election (six months before the election there had been a series of bombings of apartment buildings in Riazan and Moscow, among other cities, which the Kremlin blamed on Chechen terrorists, though many people claimed that the FSB had been responsible for the attacks). Through his domination of the media Putin was now able to portray his critics as the 'enemies of Russia' or 'enemies of the people' – terrifying phrases from the Stalin era – to justify his strengthening of state power. Outside the main cities, few people had the internet in their homes. Eight out of ten received their news from the TV.

Other oligarchs were divested of their companies. In 2003, Khodorkovsky was arrested, charged with fraud and tax evasion, and later sentenced to nine years in a Siberian labour camp. The Kremlin had been shocked by Khodorkovsky's plan to sell his shares in Yukos to the US oil giant Exxon. Although the government had been in favour of Russia's reintegration into the global capitalist system, it would not allow a foreign company to control strategic economic sectors, such as energy, crucial for security and foreign policy. Yukos was taken over by the state. Khodorkovsky's main crime was his financing of opposition groups, a contravention of the informal pact that Putin had made with the oligarchs on becoming president: summoning the businessmen to Stalin's house in Kuntsevo, he told them he would let them keep their money if they stayed clear of politics.

This was a revival of the patrimonial principle that had defined the tsar's relations with his oligarchs since at least the sixteenth century. The boyars were permitted to enrich themselves at the expense of the people only for as long as the tsar allowed them to. Putin's inner ministerial circle was aware of the tradition. Among themselves they called the companies they were meant to protect their 'grazing grounds' (*polianie*) – a modern version of the 'feeding' (*kormlenie*) system, going back to Kievan Rus, in which officials were allowed to 'feed themselves' by extracting money from the regions under their control.

Putin's next important move was to abolish elections for the regional governors, who would henceforth be appointed by Moscow. Passed in the wake of a terrorist attack on a school in Beslan, North Ossetia, in September 2004, the reform was officially justified by the need to tighten state controls against further terrorist attacks by the Chechens, whose aim, it was claimed, was 'the break-up of Russia'.[10] Meanwhile Putin imposed what he called the 'power vertical' – a concept rich with autocratic parallels from Russia's past – to centralise and strengthen his executive powers. The effect was to undermine the two potential brakes on his authority: the autonomy of the regions and the Duma parliament. Yeltsin had begun this centralising process by sending tanks to shell the Duma in 1993, when it had opposed his constitutional reforms. But Putin completed the Duma's subjugation to the president. He streamlined the party system so that in addition to his own United Russia, the loyalist parliamentary majority, there were just three other parties to manage: the Communists; the Liberal Democrats (a misnamed ultra-nationalist party); and A Just Russia, a fake party set up by the Kremlin to take votes off the Communists. The Duma had become a rubber stamp for his decrees.

The name given to this authoritarianism was 'sovereign democracy' – a term coined in 2006 by Vladislav Surkov, Putin's deputy chief of staff and principal adviser, whose approach to words was the same as Humpty Dumpty's in Lewis Carroll's *Through the Looking Glass* ('When I use a word ... it means just what I choose it to mean'). The meaning of 'sovereign democracy', as Surkov defined it, was that Russia should be free to choose its own political system and call it a 'democracy' (Putin, after all, had been elected). Any attempt by the West to verify that claim or dictate the meaning of democracy (in terms of liberal freedoms, human rights, rule of law, respect for the sovereignty of neighbouring states, and so on) was now dismissed as meddling in Russia's internal affairs. Russia was to have a form of 'managed' or 'staged' democracy in which elections would be held but their result would be decided beforehand. The Kremlin's control of the media, the legal banning or intimidation of the opposition and systematic ballot-rigging would make sure of that.

To underpin this 'Russian' version of 'democracy' Surkov argued that it was important for the Russians to reclaim the Soviet past as a positive experience. Their sovereignty depended on their own belief that the system they now had was the outcome of their history, of *every* stage of it, and that it was of their own making. They could not be truly sovereign if they thought they had been conquered or defeated in 1991, if they were made to feel that everything they had achieved as Soviet citizens had been for naught.

The Kremlin's campaign to restore pride in Soviet history began in schools. At a national conference of high-school teachers in 2007, Putin complained about the 'mess and confusion' that he perceived in the teaching of Soviet history and called for 'common standards' to be introduced in Russian schools. The following discussion then took place:

> *A conference participant*: In 1990–1991 we disarmed
> ideologically. [We adopted] a very uncertain, abstract ideology
> of human values ... It is as if we were back in school, or even
> kindergarten. We were told [by the West]: you have rejected
> communism and are building democracy, and we will judge
> when and how you have done ...
> *Putin*: Your remark about someone who assumes the posture
> of teacher and begins to lecture us is of course absolutely
> correct. But I would like to add that this, undoubtedly, is also
> an instrument of influencing our country. This is a tried and
> true trick. If someone from the outside is getting ready to grade
> us, this means that he arrogates the right to manage [us] and is
> keen to continue to do so.

In his concluding speech to the history teachers, Putin said:

As to some problematic pages in our history – yes, we've had them. But what state hasn't? And we've had fewer of such pages than some other [states]. And ours were not as horrible as those of some others. Yes, we have had some terrible pages: let us remember the events beginning in 1937, let us not forget about them. But other countries have had no less, and even more. In any case, we did not pour chemicals over thousands of kilometers or drop on a small country seven times more bombs than during the entire World War II, as the U.S. did in Vietnam, for instance. Nor did we have other black pages, such as Nazism. All sorts of things happen in the history of every state. And we cannot allow ourselves to be saddled with guilt.[11]

Four days after the conference, the Duma passed a law empowering the Ministry of Education to decide which history textbooks should be used in schools. The textbook favoured by the Ministry (*The Modern History of Russia, 1945–2006*) had been commissioned by the presidential administration, which had issued the following guidelines to the textbook's authors about how they should evaluate the leaders of the period:

Stalin – good (strengthened vertical power but no private property); Khrushchev – bad (weakened vertical power); Brezhnev – good (for the same reasons as Stalin); Gorbachev and Yeltsin – bad (destroyed the country but under Yeltsin there was private property); Putin – the best ruler (strengthened vertical power and private property).[12]

Meanwhile the Kremlin's ideologists launched a series of attacks on what they called the 'anti-patriotic elements' (a term coined by Stalin) that had tried to 'weaken Russia' by burdening the country with a sense of guilt over its own history. The implication was that anyone who dared to highlight Stalin's crimes, or other 'black spots' in the country's history, was an agent of the West. 'Russia has ceased to be the sovereign of its own historical memory, which is now in danger of being taken over by foreign inventions,' wrote Gleb Pavlovsky, an adviser to Putin, in December 2008.[13] That same month there was a raid on the St Petersburg archive of the Memorial Society, which for twenty years had pioneered research on the Stalinist repressions, collecting information on the perpetrators and victims.[14] The archive was returned by a court order, but a warning had been served.

Four years later, a law was passed requiring NGOs that received funding from abroad to register themselves as a 'Foreign Agent' – a term fraught with meanings from the Stalin era when it was used to uncover foreign spies. The Foreign Agents Law has been enforced against bodies like Memorial, whose Moscow branch was closed in 2021 on the pretext that it failed to signal its status as a 'foreign agent' on some social media sites. Other laws have been applied to silence and discredit individual historians – in one case using trumped-up charges of paedophilia to imprison a Memorial researcher in Karelia, Yuri Dmitriev, who had uncovered a mass grave at an execution site from 1937 and was working to identify the 9,000 victims, along with their executioners. Arrested in 2016, four years later, at the age of sixty-five, Dmitriev was sentenced to thirteen years in jail (later extended to fifteen years). His persecution had been instigated by a former chief of the Karelian FSB, whose relatives had worked in the KGB and MVD going back to Stalin's time.[15]

There is no law against the publication of historical research relating to the Stalinist repressions. Putin has never denied these. But he has argued for the need to balance them against the Soviet Union's achievements under Stalin's leadership – above all the victory of 1945 which assumed a sacred status in his version of Russian history.

In 2009, the United Russia Party proposed a Duma law to protect the official history of the Great Patriotic War. Passed five years later, the law introduced a new Article 354.1 (Rehabilitation of Nazism) to Russia's Criminal Code, making it a crime, with a penalty of up to five years in prison, to 'spread intentionally false information about the Soviet Union's contribution to the victory of the Second World War', including any information that was 'disrespectful of society'. The 'memory law', as it is known, was subsequently used against a number of historians, journalists and bloggers whose only crime was to draw attention to the Soviet Union's collaboration with Nazi Germany between 1939 and 1941, or to challenge the official view of the country's glorious and heroic role in the Second World War. Of the twenty-six criminal prosecutions brought to trial between 2015 and 2019, all but one resulted in convictions – the one acquittal being of a nationalist activist and writer who denied the 'so-called Holocaust' as a 'shameless swindle' perpetrated by the Jews.[16]

Putin has weaponised the memory of the war against foreign powers too. He has defended the Hitler–Stalin Pact, offending Poland and the Baltic states; compared Ukraine's nationalists to collaborators with the Nazis in the war; and criticised the British and Americans for failing to attend the celebrations in Moscow for the 75th anniversary of the victory over Nazi Germany. His harsh words on their absence (a 'moral disgrace' and 'insult' were both used in interviews) expressed the resentment long and deeply held by the Russians based on the idea spread by Soviet propagandists since the Cold War era that the Western allies had never adequately acknowledged the Soviet contribution to the victory (a resentment strengthened by the Western myth of the Second World War in which the British and Americans are seen as the heroes who defeated Germany, while the Soviet role is minimised).

The culmination of this state campaign to control the story of Russia came in 2015 with the opening in Moscow of the first of twenty permanent 'My History' parks. Spread across the country, the parks are multimedia exhibitions with internet resources widely used by schools. The exhibition halls are crowded with large groups of schoolchildren, college students and cadets from military academies. The Russian Church had first come up with the idea of the parks to promote a patriotic view of Russian history. In 2011 it had organised an exhibition in Moscow, 'Orthodox Rus', which became the model for the parks. Patriarch Kirill, the head of the Church, was a firm supporter of the Putin line on history, arguing that Russia need no longer dwell on the sins of the Soviet era, for which, he said, it had atoned. He expressed his hope that a positive assessment of the country's history in school textbooks would help it overcome the Russian 'syndrome of historical masochism' – a sense of guilt and inferiority rooted in the country's past.[17]

The main message of 'My History' is that Russia thrives when it is united by a strong leader, and when not, in times of civil war, it is vulnerable to invasion by hostile foreign powers, which are afraid of a powerful Russia and want to keep it weak or break it up. The need for a strong state to defend its borders is of paramount significance. The exhibition dwells on every opportunity to remind the Russians that throughout their country's past – from the Mongols in the thirteenth century to the Poles and Swedes in the Times of Trouble, the British and the French in the nineteenth century, the allied intervention in the Civil War, and the Nazi invasion – its enemies have tried to destroy Russia by invading it.

Every chapter in the country's story is told in a way to justify the 'patriotic policies' of the Putin government. Alexander Nevsky's victories over the invading Swedes and Teutonic Knights serve as reminders of the ever-present need to 'repel aggressions from the West'; his collaboration with the Mongols is hailed, in the words of Sergei Lavrov, Putin's foreign minister, as the 'foundation of the centuries-old traditions of Russian diplomacy' to look east (read: to China) for assistance when the country is rejected by the West (read: Western sanctions against Russia).

Russia's need for a strong leader is illustrated in the exhibits dedicated to Ivan IV, Peter the Great and Nicholas I, the tsar perhaps most favoured by Putin because of his stand against the West in his defence of 'traditional Russian principles' during the Crimean War. Modern Russia's story is a simple one in this telling – a tale of greatness undermined by pro-Western 'enemies' within but restored by great leaders. The autocratic power of the Romanovs guaranteed the progress of the country for three centuries, until the 'liberals' of 1917, egged on by their Western allies, brought the Russian Empire to ruin. The people were divided, torn apart by civil war, but Stalin reunited them and made Russia strong again.

The cycle was repeated in 1991: the state collapse was brought about by liberals, Gorbachev and Yeltsin, who were puppets of the West, but a Great Russia was rebuilt under Putin's leadership.[18] Thus ends the 'My History' version of the story of Russia.

It is a story many Russians want to hear – the over-fifties, in particular, whose outlook has been shaped by the history they were taught in Soviet schools. They resented the 'besmirching' of their country's history in the *glasnost* period. They did not want to listen to moralising lectures about how 'bad' the Stalin era was. They thought otherwise. What they knew was the story of their parents' lives, of the sacrifices they had made to build a better life for their children. Putin's version of their history enabled them to feel good as Russians once again. Their fondness for the Soviet past is perhaps a natural reaction to the loss of welfare provisions and the growth of economic insecurity after 1991. Jobs, pensions, housing and health care were all guaranteed, albeit at a basic level, by the Soviet system. But pride in Soviet achievements is not limited to those who went through Soviet schools. Since Putin came to power, there has been a general rise in nostalgia for the Soviet Union – even among those who were not yet born when it collapsed. According to a 2020 poll by the Levada Centre, three-quarters of Russians believe that the Soviet era was the 'greatest period' in their country's history.[19] Over the past twenty years, polls have shown consistently that around half the population think that Stalin was a 'great leader'.[20]

Such nostalgia is more broadly linked to the long afterlife of Soviet mentalities, which have been passed down to the young. This was the extraordinary finding of the Levada polling group. From surveys over many years, they discovered that the attitudes which they associated with the 'Soviet personality' (low material expectations, social conformism, intolerance of ethnic and sexual minorities, acceptance of authority, and so on) had not declined, as they had expected when they started out in 1991. On the contrary, such attitudes had become more pronounced and widespread in the population as a whole.[21] *Homo Sovieticus* had not died out after the collapse of the Soviet Union: he was reborn in a new form.

We can see his reincarnation in common Russian attitudes to state violence in history. According to a 2007 poll, seven out of ten people thought that Dzerzhinsky, the founder of the Cheka, had 'protected public order and civic life'. Only 7 per cent considered him a 'murderer and executioner'. More disturbing was the survey's finding that while nearly everyone was well informed about the mass repressions under Stalin – with most acknowledging that 'between 10 and 30 million victims' had been repressed unjustly – two-thirds of these same respondents still believed that Stalin had been positive for the country. Even with a knowledge of the millions who were killed, the Russians, it appears, continue to accept the Bolshevik idea that mass state violence can be justified.[22]

In the early 2010s, millions of Russians watched the TV show *The Court of Time* (*Sud vremeni*), in which figures and episodes from Russian history were judged in a mock trial with advocates presenting evidence, witnesses and a jury of the viewers who reached their verdict by voting on the telephone. The judgments which they reached do not hold out much hope for a change in Russian attitudes. Presented with the facts of Stalin's war against the peasantry and the catastrophic effects of collectivisation, 78 per cent of the viewers still believed that his policies were justified (a 'terrible necessity') for Soviet industrialisation; only 22 per cent considered them a 'crime' against the peasantry. On other issues the figures were even more emphatic. Nine out of ten viewers thought that Stalin's programme of industrialisation had saved the country; only one out of ten considered it an 'unjustified rupture' from the country's past. On the Hitler–Stalin Pact, 91 per cent believed the Soviet version, rehabilitated by Putin, that it had been necessary to give the country time to prepare for war against Hitler; only 9 per cent thought it had enabled the Nazis to invade Poland and had thus led to the Second World War. On Gorbachev's reforms, 93 per cent believed they had been a catastrophe, with more believing that his policy of *glasnost* had been a Western 'information war'. As for *Homo Sovieticus*, it turned out he was deeply missed: 94 per cent of the audience agreed that the 'Soviet personality' was a 'real historical accomplishment'. Only 6 per cent believed it was a myth.[23]

*

During his first term in office, Putin looked to further Russia's integration with the West. In interviews he spelled out his vision of the country as 'part of western European culture', and said that he was open to the possibility of Russia joining NATO and the European Union. Everything depended on how Western institutions would respond, on how NATO, in particular, would act in regions where the Russians had security concerns, historic links and sensitivities, which, if offended or ignored, might provoke an aggressive response from Moscow. 'We will strive to remain where geography and our spirit have placed us, but if we are pushed out,' Putin warned, 'we will be forced to seek other ties to strengthen ourselves.' It was a recurring pattern running right through Russian history since at least the eighteenth century. Russia wanted to be part of Europe, to be treated with respect. But if it was rejected by the West's leaders, or if they humiliated it, Russia would rebuild itself and arm itself against the West.

NATO and the EU missed an opportunity to end this historical cycle. Instead of trying to bring Russia into new security arrangements for Europe, NATO kept it isolated. The US and its North Atlantic allies acted as if the Cold War had been 'won' by them, and that Russia, the 'defeated' power, need not be consulted on the consequences of the Soviet collapse in regions where the Russians had historic interests. The effect of Western actions was to reinforce the Russians' own resentments of the West. On the back of years of anti-Western propaganda during the Cold War it did not take a lot to persuade them that a hostile West refused to recognise their country as an equal and took advantage of its current weakness to diminish it. This was the basis on which Putin built his anti-Western ideology. Inside Russia it appealed to those who had lost out from the Soviet collapse (public sector employees, low and middle-ranking officials, workers in the old state industries) and who were struggling in the market-based economy imposed, as they saw it, by the West.

In the Kremlin's version of events, the first Western insult to Russia was NATO's unilateral intervention, without UN backing,

on the side of the Kosovan Albanians in their war for independence
against Serbia, Russia's closest Balkan ally, during 1999. Fifteen
hundred Serbians, half of them civilians, were killed by NATO
aerial bombardment between March and June. Dismissing NATO's
claims that it had intervened to prevent the ethnic cleansing of
Albanians by the Serbian Milošević regime, Moscow accused NATO
of a 'flagrant violation of the UN Charter' to promote its interests in
the Balkans, which Russia saw as its own 'sphere of influence'. The
Kremlin's anger at this NATO challenge to its status in the Balkans
was based on the myth of Russia's Pan-Slav role, which, as we have
seen, had often proved illusory (in the Crimean War, for example).
But that myth was a real factor on the Russian side. It shaped the
Kremlin's attitudes and policies. NATO's failure to recognise that fact
was bound to sour its relations with Russia. NATO's intervention,
moreover, set a dangerous precedent. It would be used by Moscow
to justify its wars in Georgia, Crimea and Ukraine.

The real rupture with the West came with NATO's eastward
expansion. In the Kremlin's thinking it was linked to the spread of
US-sponsored democratic movements in its sphere of influence that
posed a threat to Russia's 'sovereign democracy'. In 1999, the Czech
Republic, Hungary and Poland were granted NATO membership.
Five years later, Bulgaria, Romania, Latvia, Lithuania and Estonia
also joined the alliance. Moscow saw this as a betrayal of a verbal
promise made by the Americans on the collapse of the Berlin Wall
that NATO would not advance 'even one inch to the east'. Many
on the US side denied giving such a guarantee, or argued that
it had been meant for eastern Germany, not for all the Warsaw
Pact countries. They argued that the newly independent states
of eastern Europe deserved NATO protection from the threat of
Russian aggression, even if a promise of some sort had been made
by other leaders in the West (in 1991, for example, Douglas Hurd,
the British foreign secretary, had assured Moscow that there 'were
no plans in NATO to include the countries of eastern and central
Europe in NATO in one form or another').[24] Whatever the reality,
NATO's eastward expansion poisoned its relations with Russia.
George Kennan, who had shaped the Cold War policy of Soviet

containment in 1946, warned that it would be a 'tragic mistake' to encroach on the territories of the former Warsaw Pact. 'It shows so little understanding of Russian history,' he told the *New York Times* in 1998. 'Of course there is going to be a bad reaction from Russia, and then [the NATO expanders] will say that we always told you that is how the Russians are – but this is just wrong.'[25]

That indeed is how events turned out. NATO's incorporation of the former Soviet satellites made it come across as an anti-Russian alliance, reinforcing age-old Russian feelings of resentment of the West. Putin voiced these resentments in a blistering attack on US global domination and its unchecked use of force in international relations at the annual Munich Security Conference on 10 February 2007. NATO's eastward expansion was 'a serious provocation' against Russia, a betrayal of international agreements. He warned that Russia, as a consequence, would no longer play by the old international rules in furthering its interests.[26] By provoking Russian aggression, NATO had created the very problem it was meant to counteract. It was as if it needed an aggressive Russia to justify its existence.

Estonia was the first to feel the pushback from Russia two months after Putin's speech. The Estonian government's removal of a Soviet war monument in Tallinn prompted Russian hackers (probably connected to the FSB) to launch a cyber-war against the Baltic state. Georgia felt the force of Russia next. Its aspiration to join NATO had been welcomed by the NATO conference in Bucharest in April 2008. But in August of that year it became embroiled in fighting against pro-Russian separatists in the breakaway enclaves of Abkhazia and South Ossetia, causing refugees to flee to neighbouring Russia. Moscow sent in planes and tanks to push the Georgian forces back, occupying a large chunk of Georgian territory, before declaring Russia's recognition of Abkhazia and South Ossetia as independent states. President Medvedev, Putin's placeman, justified the intervention by citing the precedent of NATO's support for independent Kosovo. 'In international relations you cannot have one rule for some and another rule for others,' he warned the Americans. Russia's show of strength put an end to Georgia's NATO hopes (the alliance would not admit a country under partial occupation by Russian troops). It also showed the weakness of the West, which condemned the invasion but obviously had no intention of opposing it by military means.

Putin returned for a third term as president in 2012. The economy was doing well, boosted by an all-time high in oil and natural gas prices, the country's main exports. Despite mass protests against election rigging, or perhaps because of them, Putin struck a more assertive foreign policy. He spoke of the need for Russia to restore its influence in what he called the 'Russian world' (*Russkii mir*), a concept he attached to the defence of 'traditional Russian values' within the borders of the former Soviet Union. The 'Russian world' idea had been advanced by the patriarch of the Orthodox Church to promote its spiritual inheritance from Kievan Rus, a link broken by the break-up of the Soviet Union. It was seized on by Putin, who used it as an arm of his foreign policy from 2012. The 'Russian world', he said, was a 'family' of Slavs, the Russians, the Ukrainians and the Belarusians, who shared a common history, religion and cultural inheritance from Kievan Rus. This world had been torn apart by the collapse of the Soviet Union, the 'greatest geopolitical catastrophe of the [twentieth] century', as he had described it in a 2005 address. 'As for the Russian nation,' he went on, 'it became a real drama. Tens of millions of our citizens and compatriots found themselves outside the territory of Russia.'[27]

From the concept of the 'Russian world' it was but a short step to the Pan-Slav ideologies of the nineteenth-century Slavophiles, from whom Putin drew increasingly in the formulation of his foreign policies. The Slavophiles had argued that Russia should be seen as a 'spiritual civilisation' broader than its territorial boundaries. They had called on Nicholas I to stand up to the West in the defence of the Orthodox in the Balkans and the Holy Lands during the events that led to the Crimean War. It was the sacred duty of the tsar, they said, to promote the interests of the Orthodox abroad. Starting from that principle, Putin argued that it was the mission of the Russian state to defend the 'tens of millions of *our* [sic] citizens' who had been stranded outside Russia after the collapse of the Soviet Union. Where religion had served as the pretext for Nicholas I to interfere in Ottoman affairs, language served as the president's excuse to intervene in former Soviet countries where Russian-speakers formed a large minority. The fact that they were citizens of foreign sovereign states, and identified themselves as such, did not count in Putin's view.

Like the Slavophiles, Putin envisaged Russia as a supranational 'civilisation', defined by its spiritual values, opposed fundamentally to the secular and liberal influences of the West. His thinking here was possibly derived from Danilevsky's *Russia and Europe*, written in the wake of the Crimean War, in which the Pan-Slav thinker had maintained that Russia was a distinctive multi-cultural civilisation, neither understood nor recognised by Europe, which saw it only as an aggressor state and wanted to diminish it. Russia was not part of Europe, Danilevsky argued, and should not seek its approval or measure its own progress by its 'universal' principles, which were in fact self-serving, a means for Europe to impose its values on other civilisations. Following the West could only weaken Russia, which should stand against it if it wanted to defend its own conservative and religious traditions.

Other thinkers also shaped his idea of the Russian world. The one most often cited as the 'key' to Putin's ideology is Ivan Ilyin (1883–1954), the White emigré philosopher, monarchist and fascist sympathiser, whose mystical ideas of Russia's soul and statehood influenced a wide range of Russian nationalists after 1991. More than any other country in the world, Ilyin argued, Russia had a 'heavy cross to bear' on account of its harsh climate, its vast land mass to defend and its history of suffering; but it had emerged from these ordeals with a special spiritual strength, a capacity for love and selfless sacrifice, which, if mastered by a 'national dictator', would liberate it from the Bolsheviks and lead to its national renewal as a holy empire in Eurasia. Ilyin's ideas were heavily promoted by the Church as part of its agenda to reconnect the story of post-Soviet Russia to the lost histories of the White and monarchist movements. In 2005 it organised the repatriation of Ilyin's remains from Switzerland and reburied them, along with bones of the White army general

Denikin, in Moscow's Donskoi Monastery. Ilyin's mystical ideas were disseminated in a simpler form for Putin's cause by Alexander Dugin, a professor of philosophy at Moscow University, whose most influential book, *The Foundations of Geopolitics* (1997), was used as a textbook in the Academy of the Russian army's General Staff. It mapped out a hybrid warfare strategy (combining political subversion, the weaponisation of Russian gas and oil, cyberwar and military force) to rebuild a Russian Empire in Eurasia, totalitarian in character, which would build alliances based on the rejection of the Western liberal order and US global domination.

Ukraine soon became the battlefield for this 'clash of civilisations' between Russia and the West. Although the Putin government had many times declared its recognition of Ukrainian sovereignty, it never really came round to accepting it. In Putin's view Ukraine had occupied the borderlands of 'historical' or 'greater' Russia since the times of Kievan Rus. It was an inseparable part of the 'Russian world'. Too many families, communities, were made up of both Russians and Ukrainians; the economies of the two countries were too integrated to be pulled apart. Russia's gas was piped to Europe through Ukraine. Its most important naval base was at Sevastopol in the Crimea, a mainly Russian territory assigned to the Ukrainian Soviet Republic by Khrushchev in 1954 to mark the tercentenary of Russia's union with the Cossack hetmanate. Little significance had been attached to Khrushchev's gift. There were no national boundaries in the Soviet Union. But after 1991 the loss of the Crimea was sorely felt by the Russians, who had spent their holidays at its resorts and learned at school that it was 'theirs'. Sevastopol was a Hero City, one of only twelve that had been so honoured because of their wartime role in 1941–5. A quarter of a million Russians died in the Crimean War – another war in defence of the Orthodox against the West. Crimea was the birthplace of Russia's Christianity, where Prince Vladimir had been baptised, the symbolic home of the 'Russian soul' – that, at least, was how it was presented by the propagandists of the 'Russian world'.

Putin pursued a policy of keeping Ukraine weak, divided and dependent on Russia. He regarded Russia's domination of Ukraine as a necessary measure to prevent its falling under Western influence. He feared Ukraine as a burgeoning democracy whose freedoms were a threat to his own authoritarian regime (the 'Orange Revolution' of 2004–5, in which mass protests had reversed the rigged election of the pro-Russian presidential candidate Yanukovich to secure the victory of Viktor Yushchenko, alarmed the Kremlin in particular). His strategy was reminiscent of tsarist policies towards Russia's neighbouring states, especially the Ottoman Empire. The tsars had used their military might as a means of armed diplomacy. By threatening the sultan's Balkan territories, and, if necessary, occupying them, they had forced him to concede to their demands in the Black Sea and the Holy Lands. Putin adopted the same tactics in Ukraine. Instead of the defence of the Orthodox abroad, the pretext used by the tsars to interfere in European Turkey, he invoked the defence of 'the millions' of former Russian citizens to justify his interference in Ukrainian affairs.

The Putin regime backed pro-Russian leaders in Ukraine, and made things hard for those who favoured closer integration with Europe. Divisions in Ukraine played into the Kremlin's hands. There was a historical divide between the western regions, which had been part of the Polish–Lithuanian Commonwealth and then the Austrian–Hungarian Empire, where Ukrainian was widely spoken, and the eastern regions of Ukraine, where Russian was the dominant language. Because of the Russian presence in the east, no government could take Ukraine too close to Europe without risking civil war; but the European outlook of the western provinces meant that realigning the country with Russia would be just as dangerous.

The delicate balance was upset by two developments. The first was Putin's long-term plan, which gained momentum from 2012, to include Ukraine in a Eurasian Economic Union with Russia, Belarus and Kazakhstan, among other countries of the former Soviet Union. Putin envisaged the Eurasian Union one day growing into something like the European Union under Russia's leadership – a Eurasian bloc to counteract the West. The second was the outbreak of mass protests in Kiev and other west Ukrainian cities from the autumn of 2013. Occupying Maidan Square in Kiev, the demonstrators called on the

Yanukovich government (elected fair and square in the 2010 elections) to sign an Association Agreement with the EU. Yanukovich had negotiated the agreement, only to suspend preparations for it under pressure from Moscow. Shooting at the crowds by unidentified snipers (probably special forces of the Yanukovich government) turned the protests into a revolution, the Maidan Revolution, watched by TV audiences around the world. By 22 February 2014, the protesters had gained control of Kiev. Yanukovich fled to east Ukraine, and later to Russia, while a caretaker government was formed in the Ukrainian parliament.

The Kremlin saw the revolution as an illegal coup by the opposition parties aided and abetted by the West. Putin later placed it in a long historical continuum of Western powers using Ukraine to attack Russia. The protesters were certainly encouraged by US and EU politicians – enough for the Putin government to make its propaganda claim. The Kremlin's media outlets consistently referred to the interim Ukrainian government as a 'junta', backed by 'neo-Nazis' and 'fascists', an obvious propaganda tactic to appeal to Russian nationalist feelings rooted in the memory of the war when some Ukrainians had indeed been collaborators with the Germans. They accused the government of threatening 'genocide' against the Russians in Ukraine (an alarmist claim based on an ill-judged decision by the parliament in Kiev to repeal a law protecting Russian and other minority languages). The Kremlin's version of events was readily believed by the mainly Russian-speakers of the Crimea. They staged mass protests against the new authorities in Kiev, many of them calling for a referendum on Crimea's independence from Ukraine.

Seizing on the questionable parallel with Kosovo, where NATO's intervention had secured the Albanians' right to self-determination, the Kremlin launched a new Crimean War to defend what it claimed were the same rights for the Russians of the Crimea.[28] At the end of February, Russian special forces occupied the peninsula, installed a pro-Russian government and oversaw a hurried referendum, declared illegal by the UN General Assembly, in which 97 per cent of the people voted for reunion with Russia. Even with a properly conducted plebiscite the same decision would have been reached by a large majority. But Putin did not need to play by international rules. He knew that NATO would not act to defend Ukrainian territory. Russian might had called its bluff.

The annexation of Crimea was broadly welcomed by the population in Russia. There was a sense that an unjust loss of Russian territory – a symbol of the loss of Russia's empire and great-power status in the world – had been reversed. National pride had been restored.

Putin's approval ratings reached an 80 per cent peak. This was the high point of the Putin leader cult. He had attained the status of a tsar, the embodiment of state power, above everyone and everything. People placed their trust in him, as they had in the myth of the 'true' or 'holy tsar', despite the foreign condemnation of the annexation and Western sanctions on Russia. Most believed the regime's explanation for the economic downturn that followed, which it blamed on the sanctions to rally nationalist feelings for its 'us against them' cause against the West.

The sanctions were not strong enough to deter further Russian aggression against Ukraine. Ideas of the 'Russian world' had by this point assumed a firm hold on the Kremlin's military policy, with presidential aides like Sergei Glazyev pushing for it to extend the war in the Donbass, where pro-Russian separatists were already fighting against Kiev, to stop Ukraine from turning into what he called a 'neo-Nazi' puppet state used by the Americans against Russia.[29] Soon after the Crimean invasion Putin sent in military aid to the separatist fighters in the east, later reinforcing them with unbadged Russian troops (so-called volunteers) in a war that rumbled on for the next eight years, claiming 20,000 Russian and Ukrainian lives. The warring parties failed to reach agreement on the Minsk II Accords, a peace plan brokered by the Germans and the French under which Ukraine would regain its sovereignty in the disputed eastern areas, including its control of the border with Russia, while the Donbass would be given full autonomy in a more decentralised Ukraine.

All this time the West continued buying Russian fossil fuels. In 'Londongrad', a safe British haven for the oligarchs, law firms, bankers, tax consultants, art dealers and real estate agents carried on as usual as their money launderers. Four years after its invasion of Ukraine, Russia was allowed to host the 2018 FIFA World Cup, an event that seemed to mark its rehabilitation in the international community. As Putin watched the Russian team progress to the quarter-finals, he must have felt that he had got away with his aggression in Ukraine. The Russian economy had adapted to the sanctions and had largely recovered. Thanks to sales of oil and gas, the country's foreign currency reserves had grown to $500 billion, the fourth largest in the world. It gave Putin the war chest he would need to go on fighting in Ukraine while maintaining living standards in Russia. He was not afraid of more sanctions. With Donald Trump in the White House, with the EU weakened by Brexit and with the support of right-wing populists in Hungary, France and Italy, he was surely counting on another weak response by the Western powers, should he decide to escalate the war.

That would depend on his assessment of the NATO threat to Russia in Ukraine. At the Bucharest conference in 2008, NATO had declared that, along with Georgia, Ukraine would become a member of the alliance once it met the necessary requirements (among them better measures to combat political corruption and ensure the rule of law). The declaration was opposed by several NATO leaders, especially the German chancellor Angela Merkel, who warned that it would be seen as a dangerous provocation by Russia. But George Bush forced the measure through. In his final months in the White House, he was desperate to leave a legacy of promoting US interests and democracy in the former Soviet Union. He was supported by the east European member states, which were most alarmed by Russia's growing aggression. They saw Ukraine's NATO membership as 'an important historic opportunity to cage the bear', in the words of Lech Wałęsa, the former Polish president.[30]

NATO's involvement in Ukraine set alarm bells ringing in Moscow. After the invasion of the Crimea, the alliance gave $3 billion in military aid to the Ukrainian government, helped it to modernise its weaponry and trained its troops in joint exercises in Ukraine. The war had strengthened Ukraine's national unity. But it also gave rise to a violent hatred of Russia reflected in the cult of Stepan Bandera, the Ukrainian nationalist leader who had fought on the Nazi side against the Soviet army in 1944–5. Bandera streets and squares were newly named. Statues of the partisan leader were erected in cities such as Lviv and Ternopil. The Bandera cult was a gift for Moscow's propaganda about the threat of 'Nazis' in Ukraine.

Putin saw the role of NATO in Ukraine as a direct military threat. In an hour-long address to the Russian people on 21 February 2022, he claimed that Ukraine would 'serve as an advanced bridgehead' for NATO's forces to attack Russia unless Moscow intervened. Under the guise of its training missions, NATO, he declared, was building bases in Ukrainian cities like Kharkiv, near the Russian border, from which its nuclear missiles could reach Moscow in a few minutes. 'It is like a knife to our throat,' he said.[31] From a Western point of view this seemed mad and paranoid. NATO, after all, was a defensive alliance and had no reason to attack Russia. But as Putin saw it, it was the conclusion to be drawn from his reading of the history of Russia and Ukraine.

He explained his thinking in a long historical essay, 'On the Historical Unity of the Ukrainians and the Russians', published by the Kremlin in July 2021.[32] At the time it was dismissed as a strange scholastic article written by a man obsessed with long-dead historical disputes without bearing on the current conflict in Ukraine. The esoteric influence of thinkers such as Dugin could be clearly seen in it. Now the essay can be read as Putin's historical justification for the invasion, which he launched eight months later, in February 2022. In it Putin argued, yet again, that the Russians and Ukrainians were one nation, that Ukraine was a part of 'greater Russia' (an entity at times he equated with the Soviet Union and at times with its inner Slavic core) and, as such, had no real statehood of its own. At many points throughout its history, Putin continued, Ukraine had been used by hostile foreign states – the Swedes, the Poles, the Austrians and the Germans in the First World War, the allied powers in the Civil War – to attack Russia by encouraging the Ukrainians to believe the myth of their own independent nationhood. The West today, he claimed, was doing just the same.

Much of Putin's anger was directed at the Bolsheviks, who, he claimed, had given the Ukrainians an artificial state when they formed the Soviet Union. The Ukrainian Soviet Republic had been granted New Russia, the Black Sea coastal districts from Odessa to Donetsk which had formed a province of the Russian Empire (Novorossiia) before 1917. Later, as we know, the Crimea was transferred to Ukraine as well. None of this had mattered when the USSR had existed, Putin said. But on the Soviet Union's collapse (a consequence of Lenin's 'mistaken policy' of granting the republics a right of secession) it meant that 'historic Russian lands' had been gained unjustly by Ukraine. In a clear threat to the Ukrainians, Putin claimed that, when it left the Soviet Union, Ukraine should have taken only what it had when it had joined in 1922 – the smaller rump state (without New Russia or the Crimea) claimed by the Ukrainians in 1917. It was an argument that had been made before by Russian nationalists, such as Solzhenitsyn, a major influence on Putin's thinking after 1991. The loss of Ukraine was a bitter pill for nationalists of Putin's generation to swallow. His inner circle of *siloviki* – the 'men of force' in charge of the military and state security – had all been in the KGB or the military at the time of the Soviet collapse. Having watched their bosses lose an empire, they were united by their determination to restore the 'inner empire' of Ukraine and Belarus. They blamed the Ukrainians for the break-up of the Soviet Union (their vote for independence had certainly delivered the *coup de grâce*) and resolved to punish them.

The Russians began their military build-up in March 2021. By December, over 100,000 troops were massed on the borders of Ukraine. At this point it appeared that they were meant to serve Putin's armed diplomacy. The threat of war had exposed political divisions in Ukraine, with growing opposition to Zelensky's handling of the crisis which Putin wanted to exploit. He demanded a written guarantee that Ukraine would never become part of NATO. He also wanted the alliance to remove the military assets it had deployed in eastern Europe since 1997, when NATO had agreed to station neither nuclear weapons nor military bases in the new member states. His ultimatum was rejected by the US secretary of state, Antony Blinken, who came out of a frosty meeting with Lavrov in Geneva, on 21 January 2022, able only to repeat the usual formula that 'NATO is a defensive alliance and poses no threat to Russia.' Putin saw it otherwise. A month later, he launched his invasion, claiming it was needed to prevent the threat to Russia posed by NATO in Ukraine.

Few people thought that he would launch a full-scale invasion. An incursion in the east, followed by a round of armed diplomacy, looked like the more reasonable scenario. But Putin by this point had become a victim of his own myths about the 'Russian world'. He genuinely thought that he could conquer Kiev and 'liberate' Ukraine without serious resistance – a dangerous delusion that led him to attack on every front. His decision surprised even senior Kremlin officials. It must be explained by Putin's isolation from reality. Terrified of Covid, he had spent the past two years in lockdown on his own in the Kremlin, seldom meeting anybody in person (even the President of Kazakhstan was made to spend two weeks in quarantine before Putin would see him). After twenty-two years in power, Putin had become an autocrat. No one dared to question him. He filled his offices with statues of the greatest tsars, with whom he compared himself. Hubris lay behind his reckless decision. He thought that he could score a quick and easy victory. His spies in Kiev had told him that Zelensky's government would soon collapse: it had ruined the economy and lost the support of the Ukrainians, who would welcome Russia's troops with open arms. They were too afraid to disillusion him by telling him the truth.

On 24 February, Russian forces moved into Ukraine from Belarus, from Russia in the east and from the Crimea in the south. Putin had expected his troops to be in Kiev within two days. A victory article celebrating the return of Ukraine to the 'Russian world' was published by mistake by RIA-Novosti, the state news agency, on 26 February, before being withdrawn from its site. The Russians failed to enter the Ukrainian capital. They underestimated the Ukrainians (a nation with the fighting spirit of the Cossacks in its blood) and the leadership of their president Zelensky, dressed in khaki, whose daily broadcasts gave his people self-belief and renewed strength in unity. Putin had denied that Ukraine was a nation, but his war against it had created one far more united than before.

Once their Blitzkrieg had been stalled, the Russians had no other plan to capture Kiev. They lacked the logistics to supply their forward units with sufficient ammunition, food, fuel, technical and medical support. The Russian army, it turned out, was not as good as people had thought. It relied on heavy firepower and on its sheer size to overwhelm its better-supplied and more agile opponents – a distinctly Russian way of fighting wars, as we have seen. The low morale of the conscript troops quickly became apparent. Many of those captured claimed they had not known that they would be fighting the Ukrainians; they had been told that they had come to liberate their fellow Slavs from the 'Nazis'. As the invasion force became bogged down, it resorted to bombarding cities, targeting civilian areas, blocks of flats and even hospitals, tactics developed by the Russians in Chechnya and Syria. Millions of desperate Ukrainians chose to flee by car, by train, by any transport they could find to reach safety; others took to basements to survive as best they could. The Russians carried out a number of atrocities in towns such as Bucha and Irpin where they had been met, not with open arms, but with hatred and defiance from Ukrainian residents.

These war crimes may not amount to genocide, at least in its legal sense, an accusation made by the Ukrainians, whose memory of the Soviet terror-famine, the *Holodomor*, which has been declared a genocide by the Ukrainian parliament, leads them unsurprisingly to that opinion. The rhetoric denying the Ukrainians their nationhood is certainly a part of the legal concept of a genocide under international law. But the Russian actions on the ground, although set in motion by the Kremlin's aim to remove that nation from the earth, have more to do with the post-imperial phenomenon, in which fallen empires take revenge on their former colonies. The Russian killings of civilians, their rapes of women and other acts of terror are driven not so much by the genocidal purpose of destroying the Ukrainians as a group than by the hateful urge to punish them, to make them pay in blood for their independence and freedoms, for their determination to be part of Europe, to be Ukrainians, and not subjects of the 'Russian world'.

Unable to break through the Ukrainian defences around Kiev, in the first weeks of April the Russians withdrew from the north and regrouped their armies in the east, where they prepared for a big offensive on the steppe against the best, most battle-seasoned units of the Ukrainian army, the 40,000 men who stood between them and the central regions of Ukraine. The Russian aim was to encircle the Ukrainians, destroy their army and occupy the whole of the Donbass, thus securing a land bridge between Russia and the Crimea, if not taking all of east Ukraine. Putin, it was said, was hoping to announce a victory at the annual military parade in Moscow on 9 May, Victory Day, but at the time of writing (this book went to print on 20 April) that did not appear likely. The war looked set to last for a long time.

The Putin regime sees this as an 'existential war', to quote one of its senior advisers, Sergei Karaganov, who warned that it will go on making war until it is able to claim 'a kind of a victory'.[33] But how long can the Russians bear its costs? How many dead and wounded soldiers will they accept as the necessary sacrifice to achieve this 'victory'? How many years of economic hardship can they bear? The regime likes to call upon the memory of 1941–5, when the cult of patriotic sacrifice played such an important role in the Soviet war effort, as we have seen. But today the Russians are no longer fighting for their motherland. No foreign power has invaded it. They are being made to fight on foreign soil for Putin's myth about the 'Russian world'. Is that worth the sacrifice, they might well ask?

The Kremlin has prepared the public for this war. For the past eight years its TV channels have been churning out the same old narrative about Ukraine as an evil agent of the West, full of Nazis, bent on the destruction of Russia. The message has been passed through schools and military academies, through the print media and through the weekly sermons of Patriarch Kirill, a major force behind this war (in his sermon on 6 March, the Day of Forgiveness in the Russian Orthodox calendar, he likened it to a crusade against the West whose liberal values involved celebrating the 'sin' of homosexuality in 'gay pride parades').[34] Independent polls in early April suggested that three-quarters of the population support the 'special military operation', as the Kremlin calls the war. Such polls must be taken with a pinch of salt. People are unlikely to admit their doubts to pollsters when doing so may land them in prison. But the number is believable. A similar percentage of the population, mostly in the older age groups, depends solely on the television for its news. Without access to the internet and independent sources (Facebook, Twitter, Instagram and the last independent radio and online TV stations were all closed down in the first weeks of the war) the narrative is hard for ordinary people to challenge. Putin's narrative is all the more effective because it builds on Cold War myths, which for years had told a story of the West's 'fifth column' drawn from the non-Russians in the Soviet Union. Putin is aware of the need to build his Ukraine-Nazi myth on these earlier narratives. On TV he condemns the 'scum' and 'traitors' who are more at home in Europe than in Russia, and threatens mass repressions against those 'fifth columnists', the 'enemies' of Russia, who oppose his policies. The impact of his Stalinesque discourse is, on the one hand, to encourage 'loyal' and 'patriotic citizens' to attack those speaking out against the war (attacks using violence and racist slurs, harassment and denunciations) and, on the other, to create a general atmosphere of mistrust, hate and fear, reminiscent of the Stalin years of terror, which frightens the majority into silence and complicity. This is a pattern of behaviour learned from Soviet history. The Russian people know from their collective memory, passed down through the generations, not to question the authorities, to avoid awkward moral issues, in short to accept what they are told.

How will this war end, and what sort of Russia will emerge from it? None of the possible scenarios bodes well for Russia or Ukraine. A military defeat for Russia is the first and least likely possibility, if a 'victory' for Ukraine means, as many of its leaders think it should, the expulsion of Russian troops from all its territories. Even in defeat, the Putin regime would probably survive, albeit in a more repressive form and more isolated from the international community. Putin one day will step down (he is rumoured to have cancer), but unless there is a revolution his system will continue under different leadership. With its domination of the media, its repressive forces and its reserves of foreign currency, the regime is too powerful, even for a mass-based opposition, such as we saw in support of the imprisoned leader Alexei Navalny, who tapped into a growing public mood of anger and frustration with government corruption in the late 2010s as general living standards remained low. As Russia's story shows, the autocratic state has many times survived long periods of discontent. Society has been too weak, too divided and too disorganised to sustain an opposition movement, let alone a revolution, for long enough to bring about a change in the character of state power. Today the failure of democracy is rooted in the weakness of the public sphere. Thirty years after the collapse of the Communist dictatorship, Russia remains weak in all those institutions – genuine political parties, professional bodies, trade unions, consumer organisations, civic groups and residents' associations – whose freedom of activity is the underpinning of democracy. The intelligentsia, which once assumed the role of the nation's conscience, carries little influence today. The war has further weakened it, as tens of thousands of that caste (artists, academics, journalists, scientists and IT specialists) have fled abroad instead of opposing it at home. No doubt they are hoping to return to Russia soon. But that was the hope of the émigrés who left Russia after 1917, and very few of them returned.

The second possible scenario is a stalemate, a permanently frozen conflict in Ukraine, with Russian troops in the Donbass and the east but neither side prepared to stop the fighting, and no real basis for constructive peace talks as long as the Russians occupy these territories. Eight years of war have hardened the Ukrainians' resolve not to compromise with the Russians. For even if they gave up lands for peace, what assurance could they have that Russia would not use these as a forward base to prepare a new attack? Nothing Putin says can be trusted. The Ukrainians are equally unlikely to give up on their aim of NATO membership, a key demand of the Russians. From 2019 that aim was enshrined in the Ukrainian constitution, so any decision to remove it would need to be approved by a national plebiscite or a vote in parliament, a process that would take 'at least a year' in Zelensky's estimate. Yet with every passing week the likelihood of passing such a resolution will decline, as it becomes ever clearer that NATO membership is the only guarantee of Ukraine's survival as an independent state (before the Russian invasion, 55 per cent of the population favoured joining NATO, but by the end of March that figure had risen to 72 per cent).[35]

In the end Ukraine will be forced to reach a compromise with the Kremlin. There is no other way to stop this war. The issue is to do so on terms best for Ukraine with international guarantees of its security. This means that the West must go on arming the Ukrainians until they gain the upper hand, if not complete victory. But how long can the West be counted on? For all its talk of 'standing with Ukraine', would it really risk a direct conflict with Russia, or suffer crippling shortages of oil and gas, should the Russians cut sales to the West? Putin will be counting on the weakening of the West's resolve. He reckons that its people will grow tired of the war and become more concerned by their own problems. He has begun a war whose predictable effects (spiralling inflation, food shortages in the Middle East and North Africa, both reliant on Ukrainian grain, and mass immigration from these regions into Europe) are likely in the long term to destabilise democracies. Failing that, Putin is prepared to escalate the war, using nuclear weapons if needed, because he thinks that NATO will back down to avoid a direct confrontation with Russia. Such are the lengths to which he is prepared to go to force Ukraine back into the 'Russian world'.

A Russian victory of some kind is the most likely outcome of this war, given the resources at the Kremlin's disposal. But what sort of victory can be achieved? Even if the Russians settle for the whole of the Donbass as their 'victory', they will still be left with the problem of Ukrainian insurgency and civil disobedience, not to mention the huge cost of rebuilding cities which their armies have destroyed. The Russian economy will be further weakened by sanctions. It will be set back fifty years, returning in effect to Soviet-like conditions. Isolated from the West, Russia will be forced to pivot east, a turn accelerated by the war and welcomed by a number of the Kremlin's ideologists, who believe that Russia's future lies in a Eurasian bloc, opposed to Western liberal values and US global power, with China as its main ally. With only fossil fuels, precious metals and raw materials to offer the Chinese, Russia would become the junior partner in this new relationship. But with China it would represent a dangerous threat to the West's interests in those regions of the world, from India to the Middle East, where nationalist movements and dictatorships are able to exploit their country's grievances against the West. In the Kremlin's understanding this is a war not just about Ukraine but about the ending of the US-dominated global order and economy by the growing power of Eurasia.

It is an unnecessary war, born from myths and Putin's twisted readings of his country's history. Unless it is soon stopped, it will destroy the best of Russia – those parts of its culture and society that have enriched Europe for a thousand years. The Russia that emerges from the war will be poorer, more unpredictable and more isolated in the world. It goes to show how dangerous myths can be when used by dictators to reinvent their country's past.

Russia's future is uncertain. But one thing is for sure: its history will never be the same again. The country's past will be reinvented by the Russian state as its needs change, reimagined by its people as they look to redirect its course. It may seem now as if that story was destined to conclude with Putin's reinvention of the Russian autocratic tradition. But it did not have to end that way. There were chapters in its history when Russia might have taken a more democratic path. It had strong traditions of self-rule in its medieval city republics, in the peasant commune and the Cossack hetmanates and not least in the zemstvos, which might have laid the basis for a more inclusive form of national government. There were moments when its rulers edged towards a constitutional reform, only for their liberal initiatives to be overturned by the current of events pushing Russia closer to the tragedy of 1917. And in the chaos of the revolution there were moments when the people were able to reshape the state in line with their old utopian dreams of social justice and freedom. The retelling of these stories must surely be a part of changing Russia's destiny.

Notes

ABBREVIATIONS IN THE NOTES

IRL RAN   Institute of Russian Literature, Russian Academy of Sciences, St Petersburg
NA   National Archive, London
OR RNB   Manuscript Division, Russian National Library, St Petersburg
RGASPI   Russian State Archive of Social and Political History, Moscow
RGIA   Russian State Historical Archive, St Petersburg

INTRODUCTION

1 P.-A. Bodin, 'The Monument to Grand Prince Vladimir in Moscow and the Problem of Conservatism', in M. Suslov and D. Uzlaner (eds), *Contemporary Russian Conservatism: Problems, Paradoxes and Perspectives* (Leiden, 2019), p. 306.

2 <Kremlin.ru/events/president/news/53211.> The opening can be viewed in the video embedded here: <en.wikipedia.org/wiki/Mon ument_to_Vladimir_the_Great>.

3 A. Timofeychev, 'Moscow Monument to Prince Vladimir provokes ire in Kiev', *Russia Beyond the Headlines*, 14 November 2016: <www.rbth. com/politics_and_society/2016/11/14/moscow-monument-to-prince-vladimir-provokes-ire-in-kiev_647547>.

4 <korrespondent.net/ukraine/3544735-evropeiskyi-vybor-ukrayny-sde lan-tysiachu-let-nazad-poroshenko>.

5 G. Orwell, *Nineteen Eighty-Four* (London, 2003), p. 40. The words are the Party slogan of Oceania where the 'mutability of the past' is one of the 'sacred principles' (p. 31).

6 S. Velychenko, 'Tsarist Censorship and Ukrainian Historiography, 1828–1906', *Canadian-American Slavic Studies*, vol. 23, no. 4 (1989), pp. 385–408.

7 M. Cherniavsky, *Tsar and People: Studies in Russian Myths* (New Haven, 1961), p. 229.

8 E. Rostovtsev and D. Sosnitskii, 'Kniaz Vladimir Velikii kak natsional'nsyi geroi', *Dialog so Vremenem*, issue 65 (2018), pp. 150–64.

9 On the Ukrainian appropriation of the Vladimir cult in the late nineteenth century: H. Coleman, 'From Kiev across All Russia: The 900th Anniversary of the Christianization of Rus' and the Making of a National Saint in the Imperial Borderlands', *Ab Imperio*, vol. 19, no. 4 (2018), pp. 95–129.

10 S. Solov'ev, *Istoriia Rossii s drevneishikh vremen*, 6 vols (St Petersburg, n.d.), vol. 6, p. 339.

11 E. Kantorowicz, *The King's Two Bodies* (Princeton, 1957).

I ORIGINS

1 See P. Geary, *The Myth of Nations: The Medieval Origins of Europe* (Princeton, 2002).

2 *Povest' vremennykh let*, ed. V. P. Adrianova-Peretts and D. S. Likhachev with revisions by M. B. Sverdlov (St Petersburg, 1996), p. 13.

3 C. Jarman, *River Kings: A New History of the Vikings from Scandinavia to the Silk Road* (London, 2021), p. 190. On the identity of Rörik see: S. Coupland, 'From Poachers to Gamekeepers: Scandinavian Warlords and Carolingian Kings', *Early Medieval Europe*, vol. 7, no. 1 (2003), pp. 85–114.

4 S. Franklin and J. Shepard, *The Emergence of Rus, 750–1200* (London, 1996), pp. 317–19.

5 J. Black, *G.-F. Müller and the Imperial Russian Academy* (Montreal, 1986), pp. 109–17; V. Fomin, 'Lomonosov i Miller: uroki polemiki', *Voprosy Istorii*, no. 8 (2005), pp. 21–35.

6 Z. Harris and N. Ryan, 'The Inconsistencies of History: Vikings and Rurik', *New Zealand Slavonic Journal*, vol. 38 (2004), pp. 1115–16.

7 N. Karamzin, *Istoriia gosudarstva rossiiskogo*, 3 vols (St Petersburg, 1842–3), vol. 1, p. 43.

8 See e.g. J. Nielsen, 'Boris Grekov and the Norman Question', *Scando-Slavica*, vol. 27 (1981), pp. 69–92.

9 N. Andreyev, 'Pagan and Christian Elements in Old Russia', *Slavic Review*, vol. 21, no. 1 (1962), p. 17.

10 T. Noonan, 'Why the Vikings First Came to Russia', *Jahrbücher für Geschichte Osteuropas*, New Series, vol. 34, no. 3 (1986), pp. 321–48; Franklin and Shepard, *The Emergence of Rus*, pp. 12–16.

11 Harris and Ryan, 'The Inconsistencies of History: Vikings and Rurik', pp. 120–1.

12 G. Jones, *A History of the Vikings* (Oxford, 2001), p. 164.

13 See O. Pritsak, *The Origin of Rus'* (Cambridge, Mass., 1981).

14 J. Shepard, 'The Origins of Rus' (c. 900–1015)', in M. Perrie (ed.), *The Cambridge History of Russia*, vol. 1: *From Early Rus' to 1689* (Cambridge, 2006), p. 51. On Khazar influence see: T. Noonan, 'Khazaria as an Intermediary between Islam and Eastern Europe in the Second Half of the Ninth Century: The Numismatic Perspective', *Archivum Eurasiae Medii Aevi*, vol. 5 (1985), pp. 179–204.

15 For this view see Pritsak, *The Origin of Rus'*.

16 Franklin and Shepard, *The Emergence of Rus*, pp. 99–100, 140 ff., 170 ff.

17 *The Russian Primary Chronicle*, trans. S. Cross and O. Sherbowitz-Wetzor (Cambridge, Mass., 1953), p. 198.

18 D. Obolensky, *Byzantium and the Slavs* (New York, 1994), pp. 61–2.

19 See A. Feldman, ' The Historiographical and Archaeological Evidence of Autonomy and Rebellion in Chersōn: A Defense of the Revisionist Analysis of Vladimir's Baptism (987–989)', MRes. Thesis, University of Birmingham, 2013.

20 D. Obolensky, *The Byzantine Commonwealth: Eastern Europe, 500–1453* (London, 1971).

21 Obolensky, *Byzantium and the Slavs*, p. 101.

22 S. Averintsev, 'Visions of the Invisible: The Dual Nature of the Icon', in R. Grierson (ed.), *Gates of Mystery: The Art of Holy Russia* (Fort Worth, Tex., 1993), p. 12.

23 See R. Milner-Gulland, *The Russians* (Oxford, 1997), pp. 175–6.

24 L. Ouspensky, 'The Meaning and Language of Icons', in L. Ouspensky and V. Lossky, *The Meaning of Icons* (New York, 1982), p. 42.

25 See O. Figes and B. Kolonitskii, *Interpreting the Russian Revolution: The Language and Symbols of 1917* (New Haven, 1999), pp. 74–5.

26 M. Cherniavsky, *Tsar and People: Studies in Russian Myths* (New Haven, 1961), p. 6. See further, E. Reisman, 'The Cult of Boris and Gleb: Remnant of a Varangian Tradition?', *Russian Review*, vol. 37, no. 2 (1978), pp. 141–57; F. Sciacca, 'In Imitation of Christ: Boris and Gleb and the Ritual Consecration of the Russian Land', *Slavic Review*, vol. 49, no. 2 (1990), pp. 253–60; C. Halperin, 'The Concept of the *ruskaia zemlia* and Medieval National Consciousness', *Nationalities Papers*, vol. 8, no. 1 (1980), p. 80.

27 O. Figes, *Natasha's Dance: A Cultural History of Russia* (London, 2002), pp. 320–1.

28 I. Stepanova, *The Burial Dress of the Rus' in the Upper Volga Region (Late 10th–13th Centuries)* (Leiden, 2017), p. 4.

29 N. Kollmann, 'Collateral Succession in Kievan Rus'', *Harvard Ukrainian Studies*, vol. 14, no. 3/4 (1990), pp. 377–87.

30 Franklin and Shepard, *The Emergence of Rus*, pp. 367–9.

31 D. Miller, 'The Kievan Principality in the Century before the Mongol Invasion: An Inquiry into Recent Research and Interpretation', *Harvard Ukrainian Studies*, vol. 10, no. 1/2 (1986), p. 222.

2 THE MONGOL IMPACT

1 S. Zenkovsky (ed.), *Medieval Russia's Epics, Chronicles, and Tales* (London, 1991), p. 196.

2 See also U. Büntgen and N. Di Cosmo, 'Climatic and Environmental Aspects of the Mongol Withdrawal from Hungary in 1242 CE', *Scientific Reports*, vol. 6, no. 1 (2016), which explains the retreat by shortages of resources.

3 M. Favereau, *The Horde: How the Mongols Changed the World* (Cambridge, Mass., 2021), p. 51.

4 Ibid., p. 202.

5 David Miller, 'Monumental Building as an Indicator of Economic Trends in Northern Rus' in the Late Kievan and Mongol Periods, 1138–1462,' *American Historical Review*, vol. 94, no. 2 (April 1989), pp. 360–90.

6 L. Langer, 'Muscovite Taxation and the Problem of Mongol Rule in Rus', *Russian History*, vol. 34, nos. 1–4 (2007), p. 116.

7 Ibid., p. 110.

8 Zenkovsky, *Medieval Russia's Epics*, p. 232; M. Cherniavsky, *Tsar and People: Studies in Russian Myths* (New Haven, 1961), pp. 18–22.

9 J. Blum, *Lord and Peasant in Russia: From the Ninth to the Nineteenth Century* (Princeton, 1961), p. 106.

10 G. Vernadsky, *The Mongols and Russia*, vol. 3: *A History of Russia* (New Haven, 1953), p. 378.

11 J. Fennell, *The Emergence of Moscow, 1304–1359* (London, 1968), pp. 82–9.

12 Ibid., p. 192.

13 Vernadsky, *The Mongols*, p. 260.

14 'The Scythians' (1918) in A. Blok, *Sobranie sochinenii v vos'mi tomakh* (Moscow/Leningrad, 1961–3), vol. 3, p. 360.

15 Ibid., p. 267.

16 D. Ostrowski, *Muscovy and the Mongols: Cross-Cultural Influences on the Steppe Frontier, 1304–1589* (Cambridge, 1998), p. 67.

17 N. Karamzin, *Istoriia gosudarstva rossiiskogo*, 12 vols (St Petersburg, 1851–3), vol. 5, p. 373; D. Likhachev, *Russkaya kul'tura* (Moscow, 2000), p. 21.

18 C. Halperin, *The Tatar Yoke: The Image of the Mongols in Medieval Russia* (Bloomington, Ind., 2009), p. 193.

19 S. Solov'ev, *Istoriia Rossii s drevneiskikh vremen*, 29 vols (Moscow, 1851–79), vol. 4, p. 179.

20 See C. Halperin, 'Kliuchevskii and the Tatar Yoke', *Canadian-American Slavic Studies*, vol. 34, no. 4 (2000), pp. 385–408.

21 Favereau, *The Horde*, p. 238.

22 Ostrowski, *Muscovy and the Mongols*, p. 56. See further, N. Baskakov, *Russkie familii tiurksogo proiskhozhdeniia* (Moscow, 1979).

23 N. Trubetskoi, *K probleme russkogo samopoznaniia* (Paris, 1927), pp. 41–2, 48–51.

24 Vernadsky, *The Mongols*, pp. 13, 391.

25 H. Dewey and A. Kleimola, 'Russian Collective Consciousness: The Kievan Roots', *Slavonic and East European Review*, vol. 62, no. 2 (1984), pp. 180–91.

26 G. Alef, 'The Origin and Early Development of the Muscovite Postal Service', *Jahrbücher für Geschichte Osteuropas*, New Series, vol. 15, no. 1 (1967), p. 1.

27 Ostrowski, *Muscovy and the Mongols*, p. 52.

28 M. Cherniavsky, 'Khan or Basileus: An Aspect of Russian Medieval Political Theory', *Journal of the History of Ideas*, vol. 20 (1959), pp. 459–76.

29 See D. Ostrowski, 'The Mongol Origins of Muscovite Political Institutions', *Slavic Review*, vol. 49, no. 4 (1990), pp. 525–42.

30 Karamzin, *Istoriia gosudarstva rossiiskogo*, vol. 5, p. 374.

3 TSAR AND GOD

1 D. Miller, 'The Coronation of Ivan IV of Moscow', *Jahrbücher für Geschichte Osteuropas*, New Series, vol. 15, no. 4 (1967), pp. 559–74.

2 D. Ostrowski, *Muscovy and the Mongols: Cross-Cultural Influences on the Steppe Frontier, 1304–1589* (Cambridge, 1998), pp. 171–7.

3 D. Miller, 'Creating Legitimacy: Ritual, Ideology, and Power in Sixteenth-Century Russia', *Russian History*, vol. 21, no. 3 (1994), pp. 289–315.

4 The classic work developing this thesis is E. Kantorowicz, *The King's Two Bodies* (Princeton, 1957).

5 G. Alef, 'The Adoption of the Muscovite Two-Headed Eagle: A Discordant View', *Speculum*, vol. 41, no. 1 (1966), pp. 1–21.

6 J. Martin, *Medieval Russia, 980–1584* (Cambridge, 2007), p. 261.

7 *The Correspondence between Prince A. M. Kurbsky and Tsar Ivan IV of Russia, 1564–1579*, ed. and trans. J. Fennell (Cambridge, 1955), p. 75.

8 S. von Herberstein, *Notes upon Russia. Being a translation of the earliest account of that country, entitled Rerum Moscoviticarum Commentarii*, trans. and ed. R. H. Major, 2 vols (London, 1851–2), vol. 1, p. 30.

9 R. Pipes, *Russia under the Old Regime* (London, 1974), p. 97.

10 T. Hunczak (ed.), *Russian Imperialism from Ivan the Great to the Revolution* (New Brunswick, 1974), p. ix.

11 V. Kliuchevskii, *Kurs russkoi istorii*, 5 vols (Moscow, 1987), vol. 1, p. 31. The idea of Russia's internal colonisation was originally advanced by Kliuchevsky's teacher Soloviev in volume 2 of his *Istoriia Rossii s drevneishchikh vremen* (1851).

12 M. Perrie and A. Pavlov, *Ivan the Terrible* (London, 2003), pp. 48–50.

13 See R. Skrynnikov, 'Ermak's Siberian Expedition', *Russian History*, vol. 13, no. 1 (1986), pp. 1–40.

14 I. de Madariaga, *Ivan the Terrible* (New Haven, 2005), p. 353.

15 C. Halperin, *Ivan the Terrible: Free to Reward and Free to Punish* (Pittsburgh, 2019), pp. 182–6.

16 Madariaga, *Ivan*, pp. 257–9.

17 *Correspondence*, p. 41.

18 Perrie and Pavlov, *Ivan*, p. 159.

19 See further, P. Hunt, 'Ivan IV's Personal Mythology of Kingship', *Slavic Review*, vol. 52, no. 4 (1993), pp. 769–809.

20 M. Cherniavsky, 'Ivan the Terrible as Renaissance Prince', *Slavic Review*, vol. 27, no. 2 (1968), pp. 195–211. For the comparison with Charlemagne: D. Rowland, 'Ivan the Terrible as a Carolingian Renaissance Prince', *Harvard Ukrainian Studies*, vol. 19 (1995), pp. 594–606.

21 L. Kozlov, 'The Artist and the Shadow of Ivan', in Richard Taylor and D. W. Spring (eds), *Stalinism and Soviet Cinema* (London, 1993), p. 123.

22 *Moscow News*, no. 32 (1988), p. 8.

4 TIMES OF TROUBLE

1 F. Fletcher, *Of the Russe Common Wealth* (London, 1591), p. 34.

2 M. Cherniavsky, *Tsar and People: Studies in Russian Myths* (New Haven, 1961), p. 179.

3 Ibid., pp. 114–17.

4 P. Longworth, 'The Pretender Phenomenon in Eighteenth-Century Russia', *Past & Present*, vol. 66, issue 1 (1975), p. 61.

5 M. Perrie, *Pretenders and Popular Monarchism in Early Modern Russia* (Cambridge, 1995), p. 131.

6 C. Dunning, *Russia's First Civil War: The Time of Troubles and the Founding of the Romanov Dynasty* (University Park, Pa., 2001), p. 302.

7 The idea of a 'general crisis' in seventeenth-century Europe goes back to a 1954 essay by Eric Hobsbawm ('The General Crisis of the European Economy in the 17th Century', *Past & Present*, vol. 5, issue 1 [1954], pp. 33–53). It gave rise to a series of debates on the emergence of capitalism and the problems of the state. The most important essays are collected in G. Parker and L. Smith, *The General Crisis of the Seventeenth Century* (London, 1978). On the application of the 'general crisis' theory to Russia see: P. Brown, 'Muscovy, Poland, and the Seventeenth Century Crisis', *Polish Review*, vol. 27, no. 3/4 (1982), pp. 55–69.

8 V. Kivelson, 'The Devil Stole his Mind: The Tsar and the 1648 Moscow Uprising', *American Historical Review*, vol. 98, no. 3 (1993), p. 744.

9 V. Kliuchevsky, *A Course in Russian History: The Seventeenth Century* (New York, 1994), p. 152.

10 Ibid., p. 755.

11 R. Crummey, *Aristocrats and Servitors: The Boyar Elite in Russia, 1613– 1689* (Princeton, 1983), p. 36.

12 A. Kleimola, 'The Duty to Denounce in Muscovite Russia', *Slavic Review*, vol. 31, no. 4 (1972), p. 773.

13 R. Hellie, 'The Stratification of Muscovite Society: The Townsmen', *Russian History*, vol. 5, part 2 (1978), pp. 119–75.

14 For the legal evolution of serfdom: R. Smith, *The Enserfment of the Russian Peasantry* (Cambridge, 1968).

15 O. Figes, *The Europeans: Three Lives and the Making of a Cosmopolitan Culture* (London, 2019), p. 74.

16 P. Avrich, *Russian Rebels, 1600–1800* (New York, 1972), p. 109.

17 P. Longworth, 'The Subversive Legend of Stenka Razin', in V. Strada (ed.), *Russia* (Turin, 1975), vol. 2, p. 29.

18 S. O'Rourke, *The Cossacks* (Manchester, 2007), p. 82. On the pogroms of the Civil War, see J. Veitlinger, *In the Midst of Civilized Europe: The Pogroms of 1918–1921 and the Onset of the Holocaust* (New York, 2021).

19 L. Hughes, *Russia in the Age of Peter the Great* (New Haven, 1998), p. 317.

20 S. Collins, *The Present State of Russia* (London, 1671), pp. 64–5.

21 Kliuchevsky, *A Course*, p. 343.

22 L. Hughes, *Sophia Regent of Russia, 1657–1704* (New Haven, 1990), p. 249.

5 RUSSIA FACES WEST

1 A. Schönle, 'Calendar Reform under Peter the Great: Absolutist Prerogatives, Plural Temporalities, and Christian Exceptionalism', *Slavic Review*, vol. 80, no. 1 (2021), pp. 69–89; L. Hughes, 'Russian Culture in the Eighteenth Century', in D. Lieven (ed.), *The Cambridge History of Russia*, vol. 2: *Imperial Russia, 1689–1917* (Cambridge, 2006), p. 67.

2 N. Riasanovsky, *The Image of Peter the Great in Russian History and Thought* (New York, 1985), p. 5.

3 S. Montefiore, *The Romanovs* (London, 2016), p. 82.

4 W. Fuller, 'The Imperial Army', in Lieven (ed.), *Cambridge History of Russia*, vol. 2, p. 532.

5 Hughes, *Russia in the Age of Peter the Great*, p. 29.

6 P. Bushkovitch, 'Peter the Great and the Northern War', in Lieven (ed.), *The Cambridge History of Russia*, vol. 2, p. 498. Translation changed for clarity.

7 'Peterburg v 1720 g. Zapiski poliaka-ochevidtsa', *Russkaya Starina*, vol. 25 (1879), p. 267.

8 S. Soloviev, *Istoriia Rossii ot drevneishikh vremen*, 29 vols (Moscow, 1864–79), vol. 13, p. 1270.

9 On textile manufacturing: W. Daniel, 'Entrepreneurship and the Russian Textile Industry: From Peter the Great to Catherine the Great', *Russian Review*, vol. 54, no. 1 (1995), pp. 1–25.

10 *Iusnosti chestnoe zertsalo* (St Petersburg, 1717), pp. 73–4.

11 L. Tolstoy, *War and Peace*, trans. L. and A. Maude (Oxford, 1998), p. 3.

12 Riasanovsky, *Image*, p. 80.

13 Ibid., p. 60.

14 V. Solov'ev, *Sochineniia*, 2 vols (Moscow, 1989), vol. 1, p. 287.

15 S. Dixon, *The Modernisation of Russia* (Cambridge, 2012), p. 16.

16 See further, B. Meehan-Waters, 'Catherine the Great and the Problem of Female Rule', *Russian Review*, vol. 34, no. 3 (1975), pp. 293–300.

17 H. Rogger, *National Consciousness in Eighteenth-Century Russia* (Cambridge, Mass., 1960), p. 37.

18 J. Alexander, *Catherine the Great: Life and Legend* (Oxford, 1989), pp. 11, 14.

19 R. Ovchinnikov, 'Sledstvie i sud nad E. I. Pugachevym', *Voprosy Istorii*, no. 3 (1966), p. 128.

20 R. Jones, *The Emancipation of the Russian Nobility, 1762–1785* (Princeton, 2019), p. 204.

21 P. Dukes (ed.), *Russia under Catherine the Great*, vol. 2: *Catherine the Great's Instruction (Nakaz) to the Legislative Commission, 1767* (Newtonville, Mass., 1977), p. 3.

22 See M. Bassin, 'Geographies of Imperial Identity', in Lieven (ed.), *Cambridge History of Russia*, vol. 2, pp. 45–64.

23 M. Bassin, 'Inventing Siberia: Visions of the Russian East in the Early Nineteenth Century', *American Historical Review*, vol. 96, no. 3 (1991), pp. 768–70.

24 The number of Jews is hard to estimate with accuracy. It might have been as high as 200,000 or as low as 32,000. See J. Klier, *Russia Gathers her Jews: The Origins of the 'Jewish Question' in Russia, 1772–1825* (DeKalb, Ill., 1986), p. 56.

25 W. Reddaway (ed.), *Documents of Catherine the Great* (Cambridge, 1931), p. 147; *Correspondance artistique de Grimm avec Catherine II*, Archives de l'art français, nouvelle période, 17 (Paris, 1932), pp. 61–2.

26 See further, O. Figes, *Crimea: The Last Crusade* (London, 2010), pp. 10–17.

27 S. Montefiore, *Prince of Princes: The Life of Potemkin* (London, 2000), pp. 274–5.

28 J. Blum, *Lord and Peasant in Russia: From the Ninth to the Nineteenth Century* (Princeton, 1961), p. 441.

29 Jones, *Emancipation of the Russian Nobility*, p. 293.

30 Alexander, *Catherine*, p. 283.

31 V. Semennikov (ed.), *Materialy dlia istorii russkoi literatury* (St Petersburg, 1914), p. 34.

6 THE SHADOW OF NAPOLEON

1 M. Heller, *Histoire de la Russie et de son empire* (Paris, 1997), p. 616.

2 A. Czartoryski, *Mémoires et correspondance avec l'empereur Alexandre Ier*, 2 vols (Paris, 1887), vol. 1, p. 979.

3 See M.-P. Rey, *Alexander I: The Tsar Who Defeated Napoleon* (De Kalb, Ill., 2012), ch. 7.

4 Ibid., Kindle edn, loc. 6079.

5 IRL RAN, f. 57, op. 1, n. 63, l. 57 (Sergei Volkonsky).

6 A. Ulam, *Russia's Failed Revolutions: From the Decembrists to the Dissidents* (New York, 1981), p. 5.

7 A. Sergeyev, 'Graf A. Kh. Benkendorf o Rossii v 1827–30gg. (Yezhegodnyye otchoty tret'yego otdeleniya i korpusa zhandarmov)', *Krasnyi Arkhiv*, vol. 37 (1929), pp. 131–74.

8 P. Squire, 'The Metternich–Benckendorff Letters, 1835–1842', *Slavonic and East European Review*, vol. 45, no. 105 (July 1967), pp. 368–90.

9 N. Riasanovsky, *Nicholas I and Official Nationality in Russia* (Berkeley, 1959), p. 74.

10 K. Aksakov, *Polnoe sobranie sochinenii*, 2 vols (St Petersburg, 1861), vol. 2, p. 292.

11 N. Gogol, *Pis'ma*, 4 vols (St Petersburg, n.d.), vol. 2, p. 508.

12 P. Annenkov, *The Extraordinary Decade: Literary Memoirs* (Ann Arbor, 1968).

13 V. Belinskii, *Polnoe sobranie sochinenii*, 13 vols (Moscow, 1953–9), vol. 10, p. 212.

14 A Presniakov, *Emperor Nicholas I of Russia: The Apogee of Autocracy, 1825–1855* (Gulf Breeze, Fla., 1974), p. 56.

15 S. Monas, *The Third Section: Police and Society in Russia under Nicholas I* (Cambridge, Mass., 1961), p. 240.

16 NA, FO 195/332, Colquhoun to Stratford Canning, 2 July 1849.

17 W. Bruce Lincoln, *Nicholas I: Emperor and Autocrat of All the Russias* (De Kalb, Ill., 1989), p. 321; Monas, *The Third Section*, pp. 142, 194.

18 J. and E. Goncourt, *Journal: Mémoires de la vie littéraire*, ed. Robert Ricatte, 3 vols (Monaco, 1956), vol. 2, p. 499.

19 A. Taylor, *The Struggle for Mastery in Europe, 1848–1918* (Oxford, 1959), p. 49.

20 O. Figes, *Crimea: The Last Crusade* (London, 2010), p. 8.

21 A. Zaoinchkovskii, *Vostochnaia voina, 1853–1856*, 3 vols (St Petersburg, 2002), vol. 2, p. 523.

22 Ibid., vol. 1, pp. 702–8.

23 Figes, *Crimea*, p. 442.

24 N. Danilevskii, *Russia and Europe: The Slavic World's Political and Cultural Relations with the Germanic-Roman West*, trans. S. Woodburn (Bloomington, Ind., 2013), p. 107.

25 A. Kelly, *Toward Another Shore: Russian Thinkers between Necessity and Chance* (New Haven, 1998), p. 41.

26 RGIA, f. 914, op. 1, d. 68, ll. 1–2.

27 *Materialy dlia istorii uprazdneniia krepostnogo sostoianii pomeshchich'ikh krest'ian v Rossii v tsarstvovanii Imperatora Aleksandra II*, 3 vols (Berlin, 1860–2), vol. 1, p. 114.

7 AN EMPIRE IN CRISIS

1 For more on the Bezdna incident: Daniel Field, *Rebels in the Name of the Tsar* (New York, 1976).

2 T. Emmons, 'The Peasant and the Emancipation', in W. Vucinich (ed.), *The Peasant in Nineteenth-Century Russia* (Stanford, 1968), p. 54.

3 See J. Blum, *Lord and Peasant in Russia: From the Ninth to the Nineteenth Century* (Princeton, 1961), pp. 512–14.

4 I discuss the peasant ideology in greater depth in *A People's Tragedy: The Russian Revolution, 1891–1924* (London, 1996), pp. 98–102; and *Peasant Russia, Civil War: The Volga Countryside in Revolution, 1917–1921* (Oxford, 1989), ch. 3.

5 Figes, *A People's Tragedy*, p. 105.

6 T. Shanin, *The Awkward Class* (Oxford, 1972), p. 48.

7 A. Anfimov, *Zemel'naya arenda v Rossii v nachale XX veka* (Moscow, 1961), p. 15.

8 D. Saunders, *Russia in the Age of Reaction and Reform* (London, 1992), p. 213.

9 J. Habermas, 'The Public Sphere', *New German Critique*, no. 3 (1974), p. 49.

10 Figes, *A People's Tragedy*, p. 46.

11 F. Venturi, *Roots of Revolution: A History of the Populist and Socialist Movements in Nineteenth-Century Russia* (New York, 1960), p. xxvi.

12 See R. Crews, *For Prophet and Tsar: Islam and Empire in Russia and Central Asia* (Cambridge, Mass., 2009).

13 J. Brooks, *When Russia Learned to Read: Literacy and Popular Literature, 1861–1917* (Princeton, 1985), pp. 55–6.

14 For an analysis of Russia as a 'developing society' at this time see T. Shanin, *Russia as a 'Developing Society'*, vol. 1: *Roots of Otherness: Russia's Turn of Century* (London, 1985). On similar patterns of rural migration into towns in twentieth-century India see R. Chandavarkar, '"The Making of the Working Class": E. P. Thompson and Indian History', *History Workshop Journal*, no. 43 (1997), pp. 185–7.

15 T. von Laue, 'A Secret Memorandum of Sergei Witte on the Industrialization of Imperial Russia', *Journal of Modern History*, vol. 26 (1954), p. 71.

16 D. Volkogonov, *Lenin: Life and Legacy* (London, 1991), pp. 8–9.

17 L. Fischer, *The Life of Lenin* (London, 1965), p. 329.

18 L. Lih, *Lenin Rediscovered: What Is to Be Done? In Context* (Chicago, 2008), p. 447.

19 W. Sablinsky, *The Road to Bloody Sunday: Father Gapon and the St Petersburg Massacre of 1905* (Princeton, 1976), p. 344.

20 On earlier signs of more hostile peasant attitudes towards the tsar, based on police arrest protocols of peasants denounced for anti-tsarist statements following the assassination of Alexander III in 1881,

see D. Beer, '"To a Dog, a Dog's Death!": Naive Monarchism and Regicide in Imperial Russia, 1878–1884', *Slavic Review*, vol. 80, no. 1 (2021), pp. 112–32.

21 *Voennaya Gazeta*, 13 June 1913, p. 2.

22 *Novoe Vremia*, 6 March 1914.

23 Figes, *A People's Tragedy*, p. 251.

24 P. Gilliard, *Thirteen Years at the Russian Court* (London, 1921), p. III.

25 A. Brussilov, *A Soldier's Notebook, 1914–1918* (London, 1930), p. 39.

26 F. Golder, *Documents on Russian History, 1914–1917* (New York, 1927), p. 21.

8 REVOLUTIONARY RUSSIA

1 A. Brussilov, *A Soldier's Notebook, 1914–1918* (London, 1930), pp. 93–4.

2 O. Figes and B. Kolonitskii, *Interpreting the Russian Revolution: The Language and Symbols of 1917* (New Haven, 1999), p. 24.

3 B. Pares (ed.), *Letters of the Tsaritsa to the Tsar, 1914–1916* (London, 1923), p. 157.

4 O. Figes, *A People's Tragedy: The Russian Revolution, 1891–1924* (London, 1996), p. 345.

5 L. Trotsky, *The History of the Russian Revolution* (London, 1977), p. 193.

6 G. Buchanan, *My Mission to Russia and Other Diplomatic Memoirs*, 2 vols (London, 1923), vol. 2, p. 86.

7 OR RNB f. 152, op. 1, d. 98, l. 34.

8 St Antony's College, Oxford, Russian and East European Centre, G. Katkov Papers, 'Moskovskii sovet rabochikh deputatov (1917–1922)', p. 10.

9 R. Lockhart, *Memoirs of a British Agent* (London, 1933), p. 304.

10 R. Browder and A. Kerensky (eds), *The Russian Provisional Government 1917: Documents*, 3 vols (Stanford, 1961), vol. 2, pp. 913–15.

11 F. Farmborough, *Nurse at the Russian Front* (London, 1977), pp. 269–70.

12 G. Zinoviev, 'Lenin i iiul'skie dni', *Proletarskaya Revoliutsiia*, no. 8–9 (1929), p. 62.

13 V. Lenin, *Collected Works*, 47 vols (London, 1977), vol. 25, pp. 176–9.

14 Ibid., vol. 26, pp. 19, 21.

15 *The Bolsheviks and the October Revolution: Minutes of the Central Committee of the Russian Social-Democratic Labour Party (Bolsheviks), August 1917–February 1918*, trans. A. Bone (London, 1974), p. 98.

16 Figes, *A People's Tragedy*, pp. 489–91.

17 M. Gorky, *Untimely Thoughts: Essays on Revolution, Culture, and the Bolsheviks, 1917–1918*, trans. Herman Ermolaev (New Haven, 1995), p. 95.

18 V. Lenin, *Polnoe sobranie sochinenii*, 55 vols (Moscow, 1958–65), vol. 35, p. 204.

19 RGASPI, f. 17, op. 1, d. 405, l. 1–13.

20 J. Wheeler-Bennett, *Brest-Litovsk: The Forgotten Peace* (New York, 1938), p. 269.

21 O. Figes, *Peasant Russia, Civil War: The Volga Countryside in Revolution, 1917–1921* (Oxford, 1989), pp. 150 ff.

22 O. Figes, 'The Village and *Volost* Soviet Elections of 1919', *Soviet Studies*, vol. 40, no. 1 (1988), pp. 21–45.

23 Figes and Kolonitskii, *Interpreting the Russian Revolution*, p. 152.

24 O. Figes, 'The Red Army and Mass Mobilization during the Russian Civil War', *Past & Present*, vol. 129, issue 1 (1990), pp. 206–9.

25 *Kronshtadtski miatezh: sbornik statei, vospominanii i dokumentov* (Leningrad, 1931), p. 26.

26 See I. Getzler, *Kronstadt, 1917–1921: The Fate of a Soviet Democracy* (Cambridge, 1983).

27 Lenin, *Collected Works*, vol. 33, pp. 487–502.

9 THE WAR ON OLD RUSSIA

1 N. Sukhanov, *The Russian Revolution, 1917: A Personal Record*, ed. J. Carmichael (Oxford, 1955), p. 230.

2 S. Kotkin, *Stalin*, vol. 1: *Paradoxes of Power, 1878–1928* (London, 2014), p. 432.

3 Ibid., pp. 433–41; B. Bazhanov, *Bazhanov and the Damnation of Stalin*, trans. D. Doyle (Athens, Oh., 1990), p. 40. See further, N. Rosenfeldt, '"The Consistory of the Communist Church": The Origins and Development of Stalin's Secret Chancellery', *Russian History* 9 (1982), pp. 308–24; J. Harris, 'Stalin as General Secretary: The Appointments Process and the Nature of Stalin's Power', in S. Davis and J. Harris, *Stalin: A New History* (Cambridge, 2005), pp. 63–82.

4 *Izvestiia TsK*, no. 12 (1989), pp. 193, 198.

5 N. Tumarkin, *Lenin Lives! The Lenin Cult in Soviet Russia* (Cambridge, Mass., 1997), pp. 139–49, 160–4; O. Velikanova, *Making of an Idol: On Uses of Lenin* (Göttingen, 1996), pp. 33–4.

6 See R. Conquest, *The Harvest of Sorrow: Soviet Collectivization and the Terror-Famine* (Oxford, 1986), and A. Applebaum, *Red Famine: Stalin's War on Ukraine* (New York, 2017).

7 N. Kaminskaya, *Final Judgment: My Life as a Soviet Defence Attorney* (New York, 1982), pp. 18–21.

8 On such statements and their provenance see D. Brandenberger and A. Dubrovsky, '"The People Need a Tsar": The Emergence of National Bolshevism as Stalinist Ideology, 1931–1941', *Europe-Asia Studies*, vol. 50, no. 5 (1998), p. 873.

9 O. Figes, *The Whisperers: Private Life in Stalin's Russia* (London, 2007), p. 275.

10 J. Haslam, 'Political Opposition to Stalin and the Origins of the Terror in Russia, 1932–1936', *Historical Journal*, vol. 29, no. 2 (1986), p. 396.

11 J. Getty and O. Naumov, *The Road to Terror: Stalin and the Self-Destruction of the Bolsheviks, 1932–1939* (New Haven, 1999), pp. 54–7.

12 H. Kuromiya, 'Accounting for the Great Terror', *Jahrbücher für Geschichte Osteuropas*, New Series, vol. 53, no. 1 (2005), pp. 86–101.

13 O. Khlevniuk, *Master of the House: Stalin and his Inner Circle* (New Haven, 2009), p. 174; *Istochnik*, no. 3 (1994), p. 80.

10 MOTHERLAND

1 *Izvestiia*, 29 November 1938; *Kino-Gazeta*, 2 December 1938.

2 S. Eizenshtein, 'Patriotizm – moia tema', in *Izbrannye prozvedeniia v shesti tomakh* (Moscow, 1964), vol. 1, p. 162.

3 D. Brandenberger and A. Dubrovsky, '"The People Need a Tsar": The Emergence of National Bolshevism as Stalinist Ideology, 1931–1941', *Europe-Asia Studies*, vol. 50, no. 5 (1998), p. 880.

4 See T. Martin, *The Affirmative Action Empire: Nations and Nationalism in the Soviet Union, 1923–1939* (Ithaca, NY, 2001).

5 Cited in S. Plokhy, *Lost Kingdom: A History of Russian Nationalism from Ivan the Great to Vladimir Putin* (London, 2018), p. 255.

6 O. Khlevniuk, *Stalin: New Biography of a Dictator*, trans. N. Favorov (New Haven, 2015), p. 188.

7   T. Snyder, *Black Earth: The Holocaust as History and Warning* (New York, 2016), p. 19.

8   *Pravda*, 3 July 1941, p. 1.

9   Khlevniuk, *Stalin*, p. 218.

10 *Vecherniaya Moskva*, 8 November 1941.

11 M. Djilas, *Conversations with Stalin*, trans. M. Petrovich (London, 2014), p. 40.

12 Interviews with Rebekka (Rita) Kogan, St Petersburg, June, November 2003. See O. Figes, *The Whisperers: Private Life in Stalin's Russia* (London, 2007), pp. 417–19.

13 The figures for military casualties are disputed and difficult to calculate with certainty. The figure given by the Russian Ministry of Defence is 8.7 million but higher figures (up to 14 million) have been calculated from lists of personnel in military archives. I have followed Viktor Zemskov's calculation based on counting Soviet POWs who died in forced-labour camps in Germany (V. Zemskov, 'O Masshtabakh liudskikh poter' SSSR v Velikoi Otechestvennoi Voine', *Voenno-Istoricheskii Arkhiv*, vol. 9 [2012], pp. 59–71).

14 R. McNeal, *Stalin: Man and Ruler* (London, 1988), p. 241.

15 G. Hosking, 'The Second World War and Russian National Consciousness', *Past & Present*, vol. 175, issue 1 (2002), p. 177.

16 Figes, *The Whisperers*, pp. 414–15.

17 Djilas, *Conversations with Stalin*, p. 78.

18 <marxists.org/reference/archive/stalin/works/1945/05/24.htm>.

19 Djilas, *Conversations with Stalin*, p. 45.

20 Ibid., pp. 80–1.

21 M. Ellman and S. Maksudov, 'Soviet Deaths in the Great Patriotic War: A Note', *Europe-Asia Studies*, vol. 46, no. 4 (1994), p. 671. The estimate of 28 million was made by an expert commission appointed by Gorbachev in 1989.

22 No explanation of Stalin's motives for grossly underestimating the war losses has yet been found in the archival documents. It may be that he had in mind the possibility of a new war against the West and did not want the population to be told how many had already died.

23 <soviethistory.msu.edu/1947-2/famine-of-1946-1947/>.

24 I. Stalin, *Speeches Delivered at Meetings of Voters of the Stalin Electoral District, Moscow* (Moscow, 1950), pp. 19–44.

25 *Pravda*, 9 January 1949.

26 *Pravda*, 7 November 1946.

27 L. Alexeyeva and P. Goldberg, *The Thaw Generation: Coming of Age in the Post-Stalin Era* (Boston, 1990), p. 4.

28 J. Brodsky, 'Spoils of War', in *On Grief and Reason: Essays* (London, 1996), p. 8.

29 S. Schattenberg, *Brezhnev: The Making of a Statesman*, trans. J. Heath (London, 2021), p. 186.

30 Ibid., p. 217.

31 L. Timofeev, *Soviet Peasants: Or, the Peasants' Art of Starving* (n.p., 1985).

32 *The Current Digest of the Soviet Press* (Columbus, Oh.), 27 April 1988, pp. 1–6.

II ENDS

1 See e.g. A. Ostrovsky, *Inventing Russia: The Journey from Gorbachev's Freedom to Putin's War* (London, 2018), p. 115.

2 Diane Sawyer of ABC, *World News Tonight*: <youtube.com/watch?v=fdKu09ZqVZw>.

3 See the interview with Aleksandr Mikhailov, the KGB's press officer: <icds.ee/en/25-years-after-the-moscow-putsch-what-did-eve nts-look-like-from-within-the-kgb/>.

4 A. Kolesnichenko, 'Effects of 1991 August Putsch still felt in Russia', *Russia Beyond the Headlines*, 23 August 2013: <rbth.com/polit ics/2013/08/23/effects_of_1991_august_putsch_still_felt_in_russi a_29171.html>.

5 T. Wood, *Russia without Putin: Money, Power and the Myths of the New Cold War* (London, 2018), Kindle edn, loc. 555.

6 See D. Hoffman, *The Oligarchs: Wealth and Power in the New Russia* (New York, 2001).

7 M. Gessen, *Man without A Face: The Unlikely Rise of Vladimir Putin* (New York, 2013).

8 S. Corbesero, 'History, Myth and Memory: A Biography of a Stalin Portrait', *Russian History*, vol. 38, no. 1 (2011), p. 77. Many thanks to @cdmoldes for tracking down the image.

9 V. Putin, 'Russia at the Turn of the Millennium', <government.gov. ru/english/statVP_eng_1.html>.

10 C. Belton, *Putin's People: How the KGB Took Back Russia and Then Took on the West* (London, 2020), p. 267.

11 L. Aron, 'The Problematic Pages', *New Republic*, 24 September 2008.

12 *Kommersant-Vlast'*, no. 27 (371), 16 July 2007.

13 G. Pavlovskii, 'Plokho s pamiat'iu – plokho s politikoi', *Russkii Zhurnal*, December 2008.

14 See my account in 'Putin vs. The Truth', *New York Review of Books*, 30 April 2009.

15 International Federation for Human Rights (FIDH), *Russia – 'Crimes against History'*, report published 10 June 2021, p. 29: <fidh. org/IMG/pdf/russie-_pad-uk-web.pdf>.

16 Ibid., p. 10. See further I. Kurilla, 'The Implications of Russia's Law against the "Rehabilitation of Nazism"', *PONARS Eurasia Policy Memo*, no. 331 (August 2014).

17 A. Miller, 'Adjusting Historical Policy in Russia', *Russia in Global Affairs*, no. 4 (2014): <eng.globalaffairs.ru/articles/a-year-of-frustra ted-hopes/>. See further, H. Bækken and J. Due Enstad, 'Identity under Siege: Selective Securitization of History in Putin's Russia', *Slavonic and East European Review*, vol. 98, no. 2 (2020), pp. 321–44.

18 E. Klimenko, 'Building the Nation, Legitimizing the State: Russia – My History and Memory of the Russian Revolutions in Contemporary Russia', *Nationalities Papers*, vol. 49, no. 1 (2021), pp. 72–88.

19 <themoscowtimes.com/2020/03/24/75-of-russians-say-sov iet-era-was-greatest-time-in-countrys-history-poll-a69735>.

20 <levada.ru/2021/06/23/otnoshenie-k-stalinu-rossiya-i-ukraina/>.

21 Iu. Levada, '"Chelovek sovetskii": chetvertaia volna', *Polit.ru*, 30 April 2010: <polit.ru/lectures/2004/04/15/levada.html>. See further M. Gessen, *The Future Is History: How Totalitarianism Reclaimed Russia* (New York, 2017), which discusses the phenomenon.

22 D. Khapaeva and N. Koposov, *Pozhaleite, lyudi, palachei: Massovoe istoricheskoe soznanie v postsovetskoi Rossii i Stalinizm* (Moscow, 2007).

23 For transcripts and recordings of the shows see: <kurginyan.ru>.

24 Cited in R. Braithwaite, 'NATO enlargement: Assurances and misunderstandings', European Council on Foreign Relations, 7 July 2016. On-line edition: <ecfr.eu/article/commentary_nato_ enlargement_assurances_and_misunderstandings/>.

25 T. Friedman, 'Foreign Affairs; Now a Word from X', *New York Times*, 2 May 1998.

26 <en.kremlin.ru/events/president/transcripts/24034>.

27 <en.kremlin.ru/events/president/transcripts/22931>.

28 NATO's intervention in Yugoslavia was preceded by three UN Security Council resolutions condemning Belgrade's policies. No such diplomatic efforts were made by the Russians before their invasion of Ukraine. Ninety-seven UN member states recognised Kosovo's independence, whereas only five recognised the legality of Russia's annexation of Crimea.

29 On Glazyev's influence see M. Zygar, *All the Kremlin's Men: Inside the Court of Vladimir Putin* (New York, 2016), ch. 17.

30 M. Sarotte, *Not One Inch: America, Russia, and the Making of Post-Cold War Stalemate* (New Haven, 2022), p. 184.

31 <en.kremlin.ru/events/president/news/67828>.

32 <en.kremlin.ru/events/president/news/66181>.

33 <https://www.newstatesman.com/world/europe/ukraine/2022/04/russia-cannot-afford-to-lose-so-we-need-a-kind-of-a-victory-sergey-karaganov-on-what-putin-wants>.

34 <https://www.themoscowtimes.com/2022/03/07/russian-church-leader-appears-to-blame-gay-pride-parades-for-ukraine-war-a76803>.

35 For Zelensky's comments on the timescale of a constitutional change see his fascinating interview with four Russian independent journalists: <https://www.youtube.com/watch?v=IAo1DLfqYIY>. (from 50 minutes in). For Ukrainian polls: <https://www.themoscowtimes.com/2022/02/18/ukrainians-support-for-joining-nato-hits-record-high-poll-a76442> and <https://ratinggroup.ua/research/ukraine/pyatyy_obschenacionalnyy_opros_ukraina_v_usloviyah_voyny_18_marta_2022.html>.

Picture Credits

Vladimir Putin and Patriarch Kirill at the Vladimir the Great monument in Moscow. Photo: https://mos.ru/mayor/media/photo/5454057/carousel/2/11/; photographer: Evgeny Samarin

Viktor Vasnetsov (1848–1926), *The Invitation of the Varangians...* Photo: Wikimedia Commons PD

The Church of St Sophia, Kiev, Ukraine. Photo: Ivan Nesterov/Alamy

Iconostasis inside the Dormition Cathedral, Moscow. Photo: robertharding/Alamy

Birch bark letter from Peter to Volchko, from Nerevsky, Novgorod, c. 1120–1140. 'Was it you that told Roshnet that two sorochoks are to be collected...'. Photo: www.gramoty.ru ©The National Museums Veliky Novgorod

Andrei Rublev (c. 1370–1430), *The Holy Trinity*, 1420s. Tempera on wood. Tretyakov Gallery, Moscow. Photo: Universal History Archive/Getty Images

An aerial view of the Solovetsky Monastery, Arkhangelsk Region. Photo: ITAR-TASS/Alamy

Cathedral square, Kremlin, Moscow. Photo: Ivan Vdovin/Alamy

Anonymous, attributed to Athanasius, *The Blessed Host of the Heavenly Tsar (Church Militant)*, 1552. Tempera on wood. Tretyakov Gallery, Moscow. Photo: Wikimedia Commons PD

Vasily Surikov (1848–1916), *Ermak's Conquest of Siberia in 1582*, c. 1895. Oil on canvas. State Russian Museum, St Petersburg. Photo: Universal History Archive/Getty Images

Irakli Toidze (1902–85), Mother Russia Calls, 1941. Soviet poster. Private
     Collection. Photo: Stefano Bianchetti/Bridgeman Images
United Russia party poster, Moscow, November 5, 2003. Photo: Misha
     Japaridze/AP/Shutterstock
A panel from the 'My History' exhibition. Photo: courtesy Ivan Kurilla

Index

Acknowledgements

I would like to thank the following people: Peter Straus, Melanie Jackson, Stephen Edwards and the rest of the team at RCW; Stella Tillyard and Christopher Wyld, the first readers of my early draft; Alexis Kirschbaum and her team at Bloomsbury – Jasmine Horsey, Stephanie Rathbone, Lauren Whybrow, Jonny Coward, Peter James, the copy-editor, Mike Athanson, the map-maker, Jo Carlill, the picture researcher, Catherine Best and Genista Tate-Alexander; and at Metropolitan my beloved editor, Sara Bershtel and her team – Brian Lax, Carolyn O'Keefe and Christopher Sergio.

A Note on the Author

Orlando Figes is an award-winning author and historian, who has held teaching posts at Birkbeck College, University of London and Trinity College, University of Cambridge. He was born in London in 1959 and studied History at the University of Cambridge. Figes is the bestselling author of nine books on Russian and European history, including *Natasha's Dance* and *A People's Tragedy*. His books have been translated into over thirty languages.

A Note on the Type

The text of this book is set Adobe Garamond. It is one of several versions of Garamond based on the designs of Claude Garamond. It is thought that Garamond based his font on Bembo, cut in 1495 by Francesco Griffo in collaboration with the Italian printer Aldus Manutius. Garamond types were first used in books printed in Paris around 1532. Many of the present-day versions of this type are based on the *Typi Academiae* of Jean Jannon cut in Sedan in 1615.

Claude Garamond was born in Paris in 1480. He learned how to cut type from his father and by the age of fifteen he was able to fashion steel punches the size of a pica with great precision. At the age of sixty he was commissioned by King Francis I to design a Greek alphabet, and for this he was given the honourable title of royal type founder. He died in 1561.